# The Changeling

# ARDEN SHAKESPEARE STATE OF PLAY SERIES

General Editors: Lena Cowen Orlin and Ann Thompson

*Elizabethan Narrative Poems: The State of Play*,
edited by Lynn Enterline
*Macbeth: The State of Play*, edited by Ann Thompson
*Othello: The State of Play*, edited by Lena Cowen Orlin
*The Revenger's Tragedy: The State of Play*,
edited by Gretchen E. Minton
*The Sonnets: The State of Play*, edited by Hannah Crawforth,
Elizabeth Scott-Baumann and Clare Whitehead
*Titus Andronicus: The State of Play*,
edited by Farah Karim-Cooper
*The Taming of the Shrew: The State of Play,*
edited by Heather C. Easterling and Jennifer Flaherty
*Hamlet: The State of Play*, edited by Sonia Massai and
Lucy Munro

# The Changeling

## The State of Play

*Edited by*
*Gordon McMullan*
*and Kelly Stage*

THE ARDEN SHAKESPEARE
LONDON • NEW YORK • OXFORD • NEW DELHI • SYDNEY

THE ARDEN SHAKESPEARE
Bloomsbury Publishing Plc
50 Bedford Square, London, WC1B 3DP, UK
1385 Broadway, New York, NY 10018, USA
29 Earlsfort Terrace, Dublin 2, Ireland

BLOOMSBURY, THE ARDEN SHAKESPEARE and the Arden Shakespeare logo
are trademarks of Bloomsbury Publishing Plc

First published in Great Britain 2022
Paperback edition published 2023

Copyright © Gordon McMullan, Kelly Stage and contributors, 2022, 2023

Gordon McMullan, Kelly Stage and contributors have asserted their right under the
Copyright, Designs and Patents Act, 1988, to be identified as the
authors of this work.

Cover image © Shutterstock

All rights reserved. No part of this publication may be reproduced or transmitted
in any form or by any means, electronic or mechanical, including photocopying,
recording, or any information storage or retrieval system, without prior
permission in writing from the publishers.

Bloomsbury Publishing Plc does not have any control over, or responsibility for, any
third-party websites referred to or in this book. All internet addresses given in
this book were correct at the time of going to press. The author and publisher
regret any inconvenience caused if addresses have changed or sites have
ceased to exist, but can accept no responsibility for any such changes.

A catalogue record for this book is available from the British Library.

A catalog record for this book is available from the Library of Congress.

ISBN: HB:    978-1-3501-7438-2
      PB:    978-1-3502-8843-0
      ePDF:  978-1-3502-3591-5
      eBook: 978-1-3501-7439-9

Series: Arden Shakespeare The State of Play

Typeset by RefineCatch Limited, Bungay, Suffolk

To find out more about our authors and books visit www.bloomsbury.com
and sign up for our newsletters.

# CONTENTS

*List of Illustrations* viii
*Notes on Contributors* ix
*Preface* xiv
*Series Preface* xvi

    Introduction 1
    *Kelly Stage and Gordon McMullan*

## Part One  Spaces and Places

1  Space, Gender and the Rules of Movement in *The Changeling* 23
    *Jean E. Howard*

2  Chang(el)ing Spaces: Dramatic Forms of Worlding in Late Jacobean England 42
    *Ina Habermann*

## Part Two  Collaboration and the Hospital Plot

3  A Secret Within the Castle: William Rowley and *The Changeling* 61
    *David Nicol*

4  Isabella 78
    *Douglas Bruster*

## Part Three  States of Mind

5  'The Pleasure of Your Bedlam': Mismanaging Insanity in *The Changeling*  97
   *Pascale Drouet*

6  Passions, Affections and Instinct in *The Changeling*  116
   *Jesse M. Lander*

## Part Four  Disabilities

7  *The Changeling*'s Phantom Limbs  139
   *Karen Sawyer Marsalek*

8  Disability Representation and Theatrical Form in *The Changeling* and *The Nice Valour*  157
   *Katherine Schaap Williams*

## Part Five  Actor and Audience in Jacobean Performance

9  *The Changeling*, The Boy Actor and Female Subjectivity  179
   *Lucy Munro*

10  Witnessing at the Phoenix: Early Modern Audiences at *The Changeling*  197
    *Jennifer A. Low*

**Part Six Rape and the Female Body in Contemporary Performance**

11 'What Would a Foreign Woman Be?': Sexual Borderlands, Hospitality, and 'Forgetting Parentage' in *The Changeling* on Film  217
*Courtney Lehmann*

12 Feminist Staging in Brave Spirits' *Changeling*  237
*Charlene V. Smith and Musa Gurnis*

*Selected Bibliography*  257
*Index*  262

# ILLUSTRATIONS

7.1 Pair of gloves, early seventeenth century. Image courtesy of the Metropolitan Museum of Art, 28.220.1, 2. Gift of Mrs. Edward S. Harkness, 1928. 140

7.2 Prosthetic Hand by Ambroise Paré. Illustration from *Les oeuures d'Ambroise Paré . . .: diuisees en vingt huict liures, auec les figures & portraicts, tant de l'anatomie que des instruments de chirurgie, & de plusieurs monstres* (Paris: Buon, 1585), 917. Image courtesy of *Historical Anatomies on the Web*, National Library of Medicine, National Institute of Health. 145

# NOTES ON CONTRIBUTORS

**Douglas Bruster** is Mody C. Boatright Regents Professor of American and English Literature and Distinguished Teaching Professor in the Department of English at the University of Texas at Austin. His books include: *Drama and the Market in the Age of Shakespeare* (1992), *Quoting Shakespeare* (2000), *Shakespeare and the Question of Culture* (2003), *Prologues to Shakespeare's Theatre* (2004), *To Be or Not To Be* (2007) and *Shakespeare and the Power of Performance* (2008). Notably, he is the editor of *The Changeling* in *Thomas Middleton: The Collected Works* (gen. eds. Gary Taylor and John Lavagnino). He is also editor of *Everyman* and *Mankind*, and *A Midsummer Night's Dream*.

**Pascale Drouet** is Professor in Early Modern British Studies at the University of Poitiers, France. She is the author of several monographs, including *Le Vagabond dans l'Angleterre de Shakespeare* (2003) and *De la filouterie dans l'Angleterre de la Renaissance* (2012). Her new monograph *Shakespeare and the Denial of Territory* is forthcoming. Her latest co-editions are *The Duchess of Malfi: Webster's Tragedy of Blood* (2018) and *Shakespeare et Dante* (2020). She has translated into French and edited Beaumont and Fletcher's *Philaster* (2019) and is currently translating and editing Robert Greene's *A Notable Discovery of Cozenage*.

**Musa Gurnis** is a theatre scholar and practitioner. She is the author of *Mixed Faith and Shared Feeling: Theater in Post-Reformation London*, co-published by the University of Pennsylvania Press and the Folger Shakespeare Library (2018). She is a co-editor of *Publicity and the Early Modern Stage* (2021). Her articles appear in academic journals such as

*Shakespeare* and *Shakespeare Studies*. With the director Eric Tucker, she is co-writer of the Shakespeare mash-up series *Bedlam*.

**Ina Habermann** is Professor of English Literature at the University of Basel, Switzerland. Her publications include *Staging Slander and Gender in Early Modern England* (2003) and *Myth, Memory and the Middlebrow: Priestley, du Maurier and the Symbolic Form of Englishness* (2010). She is co-editor of *Shakespeare and Space: Theatrical Explorations of the Spatial Paradigm* (2016), and her research focuses on early modern drama and theatre, middlebrow literature, gender, spatial studies and cultural topographies as well as Anglo-European Studies including Brexit. Her current research project deals with seventeenth- and eighteenth-century Anglo-Swiss relations.

**Jean E. Howard** is George Delacorte Professor in the Humanities at Columbia University where she teaches early modern literature, Shakespeare, feminist studies, and theatre history. Author of several books, including *The Stage and Social Struggle in Early Modern England* (2004); *Engendering a Nation: A Feminist Account of Shakespeare's English Histories* (1997), co-written with Phyllis Rackin; and *Theater of a City: The Places of London Comedy 1598–1642* (2007), she is also an editor of *The Norton Shakespeare* and the Bedford contextual editions of Shakespeare. Howard is completing a new book on the history play in twentieth- and twentieth-first century American and English theatre.

**Jesse M. Lander** is Associate Professor of English at the University of Notre Dame. The author of *Inventing Polemic: Religion, Print and Literary Culture in Early Modern England* (2006), he is currently working on a book about the history of emotions and the staging of the supernatural in Shakespeare's drama. In addition, he is interested in book history, textual theory and editing and has most recently co-edited, with John Tobin, The Arden Shakespeare, third series *King John* (2018).

**Courtney Lehmann** is the Tully Knoles Professor of the Humanities at University of the Pacific and the 2021 winner of the Phi Beta Kappa Excellence in Teaching Award. In addition to publishing more than forty articles and essays on Shakespeare on screen, she is the author of *Shakespeare Remains: Theater to Film, Early Modern to Postmodern* (2002) and *Screen Adaptations: Shakespeare's Romeo and Juliet* (2010), as well as co-author of *Great Shakespeareans: Welles, Kurosawa, Kozintsev, Zeffirelli* (2013). She has co-edited several collections of Shakespeare and screen criticism and currently serves on the editorial board of *Shakespeare Quarterly*.

**Jennifer A. Low**, Professor Emerita at Florida Atlantic University, is the author of *Manhood and the Duel: Masculinity in Early Modern Drama and Culture* (2003) and *Dramatic Spaces: Scenography and Spectatorial Perceptions* (2016), as well as co-editor (with Nova Myhill) of the essay collection *Imagining the Audience in Early Modern Drama 1558–1642* (2011). Her articles have been published in *Philological Quarterly, Comparative Drama, The Centennial Review* and *Poetics Today*. Her most recent essay, which concerns haptic experience and national identity in a recent Czech production of *Macbeth*, appears in *Shakespeare's Audiences* (2021).

**Gordon McMullan** is Professor of Shakespeare and Early Modern Literature at King's College London and Director of the London Shakespeare Centre. He is author of *The Politics of Unease in the Plays of John Fletcher* (1994), *Shakespeare and the Idea of Late Writing* (2007) and the collaborative monograph *Antipodal Shakespeare: Remembering and Forgetting in Britain, Australia and New Zealand, 1916–2016* (2018); and he is editor or co-editor of numerous collections of essays. He edited *Henry VIII* for the Arden Shakespeare (2000) and is a general editor of Arden Early Modern Drama and a general textual editor of the *Norton Shakespeare, 3E*, for which he edited two texts of *Romeo and Juliet*.

**Lucy Munro** is Professor of Shakespeare and Early Modern Literature at King's College London. She is author of *Children of the Queen's Revels: A Jacobean Theatre Repertory* (2005), *Archaic Style in Early Modern Literature, 1590–1674* (2013) and *Shakespeare in the Theatre: The King's Men* (2020), the editor of plays including Dekker, Ford and Rowley's *The Witch of Edmonton* (2016), and a co-investigator on the 'Before Shakespeare' and 'Engendering the Stage' projects. She is currently working on an edition of *The Insatiate Countess* for *The Complete Works of John Marston*.

**David Nicol** is an Associate Professor in the Fountain School of Performing Arts at Dalhousie University. He is the author of *Middleton and Rowley: Forms of Collaboration in the Jacobean Playhouse* (2012) and of numerous articles in *Cahiers Élisabéthains, Comparative Drama, Early Theatre, Medieval and Renaissance Drama in England, Notes and Queries, Shakespeare Bulletin* and *Studies in English Literature*. He is currently working on a scholarly edition of William Rowley's *All's Lost by Lust* for Digital Renaissance Editions.

**Karen Sawyer Marsalek** is Associate Professor of English at St Olaf College. She has contributed to the Queen's Men Editions and has published essays on early English medieval and early modern stagings of resurrection and dismembered bodies, most recently in *The Revenger's Tragedy: The State of Play* (2018). She is writing a book on remains and revenants in the repertory of the King's Men.

**Charlene V. Smith** is a director, actor, scholar and co-founder of Brave Spirits Theatre. She has an MLitt and MFA in Shakespeare and Performance from Mary Baldwin University. She is the head editor of *Rogue Shakespeare: Stagecraft and Scholarship in an Ensemble-Based MFA Company* and her article 'Margaret of Anjou: Shakespeare's Adapted Heroine' appears in *The Palgrave Handbook of Shakespeare's Queens* (2018). Her directing credits include the four plays of the Henriad, *The Changeling, 'Tis Pity She's a Whore, Coriolanus,*

*The Two Noble Kinsmen*, *Antony and Cleopatra*, *Richard III*, and co-directing the first professional modern production of *The Bloody Banquet*.

**Kelly Stage** is Associate Professor of English and Director of the Medieval and Renaissance Studies Program at the University of Nebraska-Lincoln. She is author of *Producing Early Modern London: A Comedy of Urban Space, 1598–1616* (2018) and editor of *The Roaring Girl* in *The Broadview Anthology of British Literature* (Vol. 2, 3rd ed, 2016) and in a stand-alone Babl edition (2019). She has published chapters in volumes such as *Hamlet: The State of Play* (2021) and *Representing the Plague in Early Modern England* (2011), as well as articles in *SEL: 1500–1900*, *Ben Jonson Journal*, and *English Literary Renaissance*.

**Katherine Schaap Williams** is Assistant Professor of English at the University of Toronto. Her work has been published in *ELH*, *English Studies*, *Disability Studies Quarterly*, *Early Theatre*, and in several edited collections, and she edited George Chapman, Ben Jonson, and John Marston's play *Eastward Ho* (1605) for *The Routledge Anthology of Early Modern Drama* (2020). She is the author of *Unfixable Forms: Disability, Performance, and the Early Modern English Theater* (2021).

# PREFACE

We are grateful to Ann Thompson and Lena Cowen Orlin for creating the 'State of Play' series, for their willingness to extend the series beyond the Shakespeare canon – a development pioneered by Gretchen E. Minton with a volume on another play in the Middleton canon, *The Revenger's Tragedy* – and for inviting us to edit the present volume. This collection, as with all 'State of Play' volumes, began life as a lively and engaged seminar, entitled 'The New *Changeling*', at the 2018 Shakespeare Association of America conference in Los Angeles, and we would like to thank all the contributors for their part in the seminar: Emma K. Atwood, Sarah Dustagheer, José Manuel González, Eric Griffin, Frances L. Helphinstine, Mark Kaethler, Karen Sawyer Marsalek, Avi Mendelson, David Nicol, Jamie Paris, Catherine L. Reedy, Gregory Schnitzpahn, Michael Slater and Katherine Schaap Williams. We would like especially to thank Suzanne Gossett for her participation in the seminar as a respondent: her generous readings of the papers and partnership with us were invaluable. This collection consists of a combination of essays developed from seminar papers and newly commissioned pieces that we felt would help express the direction of travel in *Changeling* criticism; some of the seminar papers, including those of Paris, Reedy, and Slater, have appeared in print elsewhere. We are hugely grateful to all of our contributors for the superb work they have done, both in writing their first drafts and in honing those drafts in the context of the collection as a whole – and above all for doing so in the immensely challenging circumstances of the Covid pandemic. Gordon wishes particularly to thank Kelly for coolly solo-chairing the supposedly co-chaired SAA seminar in 2018 when a combination of personal circumstances (family bereavement and a torn Achilles tendon) meant that he was unable to fly to LA. Kelly wishes particularly to thank Gordon for teaching her so much about assembling a collection, for his level-headed management skills and for his expertise and patience in steering a long-term project. We are grateful to everyone at Bloomsbury Arden, above all to Margaret Bartley who thought up this series in cahoots with Ann and Lena, to our commissioning editor Mark Dudgeon for his enthusiasm and patience, to Lara Bateman for responding cheerfully to our various queries, and to project manager Merv Honeywood and copy editor Judy Tither for their detailed attention to our typescript.

Throughout this collection we cite work in the Middleton canon from *Thomas Middleton: The Collected Works*, eds. Gary Taylor and John Lavagnino (Oxford: Oxford University Press, 2007) – above all, Douglas Bruster's edition of *The Changeling*. Shakespeare is cited from the relevant Arden Third Series edition. The situation for Rowley is inevitably less coherent: see individual chapters for details of editions cited.

We also refer throughout to the playhouse in which *The Changeling* received its first performances as the Cockpit/Phoenix. It began life in summer 1616 as the Cockpit, brought into existence by the actor and theatrical entrepreneur Christopher Beeston, but in March the following year it was badly damaged in a riot; reconstructed after this event, it seems to have been known interchangeably as the Cockpit or the Phoenix. (See Glynne Wickham, Herbert Berry and William Ingram, eds., *English Professional Theatre, 1530–1660*, 'Theatre in Europe, A Documentary History' (Cambridge: Cambridge University Press, 2000), 623–37.)

Pascale Drouet's essay appeared online, in an earlier, shorter form, in *Theta X – Folly and Politics*, eds. Richard Hillman and Pauline Ruberry-Blanc (Tours: Centre d'Études Supérieures de la Renaissance, 2013), 139–52: http://sceneeuropeenne.univ-tours.fr/theta/theta10. We are grateful to the editors for granting us permission to include a revised version of Pascale's essay in this collection.

# SERIES PREFACE

Arden Shakespeare
State of Play
Series editors: Lena Cowen Orlin and Ann Thompson

This series represents a collaboration between King's College London and Georgetown University. King's is the home of the London Shakespeare Centre and Georgetown is the home of the Shakespeare Association of America (SAA). Each volume in the series is an expedition to discover the 'state of play' with respect to specific works by Shakespeare. Our method is to convene a seminar at the annual convention of the SAA and see what it is that preoccupies scholars now. SAA seminars are enrolled through an open registration process that brings together academics from all stages of their careers. Participants prepare short papers that are circulated in advance and then discussed when the seminar convenes on conference weekend. From the papers submitted, the seminar leader selects a group for inclusion in a collection that aims to include fresh work by emerging voices and established scholars both. The general editors are grateful for the further collaboration of Bloomsbury Publishing, and especially our commissioning editors Margaret Bartley and Mark Dudgeon.

# Introduction

## *Gordon McMullan and Kelly Stage*

*The Changeling* is an unsettling play, haunted and haunting, that has transfixed audiences for centuries and continues to do so today, long after the vast bulk of its peers have been lost to view. It is generally held to be one of the finest tragedies of the early modern period, though one that is late enough in the era of English revenge tragedy to be parodically aware of its own generic status. Yet by way of the insistent parallels it establishes between its two plots – which normally in this collection we call 'castle plot' and 'hospital plot' – the play refuses to be solely a tragedy.[1] *The Changeling* demonstrates early modern drama's wilfully impure renegotiation of classical and vernacular models, and its embrace of hybrid dramatic technique is as significant as its generic complexity. Psychological relentlessness is perhaps its most familiar feature, but the unashamed stylization at certain key moments – the appearance of a 'medicine cabinet' that imbricates the history of science in the surveillance of women's sexuality is the most obvious, but not the only, such instance – ensures that any attempt to focus solely on psychology requires one to cut or ignore swathes of the play. The tense, taut and, in the end, disturbingly mutual relationship between two of the most prominent characters, Beatrice-Joanna and De Flores, dominates criticism of the play. Critics have understandably focused on these two characters and their sexual, pathological and theological co-destruction, which creates multiple displacements and dislocations in their private and public dealings. Yet the vortex of dysfunctional relationships imposed upon Isabella, Beatrice-Joanna's counterpart in the hospital plot, is equally expressive of social and cultural discomforts in its foregrounding of the domestic politics of coercion and of the sexual politics of the poetry of desire, demonstrated in Antonio and Franciscus' language in their attempts to seduce her. The essays here demonstrate, we believe, that critics must engage as fully with the hospital plot as with the castle plot to approach an adequate understanding of the play. In the co-dependence of the plots, the play provides a ferocious struggle between agency and inevitability that is both the apogee of early modern tragedy and evidence that the genre had already, by the early 1620s, consumed itself. It is to this savage, marvellous, challenging play that this collection attends.

The present volume's publication date falls a decade and a half after that of Gary Taylor and John Lavagnino's landmark 2007 *Thomas Middleton: The Collected Works* (referred to throughout as the *Oxford Middleton*), a major achievement that reassessed Middleton's *oeuvre* for the twenty-first century. It presented a comprehensive set of accessible modern-spelling editions of the works in the Middleton canon, situated the plays alongside his prose and other works, offered a thorough overview of a writing life and, in the process, educated critics and students alike in the remarkable range of Middleton's achievement. Works such as Suzanne Gossett's collection, *Thomas Middleton in Context,* have since followed, adding to the resurgence of critical interest in Middleton.[2] Nevertheless, *The Changeling* has not yet fully received its due. Turning back to this play at the current moment enables us, we believe, to address key developments not only in the study and teaching of one of the most frequently taught plays in the Middleton canon but in the understanding of late Jacobean theatre as a whole.

The *Oxford Middleton* also demonstrated the significance of collaboration in Middleton's career, something that is too often minimized in criticism but that increases the urgency of re-examining *The Changeling*. While Middleton's reputation underpins the *Oxford Middleton*, the fact remains that many of the 'Middleton' plays are not those of a 'solo' playwright but of 'Middleton and ...', underlining the porousness of the boundary between dramatists in an early modern London theatre industry that depended on creative cooperation and co-creation as much as on competition. As we reflect on *The Changeling*, we highlight Middleton's particularly close writing partnership with his near-exact contemporary, actor and playwright, William Rowley. Scholarly interest in collaboration by Middleton and Rowley, notably that of David Nicol, has unseated longstanding narratives about *The Changeling*'s dual plots and the presumed division of labour between the playwrights. As a result, several essays in this collection reassess the play's collaborative mix within their discussions.

Critical fields, especially in respect of frequently taught texts, tend to change at a more glacial pace than we might wish. In assembling this collection, we were keen to bring new developments and directions in the larger field of study to bear on *The Changeling*. To this end, we invited our contributors to address the play and its afterlife from a broad spectrum of current critical approaches to early modern drama, and we welcomed their reflections on the fullest range of imaginable futures for *Changeling* criticism. The essays thus express recent developments in early modern studies, exploring, for instance, Jacobean repertory, the relationship of actor (especially boy actors playing the women's roles) and audience, the implications of the 'spatial turn' and bringing into play new perspectives from disability studies and the history of the emotions. We conclude with a section that addresses the single biggest challenge, for contemporary criticism and performance, presented by *The Changeling*: its complex and unsettling representation of rape.

These approaches recognize that the critical imprint of the play over time has been considerable. There is a long history of close attention by critics to its language, structure and authorship, to its embeddedness in the politics of its Jacobean moment, to its alleged 'modernity' and to a wide range of relevant thematics. Certain essays stand out as landmarks. T.S. Eliot 'established Middleton's modern reputation' in a 1950 essay, arguing that it is 'an eternal tragedy [. . .] of the not naturally bad but irresponsible and undeveloped nature, caught in the consequences of its own action'; in 1960 Christopher Ricks outlined the symmetries of the play's verbal structure, demonstrating the double signification of several of the play's key repeated words ('blood', 'service', 'will', 'act', 'deed'); John Stachniewski, in a 1990 essay, demonstrated the centrality of the Calvinist mindset to the play's language and dramatic impetus, reading the play's obsession with the struggle between will and unconscious motivation as a precursor of psychoanalysis; a year later, Michael Neill showed the extent to which the play is a highly conscious reimagining of *Othello*; and in 1996 Marjorie Garber offered an explanation, magisterial in its playfulness, of the implications for patriarchal culture of Beatrice-Joanna's simulation of the symptoms required to pass Alsemero's virginity test.[3] Each of these is a virtuoso performance, and all are recommended to any reader wanting to develop a sense of the twentieth-century's approach to the play.

More recent interventions include Annabel Patterson's elegant introduction to Douglas Bruster's *Oxford Middleton* text and a series of incisive critical engagements with the play and its contexts by, among many others, Judith Haber, Carol Thomas Neely, Sara D. Luttfring, Tanya Pollard, Roberta Barker and David Nicol, Frances Dolan, Courtney Lehmann, Pascale Aebischer, Judith Haber, Kim Solga, Gordon McMullan, Nora J. Williams and Clare McManus, as well as essays by

Jay Zysk, Bradley Ryner and Jennifer Panek which rethink certain issues of embodiment, sexuality, marriage, performance and religion that were hallmarks of earlier phases in criticism of *The Changeling*.[4] Editions, including the New Mermaids of Joost Daalder and, later, Michael Neill as well as that of Douglas Bruster for the *Oxford Middleton,* have also served as important interventions for readers.[5] David Nicol's *Middleton & Rowley* directly addresses the collaborative nature of the play and throws down the gauntlet, challenging critics to embrace collaboration as a structure and avoid dismissing scenes thought to be Rowley's.[6] Most recently, Mark Hutchings' *The Changeling: A Critical Reader* has offered valuable contextualization of the play's textual, critical and performance history (Sara D. Luttfring, Jennifer Panek, Patricia A. Cahill), with a special nod to its engagement with Spanish contexts (Berta Cano-Echevarría), embodiment and religious representation on stage (Peter Womack), new directions in stage and film *Changelings* (Sarah Dustagheer, Nathalie Vienne-Guerrin) and teaching strategies and engagements (Nora J. Williams).[7]

The present collection engages with key debates about *The Changeling* both through reassessment of existing criticism and through new interventions. We set out to move definitively beyond two twentieth-century critical tendencies in particular: first, the treatment of Middleton as 'the early modern Ibsen', that is, as a naturalistic playwright primarily interested in psychology; and second, the dual tendency to ignore Rowley's share in the play and to focus on the castle plot. The relentless focus on Beatrice-Joanna and De Flores at the expense of the hospital plot has in our view been detrimental to the assessment of the play as a whole and of the complexity of the issues the plot raises. In reflecting on the state of the field, we note a general shift away from historical readings that begin with contemporary political intrigue, reading Beatrice-Joanna, for instance, in comparison with Frances Howard.[8] While we recognize the importance of these connections, and essays in this collection do note them, they also show that critics need not focus primarily on Beatrice-Joanna as doomed *provocateuse*. Several essays reconsider the way sexual violence and female agency have been treated in criticism of the play, shaking up the critical understanding of consent and especially rethinking the key parallel role of Isabella in the hospital plot. Several consider staging practices and theatre history to reimagine the role of the play's first audiences as well as the cultural challenges presented by performance of the play today, especially following the #MeToo movement.[9] Several offer meta-analyses of the nature and processes of performance, from the theatrical projection of a sense of place to the emergence of dramatic character from the practicalities of early modern theatre – from cue script to rehearsal to first performance – to the unveiling of the creative structures in the text that enabled boy actors playing women to develop their craft under the guidance of mentors.

This collection falls into six sections, each expressing what we believe to be, for the early twenty-first century, necessary perspectives on the play. We begin, building on the ongoing 'spatial turn' in criticism of early modern theatre, by addressing the play's locations, architectural, geographic and cultural. The collection opens with an essay by Jean E. Howard on the claustrophobic nature of *The Changeling*. She highlights the enclosed spaces that house the action, spaces that enclose further enclosed spaces within them, thereby, as Howard notes, working hand in glove with the nature of the Cockpit/Phoenix, the candlelit indoor playhouse in which the play was first performed. The theatrical space, in other words, echoed the experiences of confinement that the play plots. She argues that this 'heightened sense of confinement' underlines the 'systematic constraints differentially imposed on characters' movements within the fictional and actual stage spaces', observing that women and those incarcerated in the mental hospital are 'most subject to bodily surveillance and mobility constraint' (24). She suggests that Middleton and Rowley use theatrical space 'to expose the circumscriptions that limit how and when bodies move through space' (24), which – by aligning the audience's gaze with those of the violent spy-servants who seek to drive the action – in turn exposes the audience's implication in 'the dynamics of surveillance, confinement and abjection' (24–5) enacted on the stage before them.

Spatiality is similarly the focus of Ina Habermann's essay on 'worlding' in the play. Drawing on spatial theory, Karl Bühler's theory of language and Marie-Laure Ryan's literary critical applications, she uses 'worlding' to mean the deployment of dramatic strategies that turn the theatre space into a fictional world. 'Worlding' is especially acute in *The Changeling,* she argues, because the play 'emphasizes the creation of multiple worlds, both in terms of setting and the construction of characters' (43), thereby establishing 'a porous and precarious reality' (43) first hinted at in the frequency of asides and *double entendres* early in the play and sustained by the effort the playwrights put into the process of spatial orientation. This process is both extended and disrupted by the spatial shift that takes place in the hospital plot, in which 'the Mediterranean vanishes [...] to make room for London' (47), a shift made uncomfortable for members of the audience as they recognize that the dramatic location that is closest to 'home' is 'the mental hospital – a place where the inmates have taken leave of their reason and live in their own reality' (48). The spatial symbolism of the play derives substantially from its obsession 'with places that should be well defended and locked securely but are not' (52): Alicante's castle, the enemy already within; Alibius' mental hospital, already infiltrated by those who seek to make him a cuckold; Alsemero's cabinet, failing to keep the secrets of its science of surveillance; the marriage bed, occupied by servant not mistress; and, most disturbingly, 'the world of the living infiltrated by the ghosts of the dead' (53). The play's achievement is the extent to which it draws the audience into the shifting, betraying, multiple realities it creates.

The second section, 'Collaboration and the hospital plot', addresses the most critically neglected element of the play: the four scenes set in Alibius' mental hospital that run parallel to the story of Beatrice-Joanna, De Flores and Alsemero. A counter to the inexorably tragic castle plot, the hospital plot is technically comic – a particularly tense, uncomfortable version of comedy. This plot is Middleton and Rowley's invention – the play's primary source, John Reynolds' *Triumphs of God's Revenge,* provided them with the story only of the castle plot – and would have been, as Pascale Drouet underlines in this collection, highly topical for the first audiences, located in Bedlam Hospital in London as much as in the play's ostensible location, Alicante. Drouet details this most remarkable instance of plot counterpointing in early modern theatre, offering a series of unsettling parallels and contrasts with the castle plot that enrich a reading of the play, and – as should be clear in our aims – support the need for critics, and theatrical producers, to give the hospital plot its due.

David Nicol, as we have seen, has worked hardest to understand the collaborative nature of *The Changeling* and to ensure that it is no longer possible (*pace* the title of Marcus Thompson's film adaptation, *Middleton's Changeling*) that the play can be considered 'Middleton's' alone. As Nicol notes in his essay,

> [o]ften, [Rowley] is ignored; sometimes, he is blamed for aspects of the play that critics dislike; even when he is admired, it is typically not for his distinct contributions, but rather for his ability to merge with his collaborator into a joint figure known as 'Middleton and Rowley'. (62)

Yet Rowley too has an *oeuvre* – not as extensive as that of Middleton and not as straightforward to assess, but nonetheless a legacy that matters – and Nicol shows the difference it can make to our understanding of *The Changeling* to read it in relation to the other plays in which Rowley had a hand. In this instance, he turns to Rowley's *c.* 1619–20 tragedy, *All's Lost By Lust,* in which Spain is defeated by the invading Moors because the protagonist insists on opening a secret chamber within the fortress – believing that it contains treasure Spain needs to fund the war – but in fact reveals a set of devil figures who prophesy success for the Moors, with whom they are clearly associated in their blackness and their agency against Spain. Nicol finds in Rowley's plot a 'portrayal of Spain as a fortified castle [that] is closer to *The Changeling* than anything Middleton wrote about Spain, before or afterwards' (67), a comparison that aligns the enemies within Vermandero's fortress – his own daughter and his servant – with the Moors and devils of *All's Lost By Lust*. As Nicol notes, 'although no literal Moors appear in *The Changeling*, the racialized nature of the demonic imagery is still present', and his reading of racial politics chimes with Lucy Munro's account of aspects of racialized staging, later in the collection. Thus, new ways of understanding the play emerge when it is seen in its theatrical and repertorial contexts. It becomes clear that the central scenes of *The Changeling*'s castle plot are 'inspired by the central image in *All's Lost by Lust* of the castle whose self-destructive inhabitants have allowed hell to invade' (69). We thereby understand that the play's attitude to its Spanish location may be at least as much driven by Rowley as by Middleton, as has traditionally been supposed. In conclusion, Nicol turns the plays' key shared metaphor into an account of the collaboration that produced the play: 'If *The Changeling* is a castle, Rowley may be its hidden foundation, even if Middleton is more conspicuous to outward view' (72).

In a detailed reading of Rowley's hospital plot, Douglas Bruster offers the fullest account to date of the role of Isabella, assessing the five scenes in which she appears (silently in one) and – picking up on the wry phrase she uses in dialogue with the servant/clown/sexual-harasser figure Lollio, 'the pleasure of your Bedlam' – reading the plot as a harsh interrogation of theatrical pleasure. Isabella is assailed on all sides by men who desire her – two of Vermandero's staff, who have willingly incarcerated themselves to gain access to Alibius' jealously guarded young wife, and the foul-mouthed servant Lollio, whose desire to blackmail Isabella into sex places him in a direct parallel with De Flores in the castle plot. We might ask: will Isabella negotiate these assaults? Will she, like Beatrice-

Joanna, be blackmailed and raped by a servant? Will she be attracted to either of the young men who feign madness and accept incarceration to be near her and who both speak the conventional language of desire – though it is fiercely parodied in the play – familiar from early modern poetry? Will she stay loyal to her opportunistic and apparently unloving husband? Bruster works his way carefully through the plot, both teasing out the possibilities it offers and noting its various lacunae, not least the absence of information about what happens between Isabella's dismissal of Antonio and her bitter concluding critique of Alibius. Isabella's role is, he argues, teacherly. She seeks to educate the ignorant men with whom she shares her world in the vacuousness of their accepted conventions – the comic role of the old man who hides his young wife and is cuckolded regardless, the Petrarchan enactment of desire by wilfully abject young men – producing what Bruster acutely calls a 'rough seminar in desire' (92), one that functions, however, without the expectation that anything much will be learned.

The third section of this collection addresses 'states of mind' – that is, mentalities and passions – in the context both of the (mis)management of mental disability in the hospital plot and of the castle plot's disorientating refusal to allow the play's audience to retain ownership of their own emotions. Pascale Drouet extends the second section's emphasis on the hospital plot by outlining the local contexts in which the audience would have understood the depiction of Bedlam in the play, situating *The Changeling* by way of the English specificity of the hospital plot and of its repertory context – playwrights including Dekker, Fletcher and Webster also all dramatized Bethlehem Hospital. As she observes, the play's topicality at the time of first performance would be clear, above all, in its engagement with the mismanagement of Bedlam by its venal keeper, Helkiah Crooke. She outlines the long history of the mismanagement of the hospital, an unenlightening story of graft and callousness that played out over the period from Crooke's appointment in 1619 to his eventual dismissal by

Charles I in 1634. Drouet reads the scenes featuring Alibius and Lollio in light of the history of Crooke and his steward, noting the direct parallels with various aspects of Crooke's behaviour – the absenteeism of the keeper; the various forms of mistreatment of the patients, including undernourishment, repeated whippings and beatings; the transformation of Bedlam from hospital to theatre; the perversion of charitable practice – and analysing the playwrights' dramatization of the mental hospital for the dual purpose of entertainment and the critique of abusive practices.

The play's unforgiving depiction of the self-incarcerating would-be lovers in the hospital plot exposes the narrowness of the divide between passion and madness. Offering, like Drouet, an account that locates the play precisely in its historical moment, Jesse M. Lander turns our attention to the history of thought rather than of institutions. He examines the central role of the passions, rather than insanity per se, noting the intersections of the language of emotion with early modern philosophy and with theology – with what he calls 'a newly fashionable stoicism and a still dominant, but increasingly embattled, Calvinism' (116). He observes that the play's engagement with the former is apparent in scenes attributed both to Rowley and to Middleton, thus providing further collateral evidence for the closeness of the collaboration. For Lander, 'the play's insistence on instinct reveals that the evaluation of early modern emotions is frequently complicated by an entanglement with the supernatural or spiritual world' (117) – in other words, the play emphasizes the distinction between affections (rational emotions) and passions (inexplicable reactions) in a way that invokes both stoicism and Calvinism, undermining the former by way of the latter's foregrounding of the power of instinct and the uncomfortable proximity of the living and the dead in the play's world. Lander shows this proximity in the characterization of Tomazo, brother of Beatrice-Joanna's murdered fiancé Alonzo, and in the brief but 'sticky' appearance of Alonzo's ghost, a phenomenon that disrupts the mental frames of characters and audience alike and still unsettles audiences today, reminding us of the folly in our tendency to assume emotional universality across time.

In the fourth section, 'Disabilities', the contributors use methodologies drawn from critical disability studies to discuss the play's depiction of mental and physical states. Both examine questions of representation and of the dissembling of disability – within the narrative and without it – as well as the conceptual and physical implications of using prostheses as technological and theatrical devices. In so doing, both chapters also think more broadly about form, examining ways the hospital plot and the castle plot figure and disfigure each other. Karen Marsalek uses the tools of new materialist and disability studies to reimagine the play's physical, sexual and psychic obsession with possession through two of its key props: a leather glove and a severed finger. Examining the presence and circulation of these items on stage, Marsalek connects performances of the body and its parts with what she calls a 'system of prosthetic play' (140). In her analysis of these unique prostheses, she sees the play's characters – especially Alonzo's ghost – engaged in 'a previously unrecognized instance of "disability drag" that also structures the hospital plot of *The Changeling*' (140). In reading the gloves as a supplement, Marsalek gives Beatrice-Joanna another set of hands, rather than seeing the gloves as a vessel representing the woman's body and her violation by De Flores. The reading radically reconsiders Beatrice-Joanna's participation in her rapist's actions. In comparison, the prosthetic 'play' involved in Alonzo's severed finger – using a prosthetic to imagine absence – foregrounds the practice of 'dissembling disability'. The same premise links the castle plot to the hospital plot's patients, some of whom are imagined as disabled but all of whom are actors who dissemble. Marsalek traces the exchange of the props across the scenes and plots of the play, noting that the possession and display of hands, skin, glove and finger show the working relationship of the collaborative authors, supplemental and coextensive at once.

While Marsalek's approach brings together the two plots through the dissembling of disability, Katherine Schaap Williams reads *The Changeling*'s hospital plot specifically, and disability generally, alongside another play in the Middleton canon, *The Nice Valour* (1622). Taking on the hospital plot fully, Williams asks what it means to foreground a storyline about the supposed 'cur[ing]' of intellectual disability and mental illness. She asks what the play might 'teach us about the representation of disability in the early modern English theatre' (157)? The essay addresses *The Changeling* and *The Nice Valour* as a pair and deploys them to address madness and the early modern concept of the 'passionate' man. Williams argues that in *The Changeling* '[m]adness exceeds the dramatic character to become an aesthetic that changes the temporality of theatrical form and enables the play to experiment with performance that is not reducible to plot' (161). The chapter emphasizes 'form' that is 'out of form' (165), reading a version of 'form out of form' in the mutual construction of the two plots so as to 'challenge the assumptions that prioritize the narrative operations of plot or legibly predictive action as the primary criteria for theatrical form' (172).

The fifth section, 'Actor and audience in Jacobean performance', situates the play within the moment of its first performances so as to reconsider early modern spectatorship. While the two chapters that form this section examine different ways of 'seeing', both are concerned with certain structures of spectatorship, subjectivity, witness and judgement that concern audiences and actors both. Lucy Munro takes a deep dive into theatre history, entering obliquely by way of a description of the behaviour of boy actors in Lady Mary Wroth's *Urania* and proposing a new reading of *The Changeling* that imagines its boy actors, their relationship to their adult teachers and the staging of female subjectivity through the materials and practices of spectatorship. In her study of theatrical conventions and detailed history of theatre companies, Munro conjectures two likely actors for the roles of Isabella and Beatrice-Joanna. She goes on to examine structures in *The Changeling* that, she argues, 'suggest that its female roles were tailored to actors with varying degrees of experience or aptitude, and that the techniques that we often associate with the theatrical presentation of subjectivity, such as the aside, were carefully managed' (185). In her close attention to the construction of dialogue and action in the play – cue lines, exits and entrances, the exchange of query, repetition and response – Munro breaks down scenes to show that they inscribe the needs of apprentice actors and to demonstrate the conventions of gendered performance. She connects technique and practical performance to certain ways of engaging female spectators and representing female subjectivity, from the labyrinth to the medicine cabinet. As she notes, the actors 'create a series of subjectivity effects, moments at which their female characters are granted additional depth and complexity' (193), and she invites readers to understand gendered subjectivity through theatrical mediations.

Intensely focused on Beatrice-Joanna's final speech as a flashpoint, the next chapter explores the play through the practice of surveillance and individual performances of watching, on stage and in the audience. Jennifer Low considers the 'juridical positions' (197) of 'witness and jury member' and the conventions of 'gallows confessions', showing the play's reliance on the work of spectators (198). In attending to the early modern understanding of 'witness' and 'testimony', Low shows that 'when we ignore the overdetermined meaning of [witness], we may unintentionally conflate the legal witness with the judge or with watchers at an execution' (200). In clarifying the historical moment of the play – between what might be termed the medieval and the early modern senses of courtroom witnessing and judgement – the essay draws on the uncertainty of the individual's responsibility as witness, judge and jury in order to explore the 'conflation of legal and moral judgement' (200). Low highlights the play's persistent signifiers of surveillance throughout the performance and positions Beatrice-Joanna's final speech as comparable to a pre-execution plea, comparing the monologue to historical gallows speeches well known by 1622. However, she also calls attention to a theatrical conceit in the final act which invites the audience to reflect upon not just their judgement of Beatrice-Joanna's 'gallows' speech but also on what they have seen – witnessed – throughout the play to this point.

The sixth and final section, 'Rape and the female body in contemporary performance', brings the theatre history of *The Changeling* up to the present day and addresses the play's reassessment within certain cultural contexts of the late twentieth and early twenty-first centuries. These essays directly address the ways in which the play's deeply unsettling representation of rape has been negotiated in contemporary performance, both on stage and on screen. Courtney Lehmann's essay on film adaptations of *The Changeling* uses a framework that situates Gloria Anzaldúa's idea of '*la mestiza*' alongside Derrida's wry notion of the 'foreign' woman to address late twentieth- and early twenty-first-century film versions of the play and particularly their representation of the sexual violence at the play's core. She analyses three screen versions of *The Changeling* – those of Marcus Thompson (1998), Jay Stern (2006) and Sarah Harding (2009), the last of these relocating the action to contemporary Britain and to a context of service and arranged marriage within an affluent British Indian family. In each case, she addresses the production's dramatization of rape, examining how the films' depiction of 'extreme sexual violence [. . .] renders Beatrice-Joanna "a foreign woman" in her own body, consigning her to inhabit a "borderland"' in Gloria Anzaldúa's terms (218). She notes that all three films delete the hospital plot, reworking the centrality of discourses of insanity to that plot as the collective madness of a world wherein, in Judith Butler's terms, "what is female" is "what is injurable"' (219). In a series of precise readings of these films, Lehmann demonstrates the willing complicity of all three directors – not least, to her obvious regret, Harding – in burying the play's depiction of sexual violence, coercion and rape by making Beatrice-Joanna either responsible for or actually seeking her own degradation. None of these films comes out well from Lehmann's analysis as she demonstrates the extent to which Jacobean sexual politics is reworked through the deployment of a series of filmic tropes and traditions, each ensuring that the woman protagonist remains, in the composite sense she draws from Anzaldúa and Derrida, 'foreign'.

Musa Gurnis's and Charlene V. Smith's essay, in turn, discusses a 2018 American stage production of *The Changeling* by the Brave Spirits Theatre Company. The production was billed, and is discussed here, as a feminist re-vision of *The Changeling*, directed by Smith and with Gurnis, a cis woman, playing the role of De Flores. Born out of an especially tormented period of political and cultural fervour in the US – the flashpoint of the nomination of judge Brett Kavanagh to the US Supreme Court, despite accusations of sexual assault made against him by three women – the Brave Spirits team tapped into public outcry for their creative inspiration. The two argue that, despite the persistence of stagings that downplay the play's sexual violence, such as those Lehmann decries in film, the play nonetheless 'invites a feminist performance: it presents De Flores' misogyny as villainy and provides an incisive portrayal of the power dynamics of coercive rape as well as its psychological aftermath for survivors' (238). The two writers detail the production choices they made – including non-realistic staging choices and specific choreography – and they explain the rationale, arguing for the necessity of 'cultural translation' in creating contemporary performances of early modern plays (240). Gurnis and Smith detail the approach taken by the creative team in general and by Gurnis in particular, who radically refashioned De Flores as an unsympathetic 'incel'. In the choice to cast a woman in the role, Gurnis explains their desire to use Brechtian alienation that would give the audience a distanced perspective, allowing them to 'examine the dynamics of coercive rape' (244). More generally, she explains, 'the point of this characterization was not so much to target a specific subculture as to foreground an extreme example of the sexism that surrounds us in everyday life' (241–2). We have come a long way, obviously, from Munro's and Low's accounts of the play's very first performances, and we are reminded that the political and cultural resonances of any play that survives for centuries will necessarily modulate across time, finding new meanings in each new theatrical moment. Local specificity remains, in other words, vital for interpretation, now as much as then.

Together, the essays in this collection serve, we believe, to express the state of play in *Changeling* criticism at the present moment, opening up a series of new perspectives – from space to disability, from repertory to race – that we hope will have ongoing value for students and professional scholars alike. The contributors to this collection share an understanding that *The Changeling* is a play very firmly situated in its own moment historically and theatrically and that also speaks to the present moment. It is a play that requires us to confront a range of expectations of early modern drama, not least in respect of structural fundamentals including authorship, collaboration, genre, repertory and the modes and methods of performance in the early seventeenth century. We must also come to terms with the (perhaps surprising) similarities and the (at times jarring) differences between our own understanding and that of the play's first audiences in respect of certain questions that matter a great deal to us at the present time – rape, race, space, gender, sexuality, embodiment, disability both mental and physical – forcing us to confront some often unpalatable truths about human interactions across the centuries yet at the same time reminding us of the extraordinary ability of the best early modern plays to continue to probe, to challenge, to shock, to entertain and to keep us reimagining them for the moment we inhabit.

# Notes

1  The editors endorse the *Oxford Middleton*'s preferred terms 'castle plot' and 'hospital plot' for the play's two plotlines, agreeing that describing the hospital plot as a 'subplot'

represents a failure to acknowledge the sheer insistence of the counterpointing the playwrights achieve across both plots. Equally, we find the dated term 'madhouse plot' prejudiced and inappropriate. Where individual contributors have departed from this practice, they specify their reasons.

2   Suzanne Gossett, ed., *Middleton in Context* (Cambridge: Cambridge University Press, 2011).

3   T.S. Eliot, 'Thomas Middleton' in *Selected Essays,* 'New Edition' (New York: Harcourt Brace, 1950), 163, commented on by John Kerrigan in *Revenge Tragedy: Aeschylus to Armageddon* (Oxford: Clarendon Press, 1996), 48–9; Christopher Ricks, 'The Moral and Poetic Structure of *The Changeling*', *Essays in Criticism* 10.3 (1960): 290–306; John Stachniewski, 'Calvinist Psychology in Middleton's Tragedies', in R.V. Holdsworth (ed.), *Three Jacobean Revenge Tragedies: A Casebook* (Basingstoke: Macmillan, 1990), 226–47; Michael Neill, 'The Hidden Malady: Death, Discovery, and Indistinction in *The Changeling*', *Renaissance Drama* 22 (1991): 95–121; Marjorie Garber, 'The Insincerity of Women', in Margreta de Grazia, Maureen Quilligan and Peter Stallybrass (eds), *Subject and Object in Renaisance Culture* (Cambridge: Cambridge University Press, 1996), 349–68.

4   Judith Haber, '"I(t) Could Not Choose But Follow": Erotic Logic in *The Changeling*', *Representations* 81 (2003): 79–98; Carol Thomas Neely, *Distracted Subjects: Madness and Gender in Shakespeare and Early Modern Culture* (Ithaca, NY: Cornell University Press, 2004); Roberta Barker and David Nicol, 'Does Beatrice Joanna Have a Subtext?: *The Changeling* on the London Stage', *Early Modern Literary Studies* 10.1 (2004), 1–43; Annabel Patterson, 'Introduction' to *The Changeling*, in Gary Taylor and John Lavagnino (gen. eds), *Thomas Middleton: The Collected Works* (Oxford: Oxford University Press, 2007), 1632–6; Kim Solga, 'Playing *The Changeling* Architecturally', in *Violence Against Women in Early Modern Performance: Invisible Acts* (Basingstoke: Palgrave Macmillan, 2009), 56–76; Gordon McMullan, '*The Changeling* and the dynamics of ugliness', in Emma Smith and Garrett Sullivan (eds), *The Cambridge Companion to English Renaissance Tragedy* (Cambridge: Cambridge University Press, 2010), 222–35;

Bradley D. Ryner, 'Anxieties of Currency Exchange in Middleton and Rowley's *The Changeling*', in Julianne Vitullo and Diane Wolfthal (eds), *Money, Morality and Culture in Late Medieval and Early Modern Europe* (Aldershot: Ashgate, 2010), 109–25; Frances Dolan, 'Re-reading Rape in *The Changeling*', *Journal for Early Modern Cultural Studies* 11: 1 (2011): 4–29; Courtney Lehmann, 'Taking back the night: Hospitality in *The Changeling* on Film', *Shakespeare Bulletin* 29: 4 (2011): 591–604; Sara D. Luttfring, 'Bodily Narratives and the Politics of Virginity in *The Changeling* and the Essex Divorce', *Renaissance Drama* 39 (2011): 97–128; Tanya Pollard, 'Drugs, Remedies, Poisons, and the Theatre', in Gossett (ed.), *Thomas Middleton in Context*, 287–94; Pascale Aebischer, 'Bend it like Nagra: Mainstreaming *The Changeling* in Sarah Harding's *Compulsion*', in *Screening Early Modern Drama Beyond Shakespeare* (Cambridge: Cambridge University Press, 2013), 187–216; Jennifer Panek, 'Shame and Pleasure in *The Changeling*', *Renaissance Drama* 42.2 (2014): 191–215; Jay Zysk, 'Relics and Unreliable Bodies in *The Changeling*', *English Literary Renaissance* 45.3 (Autumn 2015): 400–24; Nora J. Williams, '"Cannot I keep That Secret?": Editing and Performing Asides in *The Changeling*', *Shakespeare Bulletin* 34. 1 (2016): 29–45; Clare McManus, '"Constant Changelings", Theatrical Form and Migration: Stage Travel in the Early 1620s', in Clare Jowitt and David McInnis (eds), *Travel and Drama in Early Modern England: The Journeying Play* (Cambridge: Cambridge University Press, 2018), 207–29.

5   Thomas Middleton and William Rowley, *The Changeling*, Joost Daalder (ed.), New Mermaids (London: A&C Black, 1990); Thomas Middleton and William Rowley, *The Changeling*, Michael Neill (ed.), revised ed., New Mermaids (London: Methuen Drama, 2019).

6   David Nicol, *Middleton & Rowley: Forms of Collaboration in the Jacobean Playhouse* (Toronto: University of Toronto Press, 2012).

7   Mark Hutchings (ed.), *The Changeling: A Critical Reader*, Arden Early Modern Drama Guides (London: Bloomsbury Arden Shakespeare, 2019).

8   The most determined attempt to locate the play in its specific historical moment is A.A. Bromham and Zara Bruzzi, *The*

*Changeling and the Years of Crisis, 1619–1624: A Hieroglyph of Britain* (London: Pinter, 1990).

9   The #MeToo movement was founded in 2006 as a social response to sexual abuse and sexual harassment, offering solidarity for women from all backgrounds who have experienced harassment, most frequently by a male colleague in the workplace. Organized mainly through social media, the movement became prominent online and in mainstream media in 2017 after a number of high-profile actresses described their experience of sexual harassment in the film industry.

# PART ONE

# Spaces and Places

# 1

# Space, Gender and the Rules of Movement in *The Changeling*

## Jean E. Howard

*The Changeling*'s opening scene evokes the sea and ocean voyages. Alsemero, a Valencian, has stopped at Alicante on his way to Malta but his intention is disrupted by the sight of the beautiful Beatrice-Joanna, daughter of Vermandero, the most prominent man in Alicante. Suddenly the onward journey is in doubt, its forward movement suspended. Jasperino, Alsemero's friend, assumes it will go forward and says: 'Come, the wind's fair with you, / You're like to have a swift and pleasant passage' (1.1.13–14), but Alsemero resists. While the exact location of the play's first encounter is not textually indicated, it occurs outside, somewhere between three key locations: the wharves from which the seamen have come to summon Alsemero to his ship, the church where Alsemero has just observed Beatrice-Joanna, and the fortress or citadel where Beatrice-Joanna and her father live. This space of encounter is one of possibility for certain characters. Some who move through it have choices about where they will go next; they could, for example, leave Alicante to pursue their lives as soldiers or merchants on the seas. Sexual attraction, however, draws Alsemero away from the port and toward the citadel, which Vermandero describes thus: 'Our citadels / Are placed conspicuous to outward view / On promonts' tops; but within are secrets' (1.1.167–9).

This looming citadel and the movements of those within it will be the focus of this essay. Critics of the play have often pointed to the slightly menacing nature of Vermandero's description, which suggests a gap between the easily perceived outward face of the fortress and the unreadable secrets hidden behind its walls.[1] I will argue that Vermandero's fortress and the house of madmen and fools that dominates the second plot are both presented as conspicuously *enclosed spaces* that hold other enclosed spaces nestled inside them. Both fortress and asylum stand in marked contrast to the open seas that represent the path not taken by Alsemero and his crew. I will suggest, further, that the sense of enclosure dictated by the play's emphasis on a rabbit warren of particularized rooms, many secured by locks and keys, is heightened for the audience by the play's first staging at the Cockpit/Phoenix theatre in Drury Lane, a small house with indoor lighting and a limited stage space. The physical space of this theatre invited spectators to be aware of how their own experience of the material playhouse mirrored the experiences of enclosure imposed on many of the play's characters. Finally, I will argue that this heightened sense of confinement draws attention to the systematic constraints differentially imposed on characters' movements within the fictional and actual stage spaces. Women and their incarcerated counterparts, the madmen and fools confined within the asylum, are most subject to bodily surveillance and mobility constraint. Ultimately, I will suggest that Middleton and Rowley's tragedy employs a radically critical dramaturgy that uses theatre space to expose the circumscriptions that limit how and when bodies move through space; I will also show how such dramaturgy challenges audiences to be critically aware of their paradoxical implication in the dynamics of surveillance, confinement and abjection apparent in the fictional world of Alicante.

## Vermandero's fortress and Alibius' asylum

As Kim Solga has suggested, Vermandero's castle 'sits queerly on the border between older, fortress-like feudal space and newer, elite Tudor structures that featured smaller rooms in "atomized" patterns with quite particular functions'.[2] On the one hand the castle is described several times as serving a protective function for Alicante, and Vermandero does not want the secrets of this fortification laid open to strangers. It is a sign of Alonzo de Piracquo's status as a welcome guest that De Flores is permitted to take him on a fatal tour of the 'full strength of the castle' (2.2.160). On the other hand, this fortress also resembles an elite house with a remarkable number of named rooms. Staged action occurs in some of these rooms; others are simply referred to in the dialogue. The most famous staged room is undoubtedly Alsemero's closet where in Act 4 Beatrice-Joanna tries out the virginity test on her waiting woman and where in Act 5 Beatrice-Joanna is imprisoned with De Flores before he kills them both. I will return to this closet repeatedly in what follows.[3]

Besides the physician's closet, Diaphanta also conducts Alsemero by a 'private way' (2.2.55) to an inner room that Beatrice-Joanna seems to control as her own private space.[4] Perhaps this is a lady's closet or cabinet parallel to Alsemero's closet. Diaphanta says to Alsemero that '[t]his place is my charge' (2.2.1), and she serves as doorkeeper, ushering in and out the love-besotted Alsemero who compares Diaphanta and women in her position as 'the ladies' cabinets' (2.2.6). This word can mean a chest for keeping valuables or secret items. Alsemero implies that Diaphanta keeps Beatrice-Joanna's sexual secrets. Certainly in this room Beatrice-Joanna attempts to keep secret from her father and husband-to-be the depth of her attraction to the visiting Valencian.[5] Here she meets Alsemero privately and, in all probability, embraces him.[6] The room, however, is less impregnable than either Beatrice-Joanna or her maid believes. Alsemero no sooner leaves than De Flores steps forward from behind the stage's centre curtain or one of the stage doors, or from the back of the upper playing area, to announce to the audience that he has seen all that has gone on and hopes to take advantage of Beatrice-Joanna's transgressive behaviour. Spying abounds both in the castle and in the asylum, making any notion of private space questionable.

There are other separately demarcated rooms referenced in Vermandero's castle. Much of 5.1, for example, is given over to speculation about what is happening between Alsemero and Diaphanta in Alsemero's bedroom. This room is never staged, but it is talked about incessantly as the site where the waiting woman disports herself in her mistress's place in the bridal bed. As this unseen off-stage scene unfolds, Beatrice-Joanna, in great distress, talks with De Flores in a room that might be either her own bedroom or the private room to which she had had Diaphanta usher Alsemero in 2.2. These two rooms may, in fact, be one and the same. Moreover, Beatrice-Joanna and De Flores hatch a scheme to light a fire in yet a third room, Diaphanta's 'chamber' (5.1.38), to which the waiting woman returns after being roused from sleep by cries of 'fire' and where she meets her death at De Flores' hands. This night-time scene (5.1) creates a sense of darkened, separate rooms, each vulnerable to discovery by prying, intrusive eyes or by the disloyalty of servants.

Finally, there are the more amorphously specified rooms in 'a back part of the house' (4.2.92) where Diaphanta and Jasperino held a private conference and from which space Jasperino heard – 'in the next room to me' (4.2.995) – the voices of De Flores and Beatrice-Joanna in conversation. Apparently, though the space of the inner castle is divided into many rooms with specific functions, their walls are porous, exposing private matters to public hearing just as De Flores and Beatrice-Joanna are exposed, later, to the prying eyes of Jasperino and Alsemero who see them in an apparently compromising posture in a 'prospect from the garden' (5.3.2).

All these locations, belonging as they do to the representation of Vermandero's castle as an elaborate elite dwelling, differ in purpose from the fortifications depicted in 3.1 when De Flores takes Alonzo on his tour of this 'most spacious and impregnable fort' (3.1.4). The pair go down a steep and narrow passage to a spot where they can view a sconce or small fortification within the warren of the castle's inner defences. It is here, in this claustrophobic secret passage, that De Flores kills Alonzo with a rapier hidden for that very purpose and then shoves the body down a drain or sewer.

Vermandero's fortress, then, is an imagined space with densely populated and carefully subdivided living spaces nestled within a foreboding set of battlements. The citadel is mirrored, spatially, by the divided spaces of Alibius' asylum. Characters speak several times of the two locked wards in which madmen and fools, respectively, are housed. In 3.3, Lollio, Alibius' assistant, suggests that the fools have their ward on the main stage and that the madmen are above, probably on the upper stage (see 3.3.126–8). Somewhere off-stage are Alibius' living quarters from which his wife, Isabella, emerges to observe and speak with her husband's charges. In both cases, the carefully delineated stage spaces are largely verbal creations. Characters speak of all the rooms enumerated above, creating a sense of them in greater or lesser detail. And yet these rooms are not evoked solely by verbal means but rely as well on the practical possibilities of the material stage at the Cockpit/Phoenix.

This theatre was, by the standards of the time, small, and this must be addressed in any account of how space was imagined and staged in the play.[7] When the Cockpit in Drury Lane at least partially burned down, it rose from the ashes as the Phoenix in 1618. Some scholars believe that Inigo Jones had a hand in its design, though there is not unanimity on this point.[8] It was at the Cockpit/Phoenix that *The Changeling* was first staged by the Lady Elizabeth's Servants in 1622. Using

Inigo Jones' drawings as a guide, Scott McMillin has estimated that such a theatre had a stage of only 350 square feet with seating for 500 to 700 spectators, one fourth of the number at the large open-air amphitheatres.[9] This stage extended into the audience, which surrounded the actors on three sides and featured an acting gallery above the main playing area, two doors at either side of the back of the stage, and a central curtained area. Unlike in the public theatres, everyone in the audience sat, just as they had done at earlier indoor theatres such as the Blackfriars, with some spectators probably sitting on stools on the stage, further reducing the size of the playing space and further increasing feelings of spatial constriction. In addition, unlike the outdoor theatres, the Phoenix would have been lit only by candles. The result would have been a more intimate theatre experience than at the Globe or the Fortune but also one with the potential to create feelings of enclosure and even claustrophobia, especially when coupled with *The Changeling's* insistent focus on the subdivided spaces of castle and asylum.[10]

Several further material aspects of the performance of *The Changeling* at the Cockpit/Phoenix contribute to its particular effects on an audience. One is the presence of a major prop: keys.[11] In the subplot, Lollio has keys which he flourishes repeatedly as he travels from ward to ward within the asylum, sometimes also brandishing a whip as he moves inmates, and sometimes Isabella, from one section of the house to another. Keys as props materially symbolize the characters' confined states, and Isabella twice protests to Lollio in 3.3 that he keeps her 'in a cage' (3.3.3) or 'pinfold' (3.3.8). Later, Lollio gives Isabella the keys to Alibius' wardrobe where she plucks out the clothing that will allow her to appear as a madwoman to her would-be lover, Antonio. Momentarily seeming to assert agency even in her imprisoned state, Isabella turns out to be doing patriarchy's work, fooling a would-be lover only to affirm her marriage to the jealous old Alibius.

Keys are equally significant in the main plot. The sense of the fortress in Alicante is partly created by the keys to the postern and other doors that De Flores must secure to open the inner fortifications for Alonzo. The most prominent keys, however, are those Alsemero has carelessly left dangling from the small room or study that houses his physician's materials. This allows Beatrice-Joanna to enter Alsemero's closet and discover his preoccupation with virginity tests. Later, having repossessed the keys, Alsemero uses them to lock Beatrice-Joanna in this same closet, where she is murdered by De Flores. People locked in enclosures is not only a metaphor in this play but a physical reality.

Perhaps most intriguing, however, is the effect of staging the main plot closet scenes in a theatre like the Cockpit/Phoenix. The theatre history debate about the presence of an inner acting area or discovery space behind a curtain at the centre of the back of the stage won't be resolved in this essay. While I assume that such a space existed, the argument that follows does not depend on this premise but, rather, focuses on the necessity for having some curtained space erected on the main stage to represent Alsemero's closet. This structure could easily have been built out from a central curtained area at the back of the stage. Inigo Jones' drawing of a private house stage indicates that a playhouse like the Cockpit/Phoenix would have had a fairly large central opening. This structure could also have been thrust out from one of the two flanking stage doors or simply been erected as a free-standing space near the tiring house wall.[12]

The most *effective* way to stage the closet, I think, would have been to have it extend out several feet beyond the central discovery area. Such a staging would have several benefits. First, it makes material – throughout the performance – the existence of a locked room meant to be foreclosed to those not invited in. Of course, as with so many other enclosed rooms in the play, this one proves porous. It is penetrated first in Act 4 by Beatrice-Joanna and Diaphanta and also by the prying eyes of the audience. In Act 5, both Beatrice-Joanna and De Flores are locked inside by Alsemero, changing his private study into a literal prison for criminals. The closet, then, is a key enclosed space, and its visual prominence would be underscored by having a curtained structure, sometimes open and sometimes closed, centrally positioned towards the back of the stage.

The second reason, however, for the staging I propose has to do with the complexity and importance of the action that occurs in that closet in Act 4. The space must include manuscripts, vials and equipment suggesting a physician's closet, and there must be room for Beatrice-Joanna and Diaphanta to converse together in full view of the audience. Most importantly, the audience must be able to observe the bodily actions by which Diaphanta proves her virginity after drinking from the bottle marked 'M': yawning, laughing and sneezing (4.1.45–50). The performance of these actions, each of which both opens the woman's facial orifices and also makes her the object of the viewer's gaze, depends for its effect on being clearly seen by everyone in the audience. It is a performative high point. If enacted in the discovery area alone, its riveting visuality would be blunted.

Moreover, when in Act 4 the curtains are first drawn back surrounding the on-stage closet, the audience would suddenly find its point of view aligned with that of patriarchal surveillance. Initially Beatrice-Joanna may appear transgressive as she invades her husband-to-be's locked closet, gaining knowledge she will need to survive the virginity test. This knowledge is important because virginity, or the appearance of virginity, secures the property value of a high-born woman in the marriage transactions arranged by her father. Beatrice-Joanna, however, fakes virginity, transgressively, if temporarily, eluding patriarchal surveillance of her sexuality.[13] Yet when Beatrice-Joanna turns the test on Diaphanta, her proxy, and watches her body for signs of the test's effects, she is herself temporarily taking on patriarchy's surveillance function, assessing the waiting woman's body for signs of its proper compliance with codes of pre-marital female virginity. The audience watches Beatrice-Joanna scrutinize Diaphanta while joining in that scrutiny; the audience's role as 'watcher' is suddenly highlighted and doubled. This moment encapsulates some of the central performative dynamics of *The Changeling:* its simultaneous emphasis on enclosure and exposure; its positing of impenetrable spaces and its revelations of impenetrability's impossibility; its tension between bold bodily self-assertion and enforced immobility and its insistence on the audience's role in closely observing the bodies before it.

The inter-imbrication of theatre audience and staged action is underscored at one other moment in the play through a highly atypical stage direction found at the beginning of Act 3: '(*In the Act time, De Flores hides a naked rapier*) (s.d. before 3.1)'.[14] De Flores does this in preparation for his eventual murder of Alonzo in the passage overlooking the inner fortifications of the castle. Intervals between acts, 'in the Act time,' were common in the private theatres, and were often the occasion for musical displays. During this interval, De Flores must have moved across the stage, perhaps among the gallants onstage who may have stood up at this pause in the stage action. This moment suggests several things: that actors and audience are intimately entangled in the Cockpit/Phoenix, sharing a limited space. It also suggests that De Flores as a character displays here an unusual and striking mobility which leads to the question: who can move freely through the rooms of Vermandero's citadel?

# The laws of movement: practised space

As has been hinted already, not everyone in Alicante moves through stage space with equal ease. Access to enclosed spaces is not equally distributed across the cast of characters; keys are given to some people and not to others; only certain groups are subject to spying and observation and their movements tracked and interrupted; escape from confinement is not an option for many, whether the 'pinfold' is the lunatic asylum or the marriage bed. How space is 'practised,' that is, turned to a social purpose, depends largely on who is attempting to act within that space.[15] To state the obvious first: un-incarcerated men, those not constrained by the labels of madmen or natural fools, move with the greatest freedom across the play's imagined spaces. Vermandero moves where he likes; grants access to other men, like Alsemero, to his castle; and has servants, like De Flores, whom he can command to move as he wishes to carry messages and do tasks within the castle space. Elite men also have the option to leave Alicante, as Alsemero might have done had he taken to his ships as the play opens. Even Tomaso de Piracquo, inquiring suspiciously after the disappearance of his brother, is not forbidden the freedom to move through the public spaces of Vermandero's citadel.

De Flores is an interesting case of male mobility, however, because as a servant to a high-ranking man, he is given privileges that come with his office, even though he himself would not in his own person be granted absolute freedom of movement. As Vermandero's retainer, for example, he obtains with ease the keys that let him into the castle's fortifications, just as Lollio has the keys to the locked doors in the asylum. As De Flores says to Alonzo: 'Yes, here are all the keys. I was afraid, my lord, / I'd wanted for the postern; this is it. / I've all, I've all, my lord' (3.1.1–3). His serviceability to Vermandero has given him intimate knowledge of all the back passages of the castle and a limited autonomy to move within them. He uses his knowledge and authority as a supposedly trustworthy servant, for example, not only to lure Alonzo to his death but to set fire to Diaphanta's chamber and then to rush there to 'scour the chimney' (5.1.89), in the process murdering the waiting woman. As is true in many domestic tragedies, to which genre *The Changeling* at least partly belongs, a servant can have enormous power to subvert as well as to confirm his master's authority.[16] Striving to access the forbidden space of the bridal bed, both Lollio and De Flores use their positions to attempt sexual liaisons with their master's wives and daughters, in one case successfully.

The great contrast to the mobility granted to elite male characters in *The Changeling*, and to some extent to resourceful servants, is the relative immobility imposed on the play's high-ranking women. To take the most obvious example, Beatrice-Joanna's movements are often dictated by her status as a virgin and a daughter of one of Alicante's leading families. She can go to church and is shown to have done so in the play's opening scene, but she is not able to meet Alsemero in a private space without subterfuge and danger. This becomes clear when De Flores is revealed to have spied on her meeting with Alsemero, gaining information that will help put her in his power. Some of the play's boldest physical acts, such as the murder of Alonzo in the bowels of the castle or Diaphanta's willing occupation of Alsemero's bed, put Beatrice-Joanna in positions of relative immobility. Because she is not a man, because she does not have the keys to the fortifications or training with weapons, and because she has had her virginity taken by De Flores, she can now only work through proxies to effect her ends, and each of these proxies thereby strengthens their control over her.

Beatrice-Joanna's own physical movements in the seemingly crowded castle are always dangerously subject to the eyes and ears of others. Her prominence makes her an object of endless observation. Tomazo de Piracquo observes every movement of her face and body, trying to discern the depth of her affection for his brother; Alsemero subjects her to a virginity test; Jasperino both eavesdrops and spies on her, reporting on her behaviour and her words with De Flores. Even when Beatrice-Joanna boldly enters her husband's closet, turning the key that he has carelessly left behind, she ends up subjecting another woman to the surveillance meant to be directed towards herself as she administers the virginity test. Part of the play's horrid fascination lies in watching Beatrice-Joanna vainly try to enhance her sphere of movement, if only through others, and to escape the forms of confinement, literal and symbolic, that the suffocating life of the castle imposes upon her as Vermandero's daughter. She ends up, of course, locked in the very closet she had once entered in an attempt to control her fate.

In the subplot, Isabella's movements are even more materially constrained, forbidden as she is by her husband even to be seen by the visitors who come to watch the patients in his asylum (1.2.52–7) and certainly not to step outside the house (3.3.1–22).[17] Within the asylum, she is largely dependent on Lollio, who holds the keys, to allow her to talk with inmates or move from ward to ward. And, like De Flores watching Beatrice-Joanna with Alsemero, Lollio spies on Isabella. When Lollio attends the madmen in an upper room, he looks down and sees Isabella speaking with, and kissing, Antonio, a nobleman disguised as a fool (3.3. 193–207). Isabella is better able to handle Lollio's subsequent requests for sex than Beatrice-Joanna is able to handle De Flores' similar demands, but she retains her married chastity at the price of remaining trapped both in a loveless marriage and inside the asylum. Ironically, as I have noted, Isabella does patriarchy's work of restraining female desire by disciplining whatever longing she herself has for freedom of movement and sexual expression. When momentarily given the key to Alibius' wardrobe, Isabella uses the opportunity to disguise herself as a madwoman and test Antonio's perspicacity as a lover. When he fails to recognize her beneath the disguise, she resumes her role as faithful wife to an old fool. In choosing not to leave Alibius, she also chooses not to leave the asylum. While she does not end up locked in a closet, she continues to endure conditions of mental, physical and sexual constriction.

Only the madmen and fools locked away in Alibius' establishment endure more obvious forms of confinement. They serve, I would argue, to render material the various constraints – physical, psychic, legal – under which all the play's subjected figures labour. When they are 'schooled' to dance at Alsemero and Beatrice-Joanna's marriage, their unfreedom extends to the very ways their bodies are allowed to move in space and not only to where they are allowed to go. Lollio assures Alibius that the inmates will behave as intended at the wedding solemnities 'as long as we are there with our commanding pizzles [whips]' (4.3.64–5). Answering to the whip, these coerced performers are an almost embarrassing literalization of the play's central kinetic trope – the hobbled mobility that deforms the lives of those lacking social power in Vermandero's castle. If in modern performance the inmates wear straitjackets, that would only drive home the point.

## The closet and the audience

The closet is the over-determined site where all the play's darkest undercurrents and themes come together. The return to the closet in 5.3 is an astonishing reprise of Beatrice-Joanna's first entrance to that space (4.1), but now she has lost all control of it. Her sexual relations with De Flores having been revealed by Jasperino and Alsemero's 'prospect from the garden' (5.3.2) and confirmed by Diaphanta before her death (5.3.55–6), Beatrice-Joanna is now reduced to the status of whore and prisoner. An enclosed arena, the closet now becomes a literal place of imprisonment, confining Beatrice-Joanna as the madmen and fools are confined in Alibius' asylum. The place where Beatrice-Joanna made her bid to control her fate now becomes the *ur*-site of enforced immobility.

The closet, however, is more than a prison; it is also a vanishing point, a site where sight is blocked. Beatrice-Joanna does not remain alone in the closet. When De Flores is confronted with her confession of adultery and of her role in Alonzo's death, he asks to join her in the closet. Crucially, exactly what happens in the closet is not revealed, only the consequence: De Flores' eventual emergence '*bringing in* BEATRICE, [*wounded*]' (s.d. following 5.3.142). Michael Neill has argued that *The Changeling* is strongly influenced by *Othello,* with Beatrice-Joanna playing the part of a fallen Desdemona and Iago's verbal denigration of Othello's wife turning to physical violence as De Flores first rapes Beatrice-Joanna and then, in the closet, stabs her. This is the act Othello could not bring himself to perform, instead strangling Desdemona in her bed.[18] But what else happens inside that closet, that black box on the playing stage, remains veiled. Through the folds of the curtain the audience can hear Beatrice-Joanna's voice crying 'O, O, O' (5.3.139) and again 'O, O!' (5.3.140). It is impossible to know whether these cries signal sexual consummation or bodily harm, pleasure or pain, or both. Through the folds of the curtain something can be heard, a cry whose meaning remains in doubt; but nothing can be seen. The secrets of the closet are not totally revealed, even when Beatrice-Joanna stumbles out, condemning herself and her poisoned blood, while De Flores speaks of the intense pleasure of their union. The closet, an enclosure within the enclosed space both of Vermandero's castle and of the Cockpit/Phoenix, does not entirely reveal its secrets, especially the meaning of the unseen events that led to the cry 'O, O, O'.

As I read the play, its revelation of the ever-narrowing sphere of Beatrice-Joanna's free movements makes possible a critique of the social conscriptions that bind her and Isabella, and also the so-called fools and madmen of Alicante who are their counterparts in subjection. This critique perhaps would have been most obvious to the women members of the audience.[19] The play shows Beatrice-Joanna to be both wilful and naïve, but her personal flaws pale beside the systemic male privilege that turns women into property and equates their worth with their intact hymens. It is a system, moreover, that turns women into self-policing conformists or rebels vulnerable to the agents and proxies upon whom they must depend for the illusion of freedom.

But what of the audience members who watch this final scene, particularly the women among them? Sitting in the galleries or on the tiny stage of the Cockpit/Phoenix, some women, I would argue, might well see themselves in Beatrice-Joanna and feel in the close confines of the Cockpit/Phoenix something of her confined state. The play's self-conscious manipulation of space thus invites sympathetic engagement with those within the fiction whose free movements are constrained. But, paradoxically, the play also puts audience members, including women, in the position of the watcher, the observer, the one who spies into the secrets of those struggling to elude surveillance. Often, the audience's gaze aligns with the eyes of Lollio, Jasperino and De Flores, servants all and spies, yet who temporarily elude their masters by subjecting others to their gaze and then to their whips, threats and sexual force. Male mastery passes down the class hierarchy. When the audience stares at the locked door of the closet in Act 5, it is positioned with those who spy upon and control women's actions and the movements of those deemed insane. The female audience members, in particular, thus experience the play's most difficult choice: to feel with the victims of surveillance or to align with those who derive their pleasure and their power from dominating them.

The final moments of the play are something of a test of audience sympathy. When Beatrice-Joanna staggers out of Alsemero's closet, the enclosed space of her body has been opened. Blood streams. A moralist would say her hot humours have been cooled, her infected blood purged. This is, in fact, what Beatrice-Joanna herself says as she asks that her poisonous blood be sluiced down the sewers of Alicante. That she has become a self-punishing subject, now less like Desdemona than like a female Othello, may say less about the justice of her self-imposed judgements than about the social pressures that make them, finally, seem inescapable. Surely there is a challenge to the audience in the sight of Beatrice's stilled body. Is this the end 'we' have desired?

# Notes

1  There is a rich critical literature on questions of space and of secrets in *The Changeling*. I have found particularly useful Bruce Boehrer, 'Alsemero's Closet: Privacy and Interiority in *The Changeling*', *The Journal of English and Germanic Philology*, 96.3 (1997): 349–68; Mariko Ichikawa, '"*Malvolio within*":

Acting on the Threshold between Onstage and Offstage Spaces', *Medieval and Renaissance Drama in England*, 18 (2005): 123–45; Joost Daalder, 'The Closet Drama in *The Changeling*, V.iii', *Modern Philology*, 89 (1991): 225–30; Lloyd Kermode, 'Experiencing the Space and Place of Early Modern Theater', *Journal of Medieval and Early Modern Studies*, 43 (2013): 1–24; Michael Neill, '"Hidden Malady": Death, Discovery, and Indistinction in *The Changeling*', *Renaissance Drama*, New Series 22 (1991): 95–121; Michelle O'Callaghan, *Thomas Middleton, Renaissance Dramatist* (Edinburgh: Edinburgh University Press, 2009), 132–53; Kim Solga, 'Playing *The Changeling* Architecturally', in Susan Bennett and Mary Polito (eds), *Performing Environments: Site-Specificity in Medieval and Early Modern English Drama* (London: Palgrave Macmillan, 2014), 56–76.

2 Solga, 'Playing *The Changeling* Architecturally', 59. The castle in *The Changeling* seems to be modelled on English architectural templates with little attempt to make it a Spanish edifice.

3 For a discussion of the role of the cabinet or closet in this play see Lucy Munro's essay, '*The Changeling*, The Boy Actor and Female Subjectivity,' in this volume.

4 Privacy is a fraught concept in the early modern period. A considerable literature focuses specifically on the closet as private in the sense of admitting circumscribed access. Alan Stewart speaks of the closet specifically as a non-public place of individual withdrawal often used to conduct business between a master and his secretary. See *Close Readers: Humanism and Sodomy in Early Modern England* (Princeton: Princeton University Press, 1997), esp. 161–87. Michelle O'Callaghan in *Thomas Middleton, Renaissance Dramatist*, 142, usefully reminds us that privacy in the period had a class valence in that only wealthier households could afford private rooms set off from more communal public rooms. I use the term in this essay to indicate spaces with limited access.

5 See Lena Orlin, *Locating Privacy in Tudor London* (Oxford: Oxford University Press, 2007), 296–7, for the idea that both men and women stored valuables in their closets or cabinets and used them for gatherings of intimates.

6 No original stage direction indicates that Alsemero and Beatrice-Joanna embrace or kiss, but at line 14 the *Oxford Middleton* editor Douglas Bruster inserts the stage direction [*They embrace.*] De Flores' subsequent comment that having watched Beatrice-Joanna with Alsemero he too will 'put in for one' (l. 60), that is, make a bid for her favours, suggests the couple have been engaging in sexually suggestive behaviour.

7 For a further account of the material affordances of this stage and their consequences for the audience's theatrical experience, see Jennifer Low's essay, 'Witnessing at the Phoenix: First Performances of *The Changeling*', in this volume.

8 Scott McMillin is one of the most judicious critics to take up the question of who designed the Cockpit/Phoenix. He is clear that the existing Inigo Jones drawing has not been directly linked to this theatre but still finds the drawing useful as suggesting how a small private theatre was laid out. See his discussion in 'Middleton's Theatres' in Gary Taylor and John Lavagnino (gen. eds), *Thomas Middleton: The Collected Works* (Oxford: Oxford University Press, 2007), 79–85.

9 Details concerning this theatre's features are taken from Scott McMillin's discussion, 81–3.

10 Boehrer in 'Alsemero's Closet' argues that the play is 'the most harrowingly claustrophobic of early English tragedies' (350). Boehrer's conclusions are based on the play's layered references to literal and figurative enclosures in which so many of the characters are entrapped. Michelle O'Callaghan in *Thomas Middleton, Renaissance Dramatist*, extends Boehrer's work by focusing also on the role played by the dim lighting and small playing area at the Phoenix.

11 On the role of keys in the play, see Boehrer, 'Alsemero's Closet', 351.

12 In her fascinating article, 'Beds on the Early Modern Stage', *Early Theatre* 19.2 (2016): 31–58, Leslie Thomson makes the case that beds were probably thrust out onto the main stage from the curtained space at the back of the stage or from one of the side doors. This is because actions played within the hypothetical discovery space could not easily be seen by the audience. By analogy, the closet in *The Changeling* would need to have been built out or shoved out from one of the openings at

the back of the stage for what went on within it to have been discernible. Thomson thinks the smallness of the Cockpit/ Phoenix may have let audiences see further into the discovery space than in larger theatres, but she does not take account of the dimness of the candle light in such a theatre nor the extent of the action that needed to be played there in the case of *The Changeling*.

13 In 'The Insincerity of Women', in Valeria Finucci and Regina Schwartz (eds), *Desire in the Renaissance: Psychoanalysis and Literature* (Princeton, NJ: Princeton University Press, 1994), 19–38. Marjorie Garber argues that attempts to police female sexual desire in the play are challenged by the possibility of the faked orgasm and by the inscrutability of female pleasure. I focus instead on the literal control of women's bodies and their vulnerability to sexual aggression as indicators of their subjected state.

14 For a discussion of this stage direction, see David Nicol, '"Exit at one door and enter at the other": The Fatal Re-Entrance in Jacobean Drama', *Shakespeare Bulletin* 37.2 (2019): 205–29.

15 For the idea of 'practised space', see Michel de Certeau, *The Practices of Everyday Life*, trans. Steven Rendall (Berkeley: University of California Press, 1984).

16 Consider the role of Michael in *Arden of Faversham*. He betrays his master, Arden, by joining with Mistress Arden in attempts to get Arden murdered. For the role of servants as what Fran Dolan calls 'dangerous familiars', see her discussion of *Arden of Faversham* in Chapter 2 of *Dangerous Familiars: Representations of Domestic Crime in England 1550–1700* (Ithaca, NY: Cornell University Press, 1994), 59–88. O'Callaghan, in *Thomas Middleton: Renaissance Dramatist*, 141, helpfully spotlights the important role of servants (Lollio, De Flores and Diaphanta) in household management and misrule in the play.

17 I agree with critics of the play who see the main and subplots as closely connected to one another rather than the separate creations of two authors who divided the work without paying much attention to how the one plot mirrors and intensifies the other. For a good discussion of the interconnections between the two plots see O'Callaghan, in *Thomas Middleton: Renaissance*

*Dramatist,* esp. 132–8, and Heather Hirschfeld, *Joint Enterprises: Collaborative Drama and the Institutionalization of English Renaissance Theater* (Amherst: University of Massachusetts Press, 2004), esp. 104.

18 De Flores' 'deflowering' of Beatrice-Joanna has in my opinion all the marks of a forced sex act. Beatrice-Joanna at first cannot comprehend the sexual demand De Flores is making of her and then begs him not to enforce that demand. When, as he takes her off to bed, he says, "Las, how the turtle pants!' (3.4.173), I read this less as a sign of her repressed desire and more as a sign of her fear. That Beatrice-Joanna comes to feel gratitude to the man who raped her for his preservation of her public honour in no way erases the forced nature of their first sexual encounter.

19 In *The Stage and Social Struggle in Early Modern England* (London: Routledge, 1994), esp. 74–93, I made the argument that the presence of women in the early modern theatre audience undoubtedly affected the kinds of plays produced for that theatre. I think that *The Changeling* was one such play, focused as it is on anatomizing with acute self-consciousness the spatial parameters informing and shaping women's lives.

# 2

# Chang(el)ing Spaces

## Dramatic Forms of Worlding in Late Jacobean England

### *Ina Habermann*

In her introduction to Douglas Bruster's edition of *The Changeling* in the *Oxford Middleton*, Annabel Patterson outlines various contemporary political subtexts to the play: an anti-Spanish and anti-Catholic agenda, a ridiculing of Prince Charles's misguided trip to Spain to woo the Spanish Infanta, the theatre company's loyalty to Elizabeth, Queen of Bohemia, the scandalous case of Frances Howard, Countess of Essex, who obtained a divorce in order to marry Robert Carr and the couple's later implication in the murder of Sir Thomas Overbury. All these topical allusions are no doubt crucial to the play's contemporary reception and may have suggested plot elements such as the virginity test, the bed trick and the murder of an inconvenient partner. Patterson also insists, however, that the play works, 'both on the page and on the stage', quite independently of these topical allusions, due to its 'ethical undecidability'.[1] In this essay I will explore why and how the play 'works' on stage, suggesting that an answer lies in *The Changeling*'s specific dramatic structure and deployment of theatrical space. To a certain extent, early modern drama always engages in 'worlding', employing dramatic and performative strategies that turn the theatrical space into a fictional world inhabited by the characters of the story. Jacobean tragedy often conjures up a teeming, corrupt, treacherous and dangerously shape-shifting world, staged both manifestly in the London playhouse and, in a phantasmagoric mode, on the stage of the mind. *The Changeling* is a particularly interesting case, however, because it emphasizes the creation of multiple worlds, both in terms of setting and the construction of characters. The first inkling one can get of this multiplicity is the play's conspicuous deployment of asides and *double entendres* that reveal a porous and precarious reality. Due to this erosion of (linguistic and social) common ground, the multiple 'possible worlds' that the characters inhabit cannot be accommodated in one coherent world. The play's possible worlds respond to an actual world so fundamentally fractured, mirroring the political climate of late Jacobean England, that the play's tragicomic potential, expressed in the hope that can be glimpsed from the characters' worlds filled with love, devotion, desire, fantasy and laughter, threatens to turn to sorrow multiplied.

## Theatrical spaces and possible worlds

Early modern theatre is, as Russell West puts it, an 'ostentatiously spatial art form', which concerns the actual playhouses situated in London as much as the dramatic settings and considerations of performance.[2] In *Shakespeare and Space*, Michelle Witen and I have argued that the early modern stage can be seen as a topological 'node', an interface that allows different temporal and spatial dimensions to merge and morph into each other, thus creating a theatrical experience where multiple dimensions of space – geographical, topographical, topological, mythical, eschatological, social, material/physical, psychological and performative/aesthetic – become entangled with each other.[3] Middleton and Rowley's tragedy is a perfect example of this ostentatious spatiality in the way it simultaneously embodies and anatomizes its late Jacobean world. The question is how exactly this is done, how entire worlds can unfold on the 'cockpits' of the early modern stage.

In his influential theory of language, Karl Bühler explains the relation between the deictic and symbolic fields of language, arguing for the existence and the importance of what he calls imagination-oriented deixis (*Deixis am Phantasma*). Generally, that is, when we show someone a place, we can point to the features we wish to draw attention to, whereas when an absent scene is evoked in language, we also see it, in front of the mind's eye, as it were, oriented towards something absent that exists in memory or even pure fantasy, while still making use of the natural deictic clues. As Bühler explains,

> the speaker and hearer of a visual description of something absent possess the same talent and resources that permit the actor on the stage to make present something that is absent, and which permit the audience to interpret what is presented on the stage as a mimesis of something absent.[4]

A spatial displacement occurs, but 'topomnestic' orientation is still possible via vectors in space, since '[t]he orientation field of the situation of present perception is exploited in all cases', and we notice 'the uncommonly easy translatability of all field values of the spatial orientation system and the linguistic deictic system from one orientation table to another'.[5] The same holds true, in fact, for temporal shifts that function in analogy to the spatial. Spatial contingency thus becomes transformed into a spatial imaginary. The necessary displacements are mainly of two kinds: the first is a *narrative* mode where the listener, reader or spectator is displaced or projected into, and thus mentally situated in, the geographical location that is imagined. The second is a *dramatic*, or theatrical mode, where the imaginary is conjured into the given order of actual perception; as Bühler puts it, 'what is absent is summoned into the present space *as in drama*' (157; italics in original). This is a crucial distinction, since in the theatre we usually do not close our eyes and allow a narrator to whisk us away in the imagination, but we accept that 'here' is now supposed to be, say, Alicante, as we invite the spatio-temporal fiction into our physical space. Ultimately, in terms of cognitive psychology, this is the basis for the ubiquitous analogy between stage and world: the stage can become a world or even contain, as I will argue with respect to *The Changeling*, multiple possible worlds.

For my discussion of possible worlds, I take my cue from Marie-Laure Ryan, who began to apply the philosophical theory of possible worlds to literary theory in the early 1990s.[6] Ryan distinguishes two main positions in possible worlds theory, the first of which grants to the actual world, where we are located, an ontologically different status, while the second position holds that the actual world has the same reality as other possible worlds and is not privileged in a modal universe – all worlds are real, while only one is actual. In Nelson Goodman's influential and radical reading to which Ryan also refers, there are even multiple competing versions of reality conceptualized as different worlds, complicating any notion of a consensual actual world.[7] Moreover, in fictions, as we apply imagination-oriented deixis, we also follow what Ryan calls the 'principle of minimal departure'.[8] If geographical and cultural references are skilfully deployed, audience members will unconsciously cooperate to enrich the setting. In *The Changeling*, both in what I will call the 'Alicante' and the 'Bedlam' settings (departing from the usual practice in this volume), audiences fill the gaps in representation with what they know from their own actual worlds, which comprises actual geographical markers as well as contemporary political resonances including the London audiences' sentiments about Spain. Thus, thinking about *The Changeling* in terms of multiple possible worlds helps us to understand how the play speaks to its audiences without assuming a naïve realism or treating the play as gruesome spectacle or one-dimensional political allegory. If we want to explore its working mechanisms more deeply, we need to follow the spatial clues that lead us to the play's specific forms of worlding.

# Setting the scene(s)

From the start, the authors of *The Changeling* go out of their way to facilitate spatial orientation. As Alsemero ponders the significance of his repeated encounter with a woman (who turns out to be Beatrice-Joanna) in 'the temple', or church, he also utters the word 'imaginary' in line 3, thus setting the keynote for the whole play's imagination-oriented deixis. The opening scene plays with spatial orientation – 'Oh sir, are you here?' (1.1.13); 'What, for Malta?' (1.1.16); 'The seamen call' (1.1.46); 'We might have come by the carriers from Valencia' (1.1.87–8); 'He's [De Flores] out of his place then now' (1.1.136), and finally 'with us in Alicante' (1.1.209). Along with this, and noting in passing that the play's villain De Flores is perceived as 'out of place' from the very start, there is a constant emphasis on perception. Beatrice-Joanna argues that '[o]ur eyes are sentinels unto our judgements, / And should give certain judgement what they see; / But they are rash sometimes' (1.1.73–5). She also asserts that some absent things can be seen in darkness, with 'intellectual eyesight' (2.1.19), and Alsemero elaborates on his view that beauty, or even the very nature of a thing, is in the eye of the beholder (1.1.116–26). Beyond this emphasis on seeing, both actually and with the eyes of the mind, the play constantly evokes physical and tactile sensations that do not easily allow audience members to forget about their own bodies present in the playhouse, and that would also affect readers.[9] Prepared in this way, the audience accepts that 'here' is a place close to Valencia from whence it is possible to reach Malta by boat, a place eventually identified as 'Alicante'. Thus, the London stage has turned into the Mediterranean, with much mention of auspicious winds, good conditions for sea voyages, seamen calling, boarding of trunks, etc. For English audiences, this would potentially be enemy territory, and it is still doubtful at the outset whether access can be granted to '[o]ur citadels' (1.1.166).

The initial scene is then balanced symmetrically with the second of the first act, introducing the hospital plot. Tellingly, the keeper is called 'Alibius', which is Latin for 'being in another place, elsewhere'. Spatial references are now exclusively English, or even specific to London – 'the town and country' (1.2.9); 'constable' (1.2.130); 'headborough, beadle, or watchman' (1.2.132-3); 'a sergeant, a jailer, and a beadle' (1.2.175); 'pillory' (1.2.204); 'chimes of Bedlam' (1.2.210), down to the name Antonio, which becomes 'Tony'. Spatial orientation thus receives a jolt – the Mediterranean vanishes in the second scene to make room for London. In theory, as regards the logic of the story, Alibius' asylum is of course located in the same city mentioned in the first scene, but the imagination-oriented deixis calls up London. From the very start, therefore, *The Changeling* introduces a split between worlds, preparing the audience for abrupt changes of scene and the existence of multiple possible worlds, which begs the question about the possible relations, and perhaps the unbridgeable gaps, between these worlds.[10] To a certain extent, the split may have been suggested to the authors by John Reynolds' source story, where Alsemero and Beatrice-Joanna live in Valencia after their marriage, De Flores coming from Alicante to visit her when her husband is away. Moreover, in Reynolds' 'histories', history V, which succeeds the source story of *The Changeling*, focuses on a man named Alibius, who murders his wife Merilla. The story is set in Venetian territory near Brescia.[11] In *The Changeling*, the split is rendered disturbing by the fact that the world which audience members are likely to recognize as closer to 'home' is the mental hospital – a place where the inmates have taken leave of their reason and live in their own reality.

The connection between the two plot lines is tenuous (see David Nicol's essay in this volume), which to my mind is deliberate. Much emphasis has been placed in criticism on the parallels, in terms of topics and imagery, between the two plots and, in recent years, under the influence of the *Oxford Middleton*, this has been generically related to the Jacobean court masque, the introduction of the antimasque and the resulting vogue for inset masques in plays. Caroline Baird presents an intricate argument about Middleton's use of the masque, arguing that 'Middleton "deconstructs" masque dramaturgy, confidently using its components and conventions to distil a play's themes. At the same time, by subverting the very device used to represent the court to the world, he subtly satirizes king and court.'[12] The two plot lines do of course speak to each other, and Baird's generic approach offers a neat and seamless reading of Jacobean tragedy's critical subversion of court culture. It may even be a reading that the authors invite, even if they cover their tracks enough not to lay themselves open to charges of high treason.

Yet I consider it important that the Alicante and the Bedlam plot are at the same time kept so carefully apart. While we see the fools and madmen rehearsing, they do not actually appear at the wedding, and Antonio and Franciscus' return is not crucial in any way to the resolution of the murder mystery. Cutting the Bedlam plot entirely, however, as has happened in performances of *The Changeling*, seriously damages the play, since it *partially* blends Alicante and London on stage, and in the minds of audiences, only to emphasize the split. This effect can be grasped more clearly perhaps when the play is contrasted with Shakespeare's *The Tempest*, where it is not possible to locate the island seamlessly in geographical terms: references to the Mediterranean and the 'New World' are blended in such a way as to produce an imaginary third space that becomes the setting for recognition and reconciliation. Although this full blending does not happen in *The Changeling*, both settings are indispensable to the play's spatial logic, and cutting the Bedlam plot produces a truncated domestic tragedy shorn of its expert performative spatiality. The insistence on multiple worlds suggests that Middleton and Rowley are on to something much more radical than just a veiled critique of the Stuart court. Once the play's strategy of deliberately fractured worlding is understood, we can also dispense with critical arguments that have been advanced about a possibly missing wedding masque scene or the substitution of the somewhat old-fashioned device of the dumb show for such a masque. In *The Changeling*, the madmen dance where they belong – in Bedlam, not in Alicante.

# Fractured worlds

As a next step, it is necessary to see that the two worlds that *The Changeling* conjures up on the stage are inhabited by characters who are also subject to conspicuous theatrical worlding. Generally, if the characters' imagination-oriented deixis seamlessly coincides with the setting, they appear very much 'at home', and the more it differs, the more they appear out of sync with their environment. In *The Changeling*, there is very little common ground, and through the split described above, the incongruence gains an ontological dimension. At the very beginning, before the setting is even established, the first place evoked by Alsemero is the 'temple', from whence he has just returned, and the 'place blest' (1.1.8), the garden of Eden. This introduces a chain of metaphysical spatial images whose trajectory in the tragedy tends towards hell, thus establishing an eschatological frame, one that does not, however, hold all characters equally.

As Ryan argues, fictions contain multiple private worlds of characters – 'wish worlds, obligation worlds, belief worlds, intention worlds (goals and plans), mock-belief worlds [. . .] and fantasy worlds'.[13] Alsemero's world is absolute; he has changed the single-minded pursuit of business and travel for equally single-minded wooing. He lives in a chivalric world of honourable men, who settle their disputes by combat, and virtuous, virginal women. This warps his judgement and ultimately makes him unsympathetic, as when, still enveloped in the raptures of his wedding night, he cares less that Diaphanta has died than that his sweetheart might catch cold. The grim joke is on him, of course, since the audience knows that it is the woman who has caused his raptures who has burnt to death. Alonzo, Beatrice-Joanna's first fiancé, is equally single-minded, with his brother Tomazo acting as his suspicious, Machiavellian, if misguided, counterpart. Vermandero, the patriarch and military veteran, shares Alsemero's chivalric ideal, though being of the older generation, he also lives in a world of memory, where good friends and lost children are still living, and his hold on the present is tenuous. Diaphanta is focused on upward mobility and pleasure, for which she pays dearly. Beatrice-Joanna – who, incidentally, is mostly addressed as 'lady' or 'Joanna' in the play, although she is 'Beatrice' in print and her full, double name is only mentioned twice – inhabits a world where she has agency. Reflecting on her own wishes and desires, and overestimating the lady's status in a chivalric frame, she hopes that she can actively achieve the desired outcome, if only through indirect influence, since as a young woman in an intensely patriarchal society she actually has no power to command.[14] Disregarding the limitations of her sex, she dares to wish and to change her mind. This attitude makes her responsive to De Flores who, appearing to confirm her world view, offers himself to her as an efficient and direct instrument of service that will make her wishes come true.

This raises the question of whose tragedy *The Changeling* actually is. Beatrice-Joanna certainly counts among the multiple candidates for 'the changeling': displaying fickleness in affection, and with a changeable name that suggests how women have come down in the world from Dante's Beatrice to brazenness and morally tainted (sexual) activity, she becomes a woman killed with kindness, changed from an almost jubilant independence and self-assertion to a party in a sado-masochistic relationship. *The Changeling* thus casts a cold eye on gender relations within a chivalric framework, revealing its underlying hypocrisy and violence. De Flores, 'up to the chin in heaven' (2.2.79), inhabits a world completely ruled by his obsession with his 'lady'. If his goal had just been, true to his name, to take her virginity, then his interest should have vanished with her changed condition, which is clearly not the case. Instead, he fully inhabits his passion and seeks 'continuance', which might well make him more attractive to Beatrice-Joanna than Alonzo, whose 'blessing / Is only mine, as I regard his name, / Else it goes from me, and turns head against me, / Transformed into a curse' (2.1.20–3). But passion is unruly and shot through with madness.

Meanwhile in London, Alibius, keeper of madmen and fools, is himself locked into a kind of madness through his jealousy – a predicament that, in Reynolds' source story, particularly afflicts Alsemero. This misogynist world view makes him incautiously rely on the completely self-centred and self-serving Lollio. The name Lollio suggests Marcus Lollius (55–2 BC) who, under the Roman emperor Augustus, was a provincial governor, consecutively, of Galatia, Macedonia and Gaul, where his legions were defeated by Germanic tribes. The character's name thus introduces a critical subtext about imperial Rome, perhaps designed to direct more educated audience members to a reflection about Stuart absolutism. Apparently, while being a capable politician and governor, Lollius exploited the provinces under his stewardship and took bribes, which would chime with the known behaviour of the keeper of Bedlam Helkiah Crooke and his steward (see Pascale Drouet's chapter in this volume). In Horace's Ode 9 of Book 4, Lollius is praised as a revenger of greedy fraud, a man of honour and wisdom. This ambivalence, traced back to deep historical space, suggests that the world of service has always been apt to produce deluded masters and self-serving stewards. Both De Flores and Lollio are smooth operators who have perverted the idea of service, but in their respective worlds they are still the heroes of their own tales. De Flores is thus insulated from the potential horror of the appearance of Alonzo's ghost; he does not manage more than a nod to Hamlet's or Macbeth's deep affliction: ''Twas but a mist of conscience. All's clear again' (5.1.60). It is as if every character is floating about in their own bubble, like the madmen, who, in Isabella's words, 'act their fantasies in any shapes / Suiting their present thoughts. [. . .] Sometimes they imitate the beasts and birds, / Singing, or howling, braying, barking; all / As their wild fancies prompt 'em' (3.3.210–15). Antonio, determined to 'tread the Galaxia to my star' (3.3.150), is also pretty far out, and Franciscus has made his own mad bubble out of a mythological world with multiple references to classical mythology. Conjuring such figures as Titania, Oberon and Tiresias, he argues for the transformative power of love, also urging the nexus of poetry, love and intoxication that Anacreon stood for in the early modern period. There is mention of Juno, 'big-bellied' (3.3.87) Luna, Hecate and the 'witches of the night' (3.3.92) – references that recall educated and refined court culture as well as the world of Shakespeare's romantic comedies, once expansive, spiritual and redemptive and now resignified as the ravings of a madman. And just in case one might think of exchanging this classical, mythological world for the modern world of science and empiricism, Alsemero's experimental machinery is ironically wiped out – not even because it intrinsically does not work, but because human beings will always find ways to fake it and to abuse and misapply the scientific apparatus. All this does not, by any stretch of the imagination, add up to a coherent world view that would enable true communication.

# Space tricks and mousetraps

*The Changeling*'s theatrical worlding is accompanied by an intricate spatial symbolism. The play is obsessed with places that should be well defended and locked securely but are not: Vermandero's castle, with the enemy already within and, halfway through the play, a corpse in the vault; Alibius' closed asylum, infiltrated by disguised gallants with easy access to the jealously guarded Isabella; the world of the living infiltrated by the ghosts of the dead; the ineffectual closet failing to keep alchemical secrets and to restrain culprits; and the bed, that should be, but is not, the most private retreat and sanctuary of virtue (see Jean Howard's essay in this volume). All these places are metonymically organized towards the ultimate enclosed space, the woman's 'mouse-hole' (3.3.91) that should be inviolate but is not. De Flores violates both Alonzo's and Beatrice-Joanna's bodily integrity, doubly in the woman's case, driven by a desire for upward mobility in a social space fractured by inequalities of class and, importantly, of gender at a time when the popular controversy over women was raging and the Frances Howard case was in people's minds. But ultimately, such rational, political explanations do not do justice to the play. Instead, the trope of madness is key to exploring the characters' solipsism expressed spatially in a radical form of worlding. Throughout, like a diamond hit by light, the play radiates striking scenic images that foster 'intellectual eyesight' (2.1.19) and extend potentially threatening agency to the material world, as in De Flores' description of ugly people who are still beautiful in the eyes of their lovers – 'Here and there five hairs, whispering in a corner, / As if they grew in fear one of another' (2.1.41–2) – or in uncanny suggestions of the material world's independent agency: 'the place itself e'er since / Has crying been for vengeance' (5.3.72–3). Perception, thought and feeling are radically spatialized as Middleton and Rowley employ imagination-oriented deixis to show us around the inner, psychic worlds of their characters in a way that is disturbingly reminiscent of the tour of the castle given by De Flores to Alonzo de Piracquo.

This leads me, finally, to the most cunning space trick of the play. In 5.1, Beatrice and De Flores, fearful of discovery, display an amazing unity of purpose and attitude (foreshadowed in the sado-masochistic exchange in 3.4). They really chime and see eye-to-eye as their worlds merge. Textually, their communion is expressed in the way they complete each other's lines in perfect understanding. Playing barley-break as a couple, as De Flores suggests, they may be 'left in Hell' (5.1.163) as Alsemero locks them into the closet, but they leave this world together within the space of two lines. The murderous villains of the play are thus vouchsafed the most perfect togetherness, which may well prompt audiences to side with them rather than with those hapless other figures perpetually at cross-purposes. Once Beatrice and De Flores have breathed their last, all the other honourable, though far from blameless, men engage in heavy-handed attempts at an allegorical interpretation of recent events, clumsily ringing the changes on the concept of 'change'. This is not, *pace* Caroline Baird, the spiritual transformation of masque applied to the public theatre. Alsemero has the last word in a lame and somewhat convoluted epilogue, but clearly the life has gone out of the play, and the words of repentance are spoken by rote. This is in stark contrast to the solemn, ringing tones and the visions of order and union that end Shakespeare's tragedies. One need only think of the congruence of community, emotion and speech evoked in *Othello*, with Lodovico's 'Myself will straight aboard, and to the state / This heavy act with heavy heart relate.'[15] *The Changeling*'s tragic ending is hardly cathartic, and the question remains: what are we to make of a late Jacobean world that has splintered into fragments, or that has mushroomed into a proliferation of private (im)possible worlds, and that grants moments of communion, fragile and doomed, only to its arch-villains – a world without intimations of Heaven, where every pleasure must be snatched from the jaws of Hell?

This reading, I suggest, sheds light on a slightly opaque passage in the play that is concerned with Alibius' announcement of the madmen's employment at the wedding:

There is a nuptial to be solemnized –
Beatrice-Joanna, his [Vermandero's] fair daughter bride,
For which the gentleman hath bespoke our pains:

> A mixture of our madmen and our fools,
> To finish (as it were) and make the fag
> Of all the revels, the third night from the first.
> Only an unexpected passage over,
> To make a frightful pleasure, that is all –
> But not the all I aim at. Could we so act it
> To teach it in a wild distracted measure,
> Though out of form and figure, breaking Time's head –
> (It were no matter, 'twould be healed again
> In one age or other, if not in this).
>
> 3.4.273–85

Alibius is not content with a brief appearance at the fag end of the revels – a little surprise effect, creating a fleeting moment of pleasurable frisson through its preposterous ugliness. Instead, he is aiming for a showstopper designed to teach through shock, performing a wild distraction that would overturn rhythm, pace, harmony, form, imagery and decorum. The effect would be to shatter people's worlds for good, burst the bubbles and change things for a long time to come. I believe that Middleton and Rowley smuggled their own ambition into Alibius' words. They do not want to transpose the court masque to the public theatre, appropriating its prestige and using it for open flattery or even a 'subtle critique' of the court. The 'all they aim at' is to use the stage for a comprehensive anatomy of the world. Perhaps reminiscent of the moment in Shakespeare's *The Tempest* where the masquers' illusions 'heavily vanish' as Prospero recalls the threat of Caliban's rebellion, this may be a bid to relinquish the increasingly ornamental function of dramatic entertainment in order to 'catch the conscience of the king'. If *The Changeling* is another 'Mousetrap', what it brings to light is the rift between a morally debauched, murderous Spain and a mad and deluded London, oblivious to the threat of Spanish infiltration. As we can see, in Alicante the damage is done: Alsemero admonishes De Flores 'O, thou shouldst have gone / A thousand leagues about to have avoided / This dangerous bridge of blood! *Here* we are lost' (5.3.79–83, my emphasis). In London, separated by a fold in space-time, the 'change is still behind' (5.3.209). In terms of my reading of the play, it makes perfect sense that the final words are directed to the audience: 'Your only smiles have power to cause re-live / The dead again, or in their rooms to give / Brother a new brother, father a child: / If these appear, all griefs are reconciled' (Epilogue 4–7). As spectators have helped to conjure the multiple worlds of *The Changeling*, complicit in the dynamics of theatrical inquiry, here and now in their actual world they need to imagine the good to bring it to life.

# Notes

1  Annabel Patterson, 'Introduction to *The Changeling*', ed. Douglas Bruster, in Gary Taylor and John Lavagnino (gen. eds), *Thomas Middleton: The Complete Works* (Oxford: Oxford University Press, 2007), 1635. For a critical assessment of this edition, see Lukas Erne, '"Our other Shakespeare": Thomas Middleton and the Canon', *Modern Philology* 107:3 (2010): 493–505. A detailed discussion of *The Changeling*'s allusions to the murder of Sir Thomas Overbury can be found in John Higgins, '"Servant obedience changed to master sin": Performance and the Public Transcript of Service in the Overbury Affair and *The Changeling*', *Journal of Early Modern Studies* 4 (2015): 231–58, and for the play's connection with 'the Spanish match', see Mark Hutchings, '*The Changeling* at Court', *Cahiers Elisabéthains*, 81 (2012): 15–24.

2  Russell West, *Spatial Representations and the Jacobean Stage: From Shakespeare to Webster* (Basingstoke: Palgrave Macmillan, 2002), 3.

3  Ina Habermann and Michelle Witen (eds.), *Shakespeare and Space: Theatrical Explorations of the Spatial Paradigm* (Basingstoke: Palgrave Macmillan, 2016).

4  Karl Bühler, *Theory of Language: The Representational Function of Language*, trans. Donald Fraser Goodwin (Amsterdam/Philadelphia: John Benjamins Publishing Company, 2011), 142. Even though Bühler's book already appeared in

1935, his theories are still highly respected in psychology and linguistics. Bühler's impact and the dissemination of his work were impaired by the fact that his career was cut short by Nazi persecution. The English translation has made Bühler's work more accessible in recent years.

5   Bühler, *Theory of Language,* 157; 148.
6   Marie-Laure Ryan, 'Possible Worlds in Recent Literary Theory', *Style* 26:4 (1992): 528–53. Ryan has continued work on the relationship between possible worlds and fictional storyworlds, though with an emphasis on narrative. See Marie-Laure Ryan, Kenneth Foote and Maoz Azaryahu, *Narrating Space/Spatializing Narrative: Where Narrative Theory and Geography Meet* (Columbus: The Ohio State University Press, 2016), and Alice Bell and Marie-Laure Ryan (eds), *Possible Worlds Theory and Contemporary Narratology* (Lincoln: University of Nebraska Press, 2019). For an idiosyncratic attempt to apply possible worlds theory to early modern drama, see Simon Palfrey, *Shakespeare's Possible Worlds* (Cambridge: Cambridge University Press, 2014). For a comprehensive introduction to the creation of imaginary worlds, see Mark J.P. Wolf, *Building Imaginary Worlds: The Theory and History of Subcreation* (New York/London: Routledge, 2012).
7   Nelson Goodman, *Ways of Worldmaking* (Indianapolis, IN: Hackett, 1978).
8   Ryan, 'Possible Worlds', 533.
9   For a queer reading of *The Changeling* that foregrounds the sense of touch see Patricia Cahill, 'The Play of Skin in *The Changeling*', *postmedieval: a journal of medieval cultural studies* 3 (2012): 391–406. See also Jay Zysk, 'Relics and Unreliable Bodies in *The Changeling*', *English Literary Renaissance*, 45:3 (2015): 400–24.
10  A.L. and M.K. Kistner also note that the division of the 'two plot locales [. . .] bifurcates the world of the play' (40); they argue, however, that a second division between fools and madmen cuts across the division between 'castle-main plot/asylum subplot' (*ibid.*), thus 'uniting the two worlds, and as a result, the play' (*ibid.*). See their essay, 'The Five Structures of *The Changeling*', *Modern Language Studies*, 11:2 (1981): 40–53.

11 John Reynolds, *The triumphs of Gods revenege [sic], against the crying, and execrable sinne of murther* (London, 1621).

12 Caroline Baird, 'From Court to Playhouse and Back: Middleton's Appropriation of the Masque', *Early Theatre*, 18:2 (2015): 58. Baird situates *The Changeling* in the context of contemporary masques commissioned by and performed at the court, also rehearsing Taylor and Sabol's argument that 'Middleton revived the choreographed dumb show to create a masque dance effect' (*Ibid.*, 74) and reading the final scene as the transformation scene of a court masque. Taylor and Sabol's argument appears in their 'Middleton, Music and Dance', in Taylor and Lavagnino (gen. eds), *Thomas Middleton: The Complete Works*, 119–81 (130).

13 Ryan, 'Possible Worlds', 543.

14 For a discussion of Beatrice-Joanna's ill-fated attempts to take control of her body see Peter Stallybrass and Anne Rosalind Jones, 'Fetishizing the Glove in Renaissance Europe', *Critical Inquiry*, 28:1 (2001): 114–32. Frances E. Dolan also discusses Beatrice-Joanna's agency, rejecting a reading of *The Changeling* as a 'rape play' in favour of a more complex take on the relationship between Beatrice-Joanna and De Flores: Frances E. Dolan, 'Re-reading Rape in *The Changeling*', *Journal for Early Modern Cultural Studies*, 11:1 (2011): 4–29.

15 William Shakespeare, *Othello*, ed. E.A.J. Honigmann, introduction by Ayanna Thompson, The Arden Shakespeare, third series, revised edition (London: Bloomsbury Arden Shakespeare, 2016), 5.2.368–9.

# PART TWO

# Collaboration and the Hospital Plot

# 3

# A Secret Within the Castle

# William Rowley and *The Changeling*

## David Nicol

The play is set in Spain. It has two plotlines. They tell of lust, adultery, revenge and murder, and they revolve around a castle with subterranean chambers and a room that conceals a secret. But the play described here is not *The Changeling*; it is William Rowley's tragedy *All's Lost by Lust*, written *c.* 1619–20 and still in the repertory of the Cockpit/Phoenix playhouse when *The Changeling* debuted there in 1622.[1] The connections between these two Spanish tragedies and their enigmatic castles have rarely been discussed by critics.[2] Thomas Middleton's attitude towards Spain has been examined in recent studies that group *The Changeling* with *The Spanish Gypsy* (1623) and *A Game at Chess* (1624) as 'Middleton's Spanish plays' or as his 'Spanish trilogy', but they have not engaged fully with the collaborative origins of the first two plays.[3] The existence of *All's Lost by Lust* thus raises the question of what Rowley's attitude towards Spain may have been and whether it complicates what *The Changeling* can tell us about Middleton. It also raises the deeper question of how, and indeed whether, we can know.

Despite Rowley's lengthy career as an actor-playwright, critics have generally treated his presence as irrelevant to interpretation of *The Changeling*. Often he is ignored; sometimes he is blamed for aspects of the play that critics dislike; even when he is admired, it is typically not for his distinct contributions but rather for his ability to merge with his collaborator into a joint figure known as 'Middleton and Rowley'.[4] To be fair, studying Rowley is not easy. Although he was a prominent performer of clown roles and one of the leaders of a playing company, most of his playwriting was collaborative and authorship attribution methodologies cannot always determine the nature of his contribution.[5] Middleton's very distinctive blend of cynicism and Calvinism is often recognizable in his plays, whereas comparatively little individuality emerges from Rowley's. One exception is the ebullient clown roles that Rowley created for himself to perform, but *The Changeling* denies us even that because it was written for Lady Elizabeth's Men, a company for whom Rowley did not act; the clown role, Lollio, appears to have been created for an actor with a quite different stage persona, as his devious and vicious personality is quite unlike the guileless plain-speakers that Rowley created for himself to play.[6]

Despite these challenges, reading the plays associated with Rowley can still provide insights into the origins of *The Changeling*. In this chapter, I begin by surveying what we know about how the play was written, including some recent challenges to received wisdom. I then focus on the Spanish castles in the two plays and propose that, no matter who wrote what in *The Changeling*, *All's Lost by Lust* inspired not only the setting but also one of the most important structural elements of its dramaturgy. This forgotten play offers an example of how the sidelining of Rowley can result in oversimplified descriptions both of *The Changeling* and of Middleton.

# How did Middleton and Rowley write *The Changeling*?

Early in 1622, Middleton and Rowley decided to dramatize the fourth tale of John Reynolds' *Triumphs of God's Revenge* and to combine its tragic narrative with a comic plot.[7] Exactly how they organized the writing process is uncertain. Nonetheless, a survey of the scholarly debate suggests that Rowley may have been more prominent in the play's creation than its critical history suggests. The earliest studies of *The Changeling*'s authorship, conducted in the late nineteenth century, began with the simple assumption that Rowley wrote the hospital plot and Middleton the castle plot. This hypothesis was founded primarily upon Rowley's career as a comic actor, but also on a distaste for the hospital plot, which critics preferred to blame on the less-admired playwright.[8] Yet these scholars soon realized that the division was not so simple. A.H. Bullen found the first and last scenes (primarily concerned with the castle plot) to be incompatible with his expectations of Middleton, citing 'the violence of the language', the 'ill-timed comic touches' and the 'metrical roughness', all of which reminded him of *All's Lost by Lust*.[9] In 1897, Pauline Wiggin expanded upon this notion in her book-length study of the two dramatists. She agreed that Rowley wrote 1.1 and 5.3 in addition to the hospital plot, finding a sharp distinction between, for example, the 'restrained dignity of the dialogue' in 3.4 and the 'invectives and violent expressions' in 5.3, and she augmented this conclusion by citing parallels of wording, plotting, thought and versification between these scenes and Rowley's plays.[10] Later studies of Rowley accepted Wiggin's conclusions, and by 1958, N.W. Bawcutt could say that the division was generally agreed on; he reinforced it further by identifying more verbal parallels with Rowley's plays, all of which appear in the scenes to which Wiggin had assigned him.[11]

Thus, although his work was disparaged, the greater part of the play was now attributed to Rowley (and, for the purposes of the present article, note that almost all of the references to the Spanish setting appear in Rowley's opening scene). However, the methodology underpinning the emerging consensus had problems. Wiggin's metrical analysis assumes that the published text accurately reflects the authors' lineation and prose/verse distinction, something modern editors doubt, while her binarist association of Rowley with crude physicality and of Middleton with poetic subtlety is simplistic, ignoring Middleton's own delight in crudity, and denigrating unjustly the rich language of the opening and closing scenes.[12]

In the 1960s and 1970s, Cyrus Hoy, David J. Lake and MacDonald P. Jackson attempted a more empirical approach by counting apparently distinctive contractions and exclamations used by the authors. An illustrative example is Hoy's discovery that in *All's Lost*, Rowley spells the contraction *'em* as *'um* eight times (along with six *'em*).[13] While Rowley was not the only playwright to use this odd spelling, it never appears in plays associated with Middleton – except for his collaborations with Rowley.[14] As such, the presence of *'um* in a passage may indicate that Rowley wrote it (although its absence cannot indicate that he didn't). Studying minutiae such as this revealed only two inconsistencies with Wiggin. One was that scene 5.2 (which combines castle plot and hospital plot material) contained no indications of authorship. The other was more unsettling to the consensus: the supposedly Rowleyan *'um* appears twice at the beginning of the supposedly Middletonian castle plot scene 4.2.

In the lines in question, Vermandero blames Alonzo's death on the missing Antonio and Fransiscus, declaring, 'The time accuses 'um, a charge of murder / Is brought within my Castle gate', and thus a 'command of apprehension / Shall pursue 'um suddenly' (10–11, 13–14; original spelling).[15] Then, just a few lines later, Vermandero uses *'em* when talking to Tomazo (31). Hoy explained this change of spelling by proposing that the first sixteen lines of 4.2 are a tiny piece of writing by Rowley at the beginning of a scene by Middleton.[16] The suggestion seems implausible at first glance – why would Rowley do that? – and has been criticized by later scholars, who felt that Hoy was torturing logic, given that he had earlier blamed compositors for the presence of *'em* in some Rowley scenes.[17] However, in an important 1979 article, Michael E. Mooney argued in favour of Hoy's suggestion, noting that 4.2.1–16 is one of the few moments at which the hospital plot and castle plot are connected causally; it is thus easy to imagine Rowley inserting these lines into an existing scene by Middleton, since the few other moments of explicit connection between the plotlines – Diaphanta's reference to Alibius (1.1.138–40), the proposed masque of madmen for the wedding (3.3.271–5), and the appearance of the hospital plot characters at the castle in 5.2 and 5.3 – all occur in scenes attributed to Rowley or in the uncertain 5.2.[18] From this evidence, and from Rowley's authorship of the opening and closing scenes, Mooney concluded that Rowley did not merely contribute writing but rather was responsible for the play's 'structural organization', the knitting together of the play.[19]

This apparent consensus among scholars using a variety of methods means that *The Changeling* is often described as a play whose authorial division is unusually well-understood.[20] Still, none of these scholars would suggest that the authors wrote their sections *entirely* separately. The two plots, though they barely connect on a causal level, are intertwined on a thematic level by parallel situations and linguistic motifs; Mooney thus assumes, at the very least, a joint pre-planning stage or a post-drafting collaborative revision.[21] Sure enough, more recent studies have complicated the division by identifying possible Middletonian language and style in the first and last scenes and in the hospital plot that may indicate a more mixed authorship.[22] The most important new contribution, Michael Slater's sceptical re-reading of previous attribution scholarship, focuses on the very idea of 'mixing'.[23] Slater identifies problematic assumptions in the stylistic studies, including the notion that one marker – such as *'um* – could indicate the authorship of an entire scene rather than simply the line in which it appears. He concludes that the evidence 'scarcely justifies the broad consensus so often asserted' and that further study using newer computer-assisted methodologies is needed, but his deeper point is that *The Changeling* is mixed, not only in authorship but also in genre and style.[24] He finds that 'if we strip away insufficient and inconsistent evidence', the established attribution ultimately descends from Wiggin's binarist approach and thus 'still rests mostly on genre and taste'; he does acknowledge that the traditional consensus describes 'a plausible way to divide the task of writing', but he insists that it is unproven and that other models are possible.[25]

Slater's work needs to be read carefully by anyone interested in the authorship of *The Changeling*. However, in decrying a binarist comic/tragic distinction between the authors, he does not acknowledge that the traditional consensus assigns to Rowley two scenes belonging to the tragic castle plot and is thus *already* complicating that distinction; he also ignores Mooney's proposition that Rowley was responsible for organizing and integrating the two storylines, a thesis that attributes to Rowley the very act of mixing. Slater appears to want Rowley to be viewed as more than just a comic writer, but because his justification is centred on the writing being ineradicably mixed, he is unable to describe any aspect of the play as characteristic of Rowley and thus pushes this already sidelined writer further into the background.[26]

But how can we study Rowley's contribution if we lack confidence in our understanding of the division of labour in the play? One approach is to read Rowley's plays, looking at the large scale rather than the small. Doing so reveals that, no matter which playwright wrote the words in question, some of Rowley's earlier work should at the very least be included among the sources of *The Changeling* and be recognized as influential upon its creation. One such work is *All's Lost by Lust*, in which Rowley's portrayal of Spain as a fortified castle is closer to *The Changeling* than anything Middleton wrote about Spain, before or afterwards. In what follows, I make no claims about who wrote what, but I do propose that thinking about the influence of *All's Lost* draws attention to dramaturgical elements that may be missed when thinking about *The Changeling* from a Middleton-centric perspective and which reveal that ideas originating with Rowley were a shaping force upon the play.

## A Rowleyan vision: fortress Spain and the dramaturgy of *The Changeling*

*All's Lost by Lust* dramatizes the Spanish legend of the eighth-century King Roderick, whose rape of Florinda (in the play called Jacinta) supposedly brought about the conquest of Spain by the Moors when her father, the general Julianus, joined them in order to be revenged.[27] The play begins with Spain preparing to confront the invaders beyond its borders: the Moors are 'ready to pass the Straits of Gibraltar, / Whose wat'ry divisions their Afric bounds / From our Christian Europe' (1.1.23–5), and Spain is already 'wasted in her noble strength' (45) after defending herself from the Turks.[28] But Roderick has a plan. 'Our treasury is / A mine unsearched,' he insists, because 'we have a castle / Supposed enchanted' (48–50). There is a secret room beneath the castle, protected by 'forbidden doors' which twenty of Roderick's predecessors have refused to open but have instead 'added each a lock to guard it more' (52–3).[29] Roderick longs to see the treasure he believes to be inside the chamber, but his lords protest that 'fatal events to Spain' are prophesied if it is opened (59).

The invading outsiders are not the true enemy, however: Spain's defences are ultimately destroyed from within, as

Roderick's rape of Jacinta becomes 'the fatal engine that hath beat down Spain' (5.5.70). Rowley links Jacinta with the besieged castle: the locked room that must not be entered is an obvious symbol of her body.[30] But if the victim is Spain, so is the villain: Jacinta cries, 'Spain has dishonoured and imprisoned me' (3.1.48–9). When Julianus learns what Roderick has done, he joins his forces with the Moorish army and invades Spain.

Tension now builds as the desperate Roderick approaches the locked door to the enigmatic chamber, vowing, 'If this door thither lead, I'll enter hell' (5.1.35). Breaking the locks, he finds inside not the hoped-for treasure but supernatural entities whom he calls 'devils' (5.2.4–23) and who perform to him a prophecy of his own defeat by the Moors. Sure enough, the invaders then capture the castle, and the King of the Moors, after betraying Julianus, becomes 'the first of Moors that e'er was King of Spain' (5.5.204). Rowley presents this moment as the triumph of the devil: following common early modern tropes, the Moors are conflated with demons, 'sooty as the inhabitants of hell' (1.1.33) and led by 'a sooty fiend' (5.2.17), so that Roderick is forced to accept that 'the Moor's a-coming, and the devil too that must / Succeed me' (34–5).[31] But although the Spaniards define themselves against these black devils, Rowley blurs the distinction.[32] Jacinta calls Roderick demonic when trying to repel his advances, telling him that love is 'the music of the spheres / Compared with gnashings and the howls below. / Can lust be called love? Then let men seek hell, / For there that fiery deity doth dwell' (2.1.107–12). The King of the Moors, surveying the climactic bloodbath, mostly inflicted by Spaniards upon Spaniards, observes dryly, 'More fruits of Christians' (5.5.55). The overwhelming impression created by *All's Lost by Lust* is thus of a self-destructive and doomed Spain that tries to protect itself behind strong defences but whose own sins permit the devil to invade and destroy it.

*The Changeling* is filled with the same imagery. Its first scene repeats the image of a castle concealing secrets. Although the castle itself derives from the source text, Reynolds' only use of it for symbolic purposes is a reference to Alsemero building 'castles in the ayre'.[33] The play instead follows *All's Lost* in using the castle to represent Spain as a besieged fortress. When Vermandero, the commander of the castle, first meets Alsemero, he suspects that his visitor may be a foreign spy: 'We,' he explains, referring to the Spanish, 'use not to give survèy / Of our chief strengths to strangers. Our citadels / Are placed conspicuous to outward view / On promonts' tops; but within are secrets' (166–9). The imagery recurs when we learn that Alsemero is Spanish and that his father died 'at Gibraltar, / In fight with those rebellious Hollanders' (185–6), referring to Spain's defeat by the Dutch at the island fortress in 1607.[34] The impression of Spain that emerges from the opening scene is, then, that of a defensive nation; its strength is on display to others, but it conceals itself behind walls.

*The Changeling* echoes *All's Lost* when it uses the castle to symbolize the body of Beatrice-Joanna.[35] It also echoes the invasion of the castle by demons: Jacinta's condemnation of lust (see above) is reworked in strikingly similar language when Alsemero tells Beatrice and De Flores to 'rehearse again / Your scene of lust, that you may be perfect / When you shall come to act it to the black audience / Where howls and gnashings shall be music to you' (5.3.114–17). Alsemero condemns the pair as 'cunning devils' (108) conquered by their 'lust's devil' (53), and Vermandero cries, 'an host of enemies entered my citadel / Could not amaze like this' (147-8); when De Flores tells him 'we are left in hell', he replies, 'We are all there. It circumscribes us here' (163–4).[36] And although no literal Moors appear in *The Changeling*, the racialized nature of the demonic imagery is still present: in addition to the 'black audience' in hell, Beatrice and Deflores are accused of wearing a 'black mask', of committing black deeds, and of being 'black fugitives' (5.3.3, 63, 193).[37] The scenes described here all seem inspired by the central image in *All's Lost by Lust* of the castle whose self-destructive inhabitants have allowed hell to invade.

The most imaginative reworking of *All's Lost*, however, can be found in the elaboration of the secret room in Roderick's castle, which became an organizing principle of the dramaturgy of *The Changeling*. The seed can be seen in *All's Lost* when Roderick contemplates the locked entrance to the mysterious room, which would have been represented in the Cockpit/Phoenix playhouse by one of the two stage doors. As he and the audience wonder what lies within, the façade of the theatre's tiring-house is imagined to be the wall concealing that secret; only when Roderick passes through it and discovers the prophecy within does he finally know himself. This image of the secret behind a wall is expanded in *The Changeling*, a play obsessed with what Michael Neill calls 'the disjunction between what is hidden and what is seen', and in which the labyrinthine castle embodies the secrets of the self.[38] In *The Changeling*, the tiring-house façade is used initially to evoke the castle's concealing fortifications, then later becomes the wall hiding Alsemero's closet, a locked room that literalizes the secret within the castle.[39] Curious as to what her new husband keeps there, Beatrice, echoing Roderick, opens the door. She discovers to her horror a well-used virginity-testing kit that reveals the falsity of Alsemero's claim to a Stoic disinterest in women.[40]

This use of the playhouse façade as a concealer of secrets recurs throughout the play. It culminates in the ambiguous cries of Beatrice and De Flores heard before De Flores reveals that he has stabbed her. But it also appears in the subplot, in which Isabella is the 'secret' that Alibius conceals (1.2.1–9) and the tiring-house façade becomes the walls of the madhouse, behind which can be heard the howling madmen who at intervals burst forth onto the stage, 'a dramatic metaphor for the invisible threat of what lies "within"'.[41] This feature of *The Changeling* has been much discussed in studies of the play, but a reading of *All's Lost* reveals that it is an expansion and deepening of an idea from that play; on a political level, the entities behind the façade derive from Rowley's Moors invading Spain; on a metaphysical level, they derive from the image of the devils fighting their way into the culpable human mind.[42]

# The importance of reading Rowley

If *All's Lost by Lust* contains a vision of Spain as a besieged castle that is echoed and deepened in *The Changeling*, then fundamental elements of the later play can be described as Rowleyan in origin, no matter who decided to elaborate upon them. And it may be significant that when Middleton finally turned his full attention to Spain in a non-collaborative play, the satirical *A Game at Chess*, he imagined it very differently. At first, similarities may seem apparent: Spain is represented by the evil Black House, a literalization of the black devil imagery in *The Changeling*.[43] But this Spain is expansive and outward looking, rather than defensive. Its 'vast ambition' is to build an empire; the Black Knight counts the White House (England) merely 'the garden for our cook to pick his salads', planning to take further morsels from France, Germany, Venice and the 'Indians and Moors' (5.3.83–103). There are no walls around this confident house; instead, the Black Knight plots 't'entrap the White Knight and with false allurements / Entice him' (4.2.78–9); Middleton thus imagines Spain not as a fortress but as a Venus fly-trap, tempting outsiders with 'sugared syllables', 'sweet-sounding airs' and 'strange delight[s]' instead of repelling them (1.1.264; 5.1.32, 37).[44] The Black House, as in the other two plays, fails because it contains the seeds of its own destruction (the Black pieces all seek their own advantage), but it is not destroyed by invading demons; rather, it is defeated by the White House, the embodiment of truth, which discovers and reveals its secrets.[45] *A Game at Chess* thus presents a very different notion of what makes Spain both dangerous and defeatable.

Our understanding of Middleton's attitude towards Spain thus needs to better acknowledge the presence of his collaborators.[46] Identifying the roots of *The Changeling* in *All's Lost* is one example of how reading the work of William Rowley can provide new insights, despite the challenges of authorship attribution. Approaching the play only through Middleton's canon, or arguing that collaborative playwrights can never be distinguished at all, obscures the complexities of early modern playwriting. If *The Changeling* is a castle, Rowley may be its hidden foundation, even if Middleton is more conspicuous to outward view.

# Notes

1. G.E. Bentley, *The Jacobean and Caroline Stage* (Oxford: Oxford University Press, 1941), 5: 1020.

2. Trudi L. Darby, 'William Rowley: A Case Study in Influence', in J.A.G. Ardila (ed.), *The Cervantean Heritage: Reception and Influence of Cervantes in Britain* (London: Legenda, 2009), 249–58, describes the two plays as evidence for Rowley's interest in Spain but draws no further conclusions.

3. Barbara Fuchs, 'Middleton and Spain', in Gary Taylor and Trish Thomas Henley (eds), *The Oxford Handbook of Thomas Middleton* (Oxford: Oxford University Press, 2012), 410; Berta Cano-Echevarría, 'New Directions: Doubles and Falsehoods: *The Changeling*'s Spanish Undertexts', in Mark Hutchings (ed.), *The Changeling: A Critical Reader* (London: Bloomsbury Arden Shakespeare, 2019), 131. For related studies of the portrayal of Spain in *The Changeling*, see A.A. Bromham and Zara Bruzzi, *The Changeling and the Years of Crisis, 1619–1624: A Hieroglyph of Britain* (London: Pinter, 1990); Annabel Patterson, 'Introduction to *The Changeling*', in Gary Taylor and John Lavagnino (eds), *Thomas Middleton: The Collected Works* (Oxford: Clarendon Press, 2007), 1634–5; Mark Hutchings, 'De Flores Between the Acts', *Studies in Theatre and Performance* 31.1 (2011): 95–111.

4. For a survey, see David Nicol, *Middleton and Rowley: Forms of Collaboration in the Jacobean Playhouse* (Toronto: University of Toronto Press, 2012), 7–15.

5. For a short biography, see David Gunby, 'Rowley, William,' in *Oxford Dictionary of National Biography* (Oxford: Oxford University Press, 2004).

6 Bentley, *The Jacobean and Caroline Stage*, 5: 1016; on the Rowleyan clown, see Nicol, *Middleton and Rowley*, 75–90.
7 On the date, see Michael Neill (ed.), *The Changeling*, revised ed. (London: Methuen, 2019), xli.
8 For examples, see Nicol, *Middleton and Rowley*, 8–9.
9 A.H. Bullen (ed.), *The Works of Thomas Middleton* (New York: Houghton Mifflin, 1885), 1: lix–lx; Frederick Gard Fleay, *A Biographical Chronicle of the English Drama, 1559–1642* (London: Reeves and Turner, 1891), 2:101 made the same attribution, but offered no reasons.
10 Pauline G. Wiggin, *An Inquiry into the Authorship of the Middleton-Rowley Plays* (Boston: Ginn, 1897), 43–51.
11 Charles Wharton Stork (ed.), *William Rowley: His All's Lost by Lust, and A Shoemaker a Gentleman, with an Introduction on Rowley's Place in the Drama* (Philadelphia: University of Philadelphia Press, 1910), 44; Arthur Symons, 'Middleton and Rowley', in A.W. Ward and A.R. Waller (eds), *The Cambridge History of English Literature, Volume 6: The Drama to 1642, Part Two*, vol. 6 (Cambridge: Cambridge University Press, 1910), 87; D.M. Robb, 'The Canon of William Rowley's Plays', *Modern Language Review* 45 (1950): 140; N.W. Bawcutt (ed.), *The Changeling* (London: Methuen, 1958), xxxix–xliv and commentary notes; he lists the relevant parallels at xl, n.1.
12 See, e.g., Neill, *Changeling*, 133–4, and Wiggin, *An Inquiry*, 43. For examples of Middletonian crudity, see Sordido and the Ward in *Women Beware Women* or the urinating Puritans in *A Chaste Maid in Cheapside*.
13 Cyrus Hoy, 'The Shares of Fletcher and His Collaborators in the Beaumont and Fletcher Canon (V)', *Studies in Bibliography* 13 (1960): 83–89.
14 See David J. Lake, *The Canon of Thomas Middleton's Plays* (Cambridge: Cambridge University Press, 1975), tables 1(g), 3(g), 4(g).
15 Hoy, 'The Shares', 87–9; Lake, *The Canon of Thomas Middleton's Plays*, 204–5.
16 Hoy, 'The Shares', 87–9.

17 Richard L. Nochimson, '"Sharing" *The Changeling* by Playwrights and Professors: The Certainty of Uncertain Knowledge about Collaboration', *Early Theatre* 5 (2002): 41–2; Michael Slater, '"Shameless Collaboration": Mixture and the Double Plot of *The Changeling*', *Renaissance Drama* 47, no. 1 (2019): 55–8. I discuss these studies in more detail later in this chapter.

18 Michael E. Mooney, '"Framing" as Collaborative Technique: Two Middleton-Rowley Plays', *Comparative Drama* 13 (1979): 132.

19 Mooney, '"Framing"', 138.

20 For examples, see Slater, '"Shameless Collaboration"', 51.

21 Mooney, '"Framing"', 136.

22 R.V. Holdsworth, 'Notes on *The Changeling*', *Notes and Queries* 234 (1989): 345–6 proposes Middletonian parallels in the first 122 lines of 5.3. Swapan Chakravorty, '"Give Her More Onion": Unriddling the Welsh Madman's Speech in *The Changeling*', *Notes and Queries* 241 (1996): 184–87, notes a Middletonian image in the subplot; Neill, *Changeling*, xxiii, n. 31 regards as Middletonian 'the high number of feminine endings' in 1.1.1–45 and 5.3.153–65 and the word 'inclinations' at 1.1.127; Douglas Bruster's textual note to 5.3.108 in Gary Taylor and John Lavagnino (eds), *Thomas Middleton and Early Modern Textual Culture: A Companion to the Collected Works* (Oxford: Clarendon Press, 2007) relates 'the use of "it" as a potentially vague substantive' to Middleton.

23 Slater's broad points are anticipated by Nochimson, '"Sharing"', but his analysis is more detailed.

24 Slater, '"Shameless Collaboration"', 58, 61, 51–3.

25 Slater, '"Shameless Collaboration"', 54, 67–71.

26 Slater, '"Shameless Collaboration"', 67–8.

27 For studies of the legend, see Elizabeth Drayson, *The King and the Whore: King Roderick and La Cava* (New York: Palgrave Macmillan, 2007) and Patricia E. Grieve, *The Eve of Spain: Myths of Origins in the History of Christian, Muslim, and Jewish Conflict* (Baltimore: Johns Hopkins University Press, 2009). No specific source for Rowley's play has been identified; see Drayson, *The King and the Whore*, 91. Darby, 'William

Rowley', 255, thinks he may simply have heard the story, since he was 'networked into a group of people who were interested in Spanish culture'.

28 Act, scene and line references to *All's Lost by Lust* refer to Stork (ed.), *William Rowley*; I have modernized the spelling.

29 As Karen Bamford notes, the subterranean location is indicated when Roderick calls the treasury a 'mine unsearched' and says he'd 'dig [. . .] through hell' (1.1.49, 66) to reach it; see *Sexual Violence on the Jacobean Stage* (New York: St. Martin's Press, 2000), 107. In addition, Roderick later refers to 'geomantic' devils inhabiting it (5.2.8).

30 Bamford, *Sexual Violence*, 107, 109–10.

31 On the conflation of blackness with the demonic, see Virginia Mason Vaughan, *Performing Blackness on English Stages, 1500–1800* (Cambridge: Cambridge University Press, 2005), 18–33.

32 Rowley may be following the English tendency to conflate Spaniards and Moors as racial others. On this trope, see Barbara Fuchs, 'The Spanish Race', in Margaret Greer, Walter Mignolo, and Maureen Quilligan (eds), *Rereading the Black Legend: The Discourses of Religious and Racial Difference in the Renaissance Empires* (Chicago: Chicago University Press, 2007), 95–8.

33 Dale B.J. Randall, 'Some New Perspectives on the Spanish Setting of *The Changeling* and Its Source', *Medieval and Renaissance Drama in England* 3 (1986): 199–200; for the passage, see Bawcutt, *Changeling*, 114.

34 For detailed studies of these lines, see Randall, 'Some New Perspectives', 190; Mark Hutchings, '"Those Rebellious Hollanders": *The Changeling*'s Double Dutch', *SEDERI* 24 (2014): 146–7.

35 For a variety of observations on Beatrice as the castle, see Mohammad Kowsar, 'Middleton and Rowley's *The Changeling*: The Besieged Temple', *Criticism* 28, no. 2 (1986): 148; Randall, 'Some New Perspectives', 200; Kim Solga, 'Playing *The Changeling* Architecturally', in Susan Bennett and Mary Polito (eds), *Performing Environments: Site-Specificity in Medieval and Early Modern English Drama* (London: Palgrave Macmillan, 2014), 65.

36 On the destruction from within, see Michael Neill, *Issues of Death: Mortality and Identity in English Renaissance Tragedy* (Oxford: Clarendon Press, 1997), 182–3. Anne Lancashire, 'The Emblematic Castle in Shakespeare and Middleton', in J.C. Gray (ed.), *Mirror up to Shakespeare: Essays in Honour of G.R. Hibbard* (Toronto: University of Toronto Press, 1984), 228–9, finds its origins in the medieval and early modern emblem of the castle as human virtue'.

37 Jamie Paris, 'Bad Blood, Black Desires: On the Fragility of Whiteness in Middleton and Rowley's *The Changeling*', *Early Theatre* 24, no. 1 (2021): 129–30.

38 Neill, *Changeling*, xxviii; for a detailed study, see his *Issues of Death*, 168–97; see also T.B. Tomlinson, *A Study of Elizabethan and Jacobean Tragedy* (Cambridge: Cambridge University Press, 1964), 192–6; Bruce Boehrer, 'Alsemero's Closet: Privacy and Interiority in *The Changeling*', *Journal of English and Germanic Philology* 96, no. 3 (1997): 349–68.

39 On the castle-like appearance of the playhouse façade and its use as an emblem of interiority, see David Bevington, *Action Is Eloquence: Shakespeare's Language of Gesture* (Cambridge, MA: Harvard University Press, 1984), 101–2, 109; on *The Changeling* specifically, see Joost Daalder (ed.), *The Changeling*, 5th impr. (London: A&C Black, 1995), xxxvii–xl. For more on the relationship between castle, closet and madhouse as 'private architectural spaces, reserved for the business of men', see Boehrer, 'Alsemero's Closet', 356–8; on the closet, see also Solga, 'Playing', 70–3.

40 On the unmasking of Alsemero, see Nicol, *Middleton and Rowley*, 62–3.

41 Neill, *Changeling*, xxviii; on the castle-like nature of the madhouse, see Tomlinson, *A Study*, 202–4.

42 On the latter point, see Daalder, *Changeling*, xxxix–xl; Neill, *Issues of Death*, 183–5.

43 Fuchs, 'Middleton and Spain', 409; on the racial connotations, see Gary Taylor, *Buying Whiteness: Race, Culture, and Identity from Columbus to Hip Hop* (New York: Palgrave Macmillan, 2005), 134.

44 On this, see Karen Britland, 'Middleton and the Continent', in *The Oxford Handbook of Thomas Middleton* (Oxford: Oxford University Press, 2012), 547–8.
45 J.W Harper (ed.), *A Game at Chess*, New Mermaids (London: Ernest Benn, 1966), xxii–xxiii; Gary Taylor, 'Introduction to A Game at Chess: A Later Form', in Gary Taylor and John Lavagnino (eds), *Thomas Middleton: The Collected Works* (Oxford: Clarendon Press, 2007), 1828.
46 *The Spanish Gypsy* involved Dekker, Ford, Middleton and Rowley; scholars continue to debate their respective contributions. For the latest study, which proposes a relatively minimal presence for Middleton and Rowley, see Brian Vickers, *The Collected Works of John Ford, Volume II* (Oxford: Clarendon Press, 2017), 186–235.

# 4

# Isabella

## *Douglas Bruster*

Isabella is a central but elusive character in *The Changeling*. Wife to Alibius, keeper of the mental hospital, she proves remarkable for staging her critique of the oppressive structures of gender, marriage and society. Unlike Beatrice-Joanna, the aristocratic heroine of the tragedy's main plot, Isabella exercises agency in a successful and theatrically comedic way. Both characters call into question assumptions – then and now – about sex and sexuality, about what women should be able do with their bodies. Yet in contrast to Beatrice-Joanna, Isabella falls largely outside critical attention, running under our radar.[1] There is a reason for this. Because the hospital plot can seem less important than the main action in Alicante's castle, Isabella and her fellow asylum characters are often cut from performance in order to emphasize the darker intrigue they counterpoint – that of Beatrice-Joanna and De Flores. But such cuts deprive audiences of Isabella's dazzling performance and her powerful perspective on the surrounding social order. As wife, hostage, object, improvisational actress and critic, Isabella both writes and reads *The Changeling* from inside the play itself. If her circumstances resemble Beatrice-Joanna's in all but the latter's privilege, unlike Beatrice-Joanna she successfully negotiates her confinement and conducts a tutorial on the nature and weakness of male fantasy. To engage with *The Changeling* without Isabella is to miss the theatrical lesson she plans and executes and so to misunderstand the play's imaginative horizon.

Before we consider Isabella as a character, we should note that most actors during the period lacked access to the full versions of the dramatic texts we read, including that of *The Changeling*. That is, working actors first read, and studied, their parts as roles, as strips of paper containing lines and cue words that could be pasted end-to-end and rolled up in the manner of a scroll.[2] Our modern word 'role', in fact, comes from the French *rôle* and refers to this very feature.[3] The actor playing Isabella (most likely a boy) would have received the part as something separate from what we consider *The Changeling*, piecing together the character's trajectory, and actor's performance, during rehearsals. Isabella, like every character in the play, existed at one time as a paper person, as words waiting to be actualized when spoken to and about other characters, as well as her own.

But one of the things that separates Isabella's role from many others in the play is her character's consciousness of theatre and of the power of theatricality itself. Like Beatrice-Joanna and Diaphanta, Isabella is aware of, and resents, the strictures upon women within the playworld's society. At so many moments, Alicante seems to accept, even to embrace, the double-standard: chastity for its women and sexual conquest for its young men. If Beatrice-Joanna works up a play-within-the-play in the main plot – a play that has Diaphanta take Beatrice-Joanna's place in bed – it is, as we will see, a much more selfish use of theatricality than Isabella's own play-within-the-play, which winds up teaching rather than taking.

If roles were originally detached things, separated by copyists from play manuscripts, so were a dramatic story's multiple plots. Isabella and the hospital plot can seem separable from *The Changeling* because they exist in another place, socially and textually. That 'place' is traditionally known as a subplot, a feature in many literary texts and common to most plays at the time *The Changeling* was written. Early modern plays, that is, often made use of multiple plots, alternating scenes, places and characters, all involved with divergent places and interests.[4] This feature is familiar from Shakespeare's plays, and *The Changeling* follows that model in giving us two stories and two places: the castle plot, which focuses on Beatrice-Joanna, De Flores and Alsemero; and the hospital plot, which focuses on Isabella, Alibius, Lollio and two suitors who pursue Isabella while in disguise.

As I mentioned above, the hospital plot is often cut entirely in performance to keep production time and expenses down and to focus on what seems the more important story – that of Beatrice-Joanna. One assumption that drives such a decision (that is, that Beatrice-Joanna's is the more pressing story) is the belief that tragedy is more important than comedy. The prefix 'sub-' in *subplot* reminds us that the characters and action in such a plot are not only socially lower than the figures in a play's main plot, but that their actions – often ending comedically – are also less consequential. But if we remember that this is merely an assumption, and an assumption that causes us to lose sight of what the hospital plot does for *The Changeling*, we will be in a better position to understand this story's contribution and thus the play.

We hear about Isabella before we see her. Just as Beatrice-Joanna is described in the romantic vision of Alsemero opening the play—''Twas in the temple where I first beheld her' (1.1.1) – so is Isabella introduced at a distance and over 300 lines before we see and hear from her. In dialogue with Lollio, his foolish servant, Alibius, Isabella's husband, mentions her as his first and most pressing concern: 'Lollio, I must trust thee with a secret, / But thou must keep it (1.2.1–2). The chord rung here will resonate throughout the hospital scenes: Alibius is a jealous older man who wants to keep his wife 'secret', safely away from those who might be attracted by her youth and beauty. Alibius is a potential cuckold, a common figure in Italianate comedy and its English derivatives. Having married a much younger woman, Alibius has almost set the stage for his wife to sleep with another – younger – man. Literature had long recorded warnings about pairing those of different ages, those 'misgraffèd in respect of years', as Lysander says in *A Midsummer Night's Dream*.[5] Alibius realizes as much and sees the likely end of this story. He shares his fears:

> Gallants I do observe
> Of quick enticing eyes, rich in habits,
> Of stature and proportion very comely:
> These are most shrewd temptations, Lollio.
>
> 1.2.54–7

Much of the hospital plot centres on the jealous confinement of Isabella and on her response to it. Less often remarked on is her awareness of, and response to, what Alibius rightly senses are 'shrewd temptations'.

Who is this Isabella, this woman to be kept a 'secret' and thus removed from not only young men's 'quick enticing eyes' but from her own 'temptations' of infidelity? Her name itself would have seemed generic to early audiences. That is, 'Isabella' is something of a cliché in drama of this time, an all-purpose name – like the male 'Antonio' (also used in *The Changeling*) – employed by English plays to convey a Mediterranean flavour. Beginning with *The Spanish Tragedy* in 1587 and continuing through the closing of the playhouses in 1642, there were at least twenty-five Isabellas in early modern dramatic texts, including in another play by Thomas Middleton (*Women Beware Women* (1621)) and as a pseudonym in John Fletcher and William Rowley's *The Maid of the Mill* (1623), where Ismena comes to be known as 'Isabella' when wooed by yet another of early modern drama's Antonios.

But we should start by admitting that, for the great majority of the play in performance, she is not even 'Isabella'. That is, not only is her appearance delayed for over 300 lines after we first hear mention of her, but her name is spoken only once, and some distance into the play itself, when Alibius calls her 'my sweet Isabella' (3.3.270). Before this lone reference, she is called 'a wife' (1.2.7) who is 'young' (1.2.16) in contrast to her husband's age (1.2.19). Alibius then refers to her with a common sexual metaphor, describing her as a 'ring' that he would keep on his 'own finger' (1.2.24) so that 'one or other' will not 'be thrusting into't' (1.2.30–1). (There is a parallel to the grisly sequence of the ring in the De Flores/Beatrice-Joanna plot). He quickly asks Lollio to watch Isabella's 'treadings' (1.2.38), a word that literally means steps, or walking, but was often used as a metaphor for bird sex, as in the Clown's discourse in *Fortune by Land and Sea* (1623):

> I found your son Philip like a Cock-sparrow billing: if I had stayed but a little longer, I might have taken him and his hen treading. I know not whether it be St. Valentine's day or no, but I am sure they are coupled.
>
> 1.2[6]

Isabella has a ring; Isabella has treadings. Coming in close sequence, these lines give us Alibius' nightmare of dispossession; his blunt images paint Isabella as an object of pornographic fantasy.

And not only his. Isabella, again, is spoken *about* before she speaks, and it is important to notice how *The Changeling* prepares for her entrance. She will first be 'my mistress' in Lollio's discourse (1.2.60), and this is of course a respectful formality. In fact, Lollio uses this phrase when speaking about Isabella with a visitor in a circumstance that will become crucial to the play's hospital plot. In brief, someone has come to the hospital inquiring about lodging (institutionalizing, in modern terms) a young gentleman who appears to have been born mentally deficient (a 'fool', in early modern terms). We soon learn that neither this young gentleman – named Antonio or 'Tony' – nor his rival for Isabella's affections – a gallant named Franciscus, and apparently 'mad' – is actually what he appears to be: both young men feign mental decentring (Tony, foolishness; Franciscus, a theatricalized madness) in order to gain access to and then, each hopes, seduce Isabella, whose beauty, we learn in hindsight, has set their separate plots in motion from before the action of the play.

Significantly, Lollio hints at the fulfilment of Alibius' worry as he accepts a gratuity from the visitor ('Pedro') to care for the apparently foolish Tony. When Pedro says, 'Let him have good attendance and sweet lodging,' Lollio replies: 'As good as my mistress lies in, sir' (1.2.119–20). Because Lollio is always snickering in his observations, always opportunistic in his relation to both Alibius and Isabella, this line sticks in our heads: '*As good as my mistress lies in*'. Understood literally, it refers merely to equivalence: Lollio assures his visitor that Tony will have a good bed. Understood sexually, though, it places Tony in bed *with* Isabella, and nearly 500 lines before we first meet her.

It is worth pausing over this sardonic preparation because we haven't yet seen or heard from Isabella. We know that Lollio and Alibius know her, and we find out that both Antonio ('Tony') and Franciscus have already seen her, desire her and have engaged in their elaborate ruses in order to attempt to seduce her. Like Beatrice-Joanna in the play's castle plot, Isabella is an object of multiple men's desires (there, Alsemero, De Flores and Piracquo). However intentionally, the play heightens Isabella's power by treating her at a distance. Described before we see her, with Alibius apparently terrified of a scenario that Lollio nonetheless hints he (Lollio) can make happen ('As good as my mistress lies in'), Isabella comes to us as the name of a character so fiercely desired, and wanted in such conflicting ways – as a young spouse to be kept 'secret', as a mistress to be pimped out, as a beautiful wife to be seduced – that she evidently must disappoint, even thwart, those desires.

None of this could be known to the actor playing Isabella from the paper role itself. That is, only in rehearsal would the performer be privy to what is essentially a conspiracy regarding Isabella's body: Alibius coveting it; Lollio hinting he can provide access to it; and Antonio and Franciscus and Lollio hotly wanting it.[7] Only in rehearsal, that is, will the Isabella-actor hear, and see, pieces of the larger puzzle that her character can't see, and hear, from the words she speaks. It is for this reason that character (hers and others) is simultaneously social and linguistic. Social, in the sense that characters are built by and in relation to their circumstances, including the desires and agency and action of other characters; and linguistic, in the sense that what they say – the style of their utterances and hence the through-line of their discourse – forms the basis of who we take them to be.

If the performer behind Isabella understands the social relations of her role only in hindsight, and only when the story has already been unfolded once in the playhouse, the role itself gives her, and by extension the audience and reader, a patterned set of cues from which the performance can take meaning. We have seen that the 'where' of Isabella's character in *The Changeling* is important: the play delays her entrance for some time and then (as we will see) affords her room and material for a bravura performance. In addition to that focused performance, however, it also enlists her in a silent ('Dumb Show') spectacle in which she accompanies Beatrice-Joanna in a foreboding procession: '*Beatrice the bride following in great state, accompanied with Diaphanta, Isabella, and other Gentlewomen*' (4.0.9–11). Where Isabella's social rank places her as an attendant in this bridal train, she will largely avoid the dangers that follow Beatrice-Joanna, and does so by setting the conditions for an erotic relationship. As we will see, these conditions are posed as a test, a kind of riddle, to vet the suitors; their failure to pass the test confirms a danger averted. We last see Isabella late in the play, delivering the third-to-last speech in *The Changeling*, one that rebukes her husband for his own failure.

Leading up to that moment, however, are two scenes (3.3 and 4.3) in which a bored Isabella experiences the potentially tempting seductions of two young 'gallants' and, after setting them an examination, humiliates them for their lack of vision. As we will see, these two scenes offer a lesson for the suitors, a lesson that punishes them less for any immorality ('it is wrong to sleep with another man's wife') than for their lack of wit ('it's too bad that you're so blind'). As such, Isabella repeats a logic from the *fabliau* of earlier centuries: a genre of short tales, familiar to us from Chaucer, that emphasize sexuality, cunning, tricks and wordplay. Rooted also in the early modern era, however, Isabella's fabliau-like trickery is closest to the way in which Miguel de Cervantes' *Don Quixote* deconstructs the inflated language and ideas of medieval chivalry. In this respect, her performance in *The Changeling* offers pointed commentary on the politics of gender, as well as the role that literary paradigms such as romance and Petrarchanism play in the worlds inside and outside the playhouse.

Before looking at the practicalities of Isabella's role and performance, a brief summary of the action of *The Changeling* as it relates to her character:

**1.2** Isabella is discussed by Alibius and Lollio; we meet Antonio ('Tony'), the 'fool' and first of Isabella's two suitors.

**3.3** Isabella appears with Lollio; she is introduced to Franciscus, the 'madman' and second of her two suitors. This madman comes on too strongly, and is replaced with Tony, the fool. When Lollio is twice distracted and drawn off stage, Tony drops his foolish disguise and reveals himself as a would-be lover. Lollio actually observes the second pass that Tony makes, and, after leading him away, returns to make his own pass at Isabella – who shuts him down just as Alibius, her husband, enters.

**4.1** Isabella appears (silently) in Beatrice-Joanna's bridal procession.

**4.3** Isabella enters, with Lollio, and opens a letter he has delivered, reading it aloud. It is from Franciscus, and while the outside is full of mythological nonsense, the inside features the lofty language of love. Lollio quickly senses his opening, and suggests blackmail: if she takes either suitor as a lover, she'll have to sleep with him (Lollio), too. She agrees, and asks for the key to Lollio's wardrobe for a purpose unknown. After she exits, Alibius enters and Lollio makes cuckold jokes to his face. When Tony re-enters, he is soon accosted by

Isabella – disguised as a madwoman spouting mythological nonsense and touching Antonio in a fashion that, not recognizing Isabella, disgusts him. She reveals herself, and exits despite his protestations.

5.3 Isabella appears in the play's final scene to be a witness to its horrors, and delivers a verdict that shames Alibius for his jealous behaviour.

The trajectory described in this summary is one that sees Isabella grow in awareness and authority, from the distant and unknowable object of desire to its subject and stage manager before becoming a choric commentator.

We see this trajectory, and the growth it involves, in the language of Isabella's role. While character is shaped strongly by other elements of framing within a play – the real and understood network of social relations in which a dramatic figure is embedded – the words and phrases a character speaks leave an indelible impression upon audience members and readers. It is in this respect that *character* as an idea most closely conveys its history as word, a history in which 'character' could mean not only 'any of the simple elements of a written language, as a letter of an alphabet' (*OED* 'character' *n.* 3.a) but also '[a] particular person's style of handwriting' (*OED* 4.b). The written elements of Isabella's role build to a style that *is* her character. Isabella's character – the sum total of her time in *The Changeling* – is of course determined by the words recorded on the dramatic role that comprised her part.

Isabella's first speech pushes back on her confinement by her jealous husband, confinement that puts her at the mercy of their servant, Lollio:

> Why, sirrah? Whence have you commission
> To fetter the doors against me? If you
> Keep me in a cage, pray whistle to me,
> Let me be doing something.

3.3.1–4

The word 'sirrah' is a social separator: withholding the more formal 'sir,' Isabella asserts her superiority to Lollio. But through much of her introduction to us, Isabella will nonetheless be sexualized, her lines – like 'Let me be doing something' – serving to set up dirty jokes, such as Lollio's retort: 'You shall be doing, if it please you; I'll whistle to you if you'll pipe after' (3.3.5–6). Acting as Alibius' man, Lollio has the power of the key, and Isabella is forced to wonder just whose idea her confinement is: 'Is it your master's pleasure, or your own, / To keep me in this pinfold?' (3.3.7–8). After an additional dirty joke that ends with him saying 'you might be pounded in another place' (3.3.10–11), Lollio somewhat mischievously plants a thought in Isabella's mind when alleging that Alibius has said 'you have company enough in the house, if you please to be sociable, of all sorts of people' (3.3.13–14). The word 'please' here circles us back to Isabella's own 'pleasure' and we perhaps recall, too, De Flores' utterance from only slightly earlier in the play; after Beatrice-Joanna touches his face, he gushes, in a sexualized aside: '"Tis half an act of pleasure / To hear her talk thus to me' (2.2.86–7).

Whose pleasure is Isabella's story going to centre on? As though rising to Lollio's bait, she asks to see the handsome madman:

> You're a brave, saucy rascal! Come on, sir:
> Afford me then the pleasure of your Bedlam.
> You were commending once today to me,
> Your last-come lunatic – what a proper
> Body there was without brains to guide it,
> And what a pitiful delight appeared
> In that defect, as if your wisdom had found
> A mirth in madness. Pray, sir, let me partake
> If there be such a pleasure.
>
> 3.3.23–31

Repeating the word 'pleasure' twice more, she also switches from 'sirrah' to 'sir' in beseeching Lollio to display the new resident of the asylum. The language of paradox she uses ('pitiful delight', 'mirth in madness') reminds us of similar oppositions in *A Midsummer Night's Dream* ('Merry and tragical? Tedious and brief?'), and it is perhaps no coincidence that Franciscus (the gallant disguised as a madman) addresses Isabella with just that story:

> Hail, bright Titania!
> Why standst thou idle on these flow'ry banks?
> Oberon is dancing with his Dryades;
> I'll gather daisies, primroses, violets,
> And bind them in a verse of poesy.
>
> 3.3.54–8[8]

Like Antonio/Tony, the counterfeit fool, Franciscus will address Isabella with the artificial language of love poetry – mythological, Petrarchan and Shakespearean.

After some stage comedy with Lollio and after singing verses of love poetry to Isabella, Franciscus is replaced onstage by Tony. Lollio again frames Isabella in sexualized language, assuring her, regarding Tony, that she 'may play with him, as safely with him as with his bauble' (3.3.115–16). She begins a conversation with Tony, declining to accept Tony's description of her as one of his 'cousins' (3.3.119); she is only too aware of the term's secondary meaning of 'prostitutes,' and sets a boundary with him. Even so, when Lollio leaves her alone with Tony, she is perhaps surprised – 'Ha!' – when he reveals himself as not 'foolish' at all, but an amorous suitor: 'The truest servant to your powerful beauties, / Whose magic had this force thus to transform me' (3.3.132; 134–5). Antonio/Tony probably kisses Isabella – 'one arrow', he says, from love's bow – for she remarks: 'A forward fool too!' (3.3.148). When Tony defines himself as 'a gentleman that loves you', Isabella puts him in his place without punishment:

> When I see him, I'll speak with him. So, in the mean time,
> Keep your habit; it becomes you well enough.
> As you are a gentleman, I'll not discover you;

That's all the favour that you must expect:
When you are weary, you may leave the school,
For all this while you have but play'd the fool.

                                          3.3.154–60

Isabella's boundaries with Tony seem to get altered almost as soon as Lollio returns. For when the servant inquires how Isabella likes the fool, she answers, in Antonio's earshot, 'If he hold on as he begins, he is like to come to something' (3.3.168–9). To a hopeful lover like Antonio, this is promising, and when Lollio inquires whether he should dismiss the fool, Isabella decisively remarks 'By no means! – Let him stay a little' (3.3.180).

During this sequence, Lollio is only temporarily absent from view, for a stage direction in the original text reads '*Enter Lollio above*' (s.d. 3.3.193). From this vantage, Lollio watches Antonio/Tony kiss, or at the very least attempt to kiss, Isabella. Ever the practical joker, Lollio makes the sound of a cuckoo (3.3.207) – intimating Alibius' cuckoldry – before bringing on, above, a parade of madmen. Re-entering to finally part Isabella from Antonio, Lollio remarks that 'I do not think but he will put you down one of these days' (3.3.228–9), continuing the narrative of infidelity that he, Alibius, Franciscus and Antonio have crafted for Isabella, each in his own manner.

It is at this point that Isabella seems to catch herself, remarking, in one of her most poetic passages:

Here the restrainèd current might make breach,
Spite of the watchful bankers. Would a woman stray,
She need not gad abroad to seek her sin;
It would be brought home one ways or other.
The needle's point will to the fixèd north,
Such drawing arctics women's beauties are.

                                          3.3.230–5

Isabella has accurately anticipated the consequences of straying in *The Changeling*'s pervasive sexual economy. Lollio re-enters the stage and tries to kiss her, effectively suggesting sexual blackmail by reciting the words of Antonio's wooing (which he has overheard) and trying to 'lay' his hand on Isabella's genitals: 'Thou hast a thing about thee would do a man pleasure' (3.3.255–6). As Isabella recognizes, the 'pleasure' in this society is largely reserved for men. She insists that Lollio remain silent about this matter or suffer violence, and at this moment Alibius enters. The conflict is postponed without resolution: will Isabella choose Franciscus, Antonio or neither? And how will she deal with Lollio's blackmail? These are real questions, for in the castle plot of *The Changeling*, Beatrice-Joanna has already had sex with De Flores (before we have seen Isabella), and the consequences of this action for the aristocrat and her world are severe.

Before we next hear from Isabella, we see her take part in Beatrice-Joanna's silent bridal procession (s.d. 4.1.0), but when 4.3 opens she finds herself absolutely deluged with words – the written words of Franciscus (the false madman), who has sent her a letter. Its outside is mythological nonsense; its (secret) inside offers nonsense of a different kind: sweet language that solicits her love. When she finishes reading the letter aloud, Lollio is quick to reiterate his demands: 'If I find you minister once and set up the trade, I put in for my thirds' (4.3.36–7). The assumption seems to be that Isabella must be willing to sleep with all three hospital suitors: Antonio, Franciscus and Lollio. Surprisingly, perhaps, Isabella reassures him: 'The first place is thine, believe it, Lollio, / If I do fall –' (4.3.39–40). But in hindsight we learn that she can make this promise ('believe it, Lollio') because she has no intentions of having sex with either of her suitors. Instead, she seeks Lollio's 'counsel,' asking him: 'how shall I deal with 'em?' (4.3.44). Lollio takes this suggestively, leading an apparently impatient Isabella to rephrase things: 'Nay, the fair understanding: how to use 'em' (4.3.46). 'Abuse 'em!', Lollio retorts (4.3.47), and that is precisely what Isabella does.

In what remains one of the most striking examples of agency from a female character in early modern English drama,

Isabella declares that 'I'll practise' and requests the key to Lollio's wardrobe (4.3.50–1). To say that she will *practise* places her in the company of shape-shifting Vice figures: this is a verb and a noun that stage villains use as a synonym for 'plot'. Lollio seems to assume that this means Isabella is plotting to have sex widely, for he teases Alibius that Isabella 'takes some pleasure in the house' (4.3.75), repeating the play's coded term for sexuality. But Isabella has another kind of practice in mind, as when she next appears it is in the guise of a madwoman. Apparently having learned performance tricks from living in the asylum, as well as from Franciscus' mad act, Isabella has a rough play in mind for Antonio, one consisting of three decentred speeches, which for convenience are joined here:

> Hey, how she treads the air: Shoo! shoo! t'other way! He burns his wings else. [*She pulls Antonio down*] Here's wax enough below, Icarus, more than will be cancelled these eighteen moons.
>     [*She rises, (singing)*] He's down, he's down,
>         What a terrible fall he had!
> Stand up, thou son of Cretan Dedalus,
> And let us tread the lower labyrinth;
> I'll bring thee to the clue. [*She raises him*]
>
> .   .   .   .   .   .   .   .
>         Art thou not drowned?
> About thy head I saw a heap of clouds
> Wrapped like a Turkish turban; on thy back, [*She touches him*]
> A crook'd chameleon-coloured rainbow hung
> Like a tiara down unto thy hams. [*She kneels*]
> Let me suck out those billows in thy belly;
> Hark how they roar and rumble in the straits!
> Bless thee from the pirates.
>
> .   .   .   .   .   .   .   .
>
> Why shouldst thou mount so high as Mercury
> Unless thou hadst reversion of his place?

> Stay in the moon with me, Endymion, [*She touches him*]
> And we will rule these wild rebellious waves
> That would have drowned my love.
>
> 4.3.107–29

Isabella's play-within-the-play exposes this lover for the superficiality of his attraction to her. At the end of these speeches she concludes: 'I have no beauty now / Nor never had, but what was in my garments' (4.3.137–8). But the prelude to this dismissal sees Isabella exercise an astoundingly direct performance of sexual agency. Just as Lollio had violated her bodily integrity earlier when he placed his hand on her crotch, the 'thing about thee would do a man pleasure' (3.3.256), Isabella clearly and repeatedly gropes Antonio. The cues are within the role itself, for she uses the Icarus scenario to speak of 'wax' (a word that could connotate sexual fluids) and seems to touch his 'back' and 'hams' and 'belly' as she molests him and suggests she 'suck out those billows in thy belly'. Antonio responds angrily, demanding that she keep her hands off him. The comeuppance Isabella delivers is as delightful as it is theatrical, for it shows her suitor – and, at the same time, the audience and readers – what it is like to be the object of an artificial language and aggressively physical pursuit.

Late in *The Changeling*, Isabella reproves her husband for his own foolishness in relation to desire:

> You are a jealous coxcomb; keep schools of folly,
> And teach your scholars how to break your own head.
>
> 5.3.211–12

Her final words are on target. A teacher in her marriage as well as in the world of *The Changeling*, Isabella provides, through her rough seminar in desire, the play's sharpest insights on the social and personal implications of sexuality. Her 'treadings', in the end, are at and on a system stacked against her. To miss her performance is to miss this point.

# Notes

1 For an earlier treatment of Isabella's character, see Joost Daalder, 'The Role of Isabella in *The Changeling*,' *English Studies* 73.1 (1992): 22–9. See also Cristina Malcolmson, '"As tame as the ladies": politics and gender in *The Changeling*', *English Literary Renaissance*, 20.2 (1990): 320–39.
2 For an introduction to the form and function of theatrical roles during the early modern period, see Simon Palfrey and Tiffany Stern, *Shakespeare in Parts* (Oxford and New York: Oxford University Press, 2010).
3 *Oxford English Dictionary*, 'role' *n*.
4 A classic description of the multiple plot in early modern drama is Richard Levin, *The Multiple Plot in English Renaissance Drama* (Chicago: University of Chicago Press, 1971).
5 William Shakespeare, *A Midsummer Night's Dream,* ed. Sukanta Chaudhuri (London: Bloomsbury Arden Shakespeare, 2017), 1.1.137.
6 Thomas Heywood and William Rowley, *Fortune by Land and Sea* (London, 1655), p. 9. I have emended the punctuation of the original.
7 For discussion of the original casting of Lollio's role, see Lucy Munro, '*The Changeling*, the Boy Actor and Female Subjectivity' in this volume.
8 Shakespeare, *A Midsummer Night's Dream,* 5.1.58.

# PART THREE

# States of Mind

# 5

# 'The Pleasure of Your Bedlam'

# Mismanaging Insanity in *The Changeling*

## *Pascale Drouet*

Early modern playwrights were fascinated by insanity. Robert Rentoul Reed observes 'an abnormally extensive use of madness upon the Jacobean stage'.[1] Both Ophelia, a 'document in madness', and Lear, '[a]s mad as the vexed sea', come to mind.[2] But other playwrights take the lion's share of the dramatic appropriation of another 'stage', that of the Hospital of Bethlehem in London, also known as Bedlam asylum. Thomas Dekker and Thomas Middleton's *The Patient Man and the Honest Whore* (i.e. *The Honest Whore, Part One*) (1604), Dekker and John Webster's *Northward Ho!* (1605), Webster's *The Duchess of Malfi* (1614), John Fletcher's *The Pilgrim* (1621) and Middleton and William Rowley's *The Changeling* (1622) all dramatize hospital inmates, whether genuinely insane or counterfeit. In contrast to *Hamlet* and *King Lear*, and with the exception of Ferdinand's lycanthropy in *The Duchess of Malfi*, these plays do not explore individual characters' disturbed psyches but rather highlight the way madmen are *socially*, that is, *institutionally*, dealt with. The treatment of lunatics in the sixteenth and seventeenth centuries was as brutal as it was ineffective. 'Society', as Gámini Salgádo notes, 'was not prepared to put up with a poor man who was insane and so he was treated in much the same way as witches, whores, vagrants and others whose conduct was likely to be socially nonconformist'.[3] As William C. Carroll observes,

> [o]nce they were inscribed in the discourse of poverty [. . .] the London mad could be classified as a social rather than a psychological problem, and official management could turn from the untreatable 'mind diseased' to the more easily managed body.[4]

The 'official management' was that of the asylum of Bedlam, whose bad reputation was, early in the reign of James I, firmly established.

*The Changeling*, with its hospital plot, is one of the most famous Jacobean 'madhouse plays'. As Michael Neill points out, 'much of the play's early reputation seems to have depended on what is nowadays often dismissed as its inferior subplot'.[5] The first record of its performance at Whitehall dates back to January 1623, but it is likely to have been performed as early as 1622 at the Cockpit/Phoenix theatre, a private, indoor playhouse which lent itself to an atmosphere of confinement and claustrophobic effects, heightening the experience of enclosure, as Jean E. Howard shows in her chapter in this volume.[6] Whatever the precise date of composition, it seems significant that the play was performed *after* 'The Petition of the Poor Distracted People in the House of Bedlem [*sic*]', a 1620 'pamphlet or broad-sheet' 'licensed at Stationers' Hall', which also means *after* the appointment of Dr Helkiah Crooke – one of James I's private court physicians – as keeper of

Bethlehem Hospital in 1619.[7] The timing suggests a clear topical connection between Dr Crooke and the play's Dr Alibius.

To begin with, I will offer a brief diachronic survey of the hospital of Bethlehem from its creation in 1247 to Rowley and Middleton's days so as to develop an understanding of the sorry state the asylum was in and of the Jacobean audience's shared knowledge and expectations as spectators. I will then trace and analyse topically resonant allusions to the mismanagement of Bedlam – that is, to elements exposing the predominance of financial motives over medical competence and concern over charges of embezzlement, neglect, exhibition and exploitation. I will conclude by noting the broad scope of Middleton and Rowley's satire, extending my analysis from socio-political to religious criticism, from hospital plot to castle plot, from clinical to human folly – while noting that such distinctions may prove more permeable than firmly established.

# Bethlehem Hospital from 1247 to the Jacobean era

Originally, Bedlam was a priory, established in 1247 for the bishop of St Mary of Bethlehem. In 1330, it was converted into 'The Hospital of St Mary of Bethlehem', and it became more specifically a 'hospital for lunatics' in 1402. Things changed with the Reformation. In 1536, George Boleyn, who was then governor of the hospital, was beheaded; he was succeeded by Bishop Bonner, then by Sir Peter Mewtys, one of Henry VIII's confidential agents: two years after the appointment of Mewtys, 'the citizens set themselves to try and save from the greed and callousness of the king some of the London hospitals, of which Bethlehem was one'.[8] In 1538, the Mayor of London, Sir Richard Gresham, petitioned the King to regard favourably the religious houses that had been founded 'only for the relief and comfort of poor and impotent people unable to help themselves'.[9] As Edward G. O'Donoghue observes, the Mayor carefully calculated his appeal to Henry VIII, being both diplomatic and persistent: 'They were not founded for the maintenance of canons, priests, and monks to live in pleasure, nothing regarding the miserable people lying in every street, offending every clean person passing by their filthy and nasty savours.'[10] It took no less than eight years for Henry VIII to agree, just before his death in 1546, to grant Bethlehem to the City of London, provided the City would pay for maintenance and restoration work. From 1547 to 1556, the hospital for lunatics was administered by the court of aldermen; in late 1556, it was transferred to the governors of Christ's Hospital; and in 1557, it was placed under the management of Bridewell, the London house of correction, which over time would also develop a bad reputation. Funding priority never seems to have been given to the asylum: as O'Donoghue puts it, 'Bethlehem has always been the Cinderella among her disdainful sister hospitals'.[11]

Notorious mismanagement of Bedlam was brought to light in James I's reign. An inquiry held at Guildhall in 1618 revealed that Thomas Jenner, the keeper of the hospital, was 'unskilful in the practice of medicine' and possibly 'guilty of harshness and neglect towards his patients'.[12] He was consequently dismissed, in spite of protests and appeals. His successor looked different at first glance: Dr Helkiah Crooke, 'physician and anatomist', had shown an early interest in the problems of mental illness with his *Paramthion: Two Treatises of the Comforting of an Afflicted Conscience* (1598) and, as William Birken notes, he had 'burst into public awareness in 1615 with the publication of *Microcosmographia: a Description of the Body of Man*', a successful book reprinted in 1616 and 1618.[13] Thus, when the hospital was placed under his direction in 1619, he appeared trustworthy. As Crooke intended to reform the hospital, he immediately wrote a petition to James I, in which he urged that Bedlam should be freed from the supervision of Bridewell, alleging that the union of Bedlam and

Bridewell had been a disaster since 1557.[14] Indeed, the governors of Bridewell, who were also responsible for Bedlam, seem to have been unconcerned with asylum matters. According to Patricia Allderidge, Crooke had 'laid his finger with singular precision on both the cause and the symptom of Bethlem's trouble over the preceding 100 years'.[15]

The King, however, interpreted Crooke's demand as a threat to the jurisdiction he claimed over Bedlam and rejected it. Ken Jackson points out that 'by 1622 the Crown was asserting its control over all charitable practices'.[16] As a result, according to Jackson, 'the exchange between the Court of Aldermen and James was a very real struggle between social actors to determine the nature and government of a charity'.[17] For O'Donoghue, the King's rejection might explain why Crooke lost interest in the hospital and let it go – until he was forced to defend himself against the City's charges of corruption. Already by 1620, 'The Petition of the Poor Distracted People in the House of Bedlem' pointed to serious abuses. The court records of the period reveal the case of 'a father complaining to the governors that for want of proper attention his daughter's foot was rotting away,' and 'in 1622, there were charges made against the servants of showing unnecessary harshness towards a patient'.[18] In 1625, Crooke's misdemeanours were investigated, and he was finally dismissed in 1634, after investigating commissions under Charles I demonstrated the extent of his mismanagement.

# Crooke and Alibius

The charges of mismanagement against Crooke – mainly, in Birken's words, 'lining his own pockets with fees and contributions that should have gone to patient care' – may have inspired Middleton and Rowley in their dramatic portrait of Alibius.[19] In the play, Alibius makes money out of insanity and is after his patients' inheritances. The patients' relatives are blindly ready to pay him handsomely, so that their fools may have 'good attendance and sweet lodging' (1.2.119). What matters to the doctor is that his inmates come from rich families and stand to be heirs to their fortunes. Hence his question: 'is there not one incurable fool / That might be begged?' (4.3.221–2). Neill explains: 'In cases where an heir was legally declared a congenital idiot, his estate passed to the management of the crown; anyone who wished to enjoy its revenue could "beg a fool" – i.e. apply through the Court of Wards to be made his guardian.'[20] In the later Caroline reports, what is exposed is no less than embezzlement: 'it was proved by the commissioners of 1632 and 1633 [...] that legacies, fees from patients' friends, and other moneys [sic] went without reference to the steward's bills into the bulging pockets of Dr Crooke'.[21] The commissioners also found that Crooke's steward appropriated the regular supply of food and drink put at the disposal of the hospital by the Mayor and sheriffs. O'Donoghue describes the situation as follows: '[T]he steward and his wife – left with little but the bones by Dr Crooke – proceeded to take the choicest bits for themselves and to sell the remainder, which had cost them nothing, to their helpless prisoners at six times its value.'[22] In *The Changeling*, Lollio, Alibius' man, seems innocent of such practices – although he does extort extra money from the patients' kin, as his remark to Pedro testifies: 'Sir, an officer in this place may deserve something; the trouble will pass through my hands' (1.2.94–5). But the madmen's off-stage disjointed cries suggest that they are hungry and undernourished: 'the bread's too little!' (204–5), 'Give her more onion' (207), 'her parmesant, her parmesant!' (213–14). Their cries may echo the First Madman's voice of starvation in *The Patient Man and the Honest Whore*, a city comedy that Middleton had co-written with Dekker eighteen years earlier: 'I am starved and have had no meat, by this light, ever since the great flood' (Scene 15.247–9); 'these are my ribs – you may look through my ribs – see how my guts come out – these are my red guts, my very guts, O, O!' (252–4). Hunger fuels insanity, as Piero Camporesi has shown:

> The most effective and upsetting drug, bitterest and most ferocious, has always been hunger, creator of unfathomable disturbances of mind and imagination. Further lifelike and convincing dreams grew out of this forced hallucination, compensating for the everyday poverty.[23]

Undernourishment thus led to both physical and psychic degradations.

It is not clear whether the lunatics are underfed in *The Changeling*, but their abnormal behaviours, which hunger may accentuate, are never examined from any medical perspective in the hope of curing or at least alleviating them. Among Crooke's numerous misdemeanours was the fact that he 'only appeared at the hospital on quarter days'.[24] For O'Donoghue, this invites a comparison with another doctor, Timothy Bright, the author of *A Treatise of Melancholy* (1586). '[W]hile he [Bright] was writing his book,' he notes, 'he was neglecting his patients at St Bartholomew's, from which he was practically dismissed,' and he asks: 'Is Dr Crooke another example of the physician who sacrifices the responsibilities of his office and salary to more congenial pursuits and society?'[25] Likewise, in *The Changeling*, the aptly-named Alibius – his name means 'being in another place' – is persistently absent from his private asylum.[26] His man Lollio laments, 'Would my master were come home! I am not able to govern both these wards together' (3.3.183–5). But it seems obvious from the beginning of the play that the doctor neither 'governs' his hospital nor 'cures' his fools and madmen, although he claims he does:

> I do profess the cure of either sort;
> My trade, my living 'tis, I thrive by it.
> But here's the care that mixes with my thrift:
> The daily visitants that come to see
> My brainsick patients I would not have
> To see my wife.
>
> 1.2.49–54

With his obsessive fear of being turned into a cuckold, Alibius seems more concerned with his wife's possible succumbing to 'most shrewd temptations' (1.2.57) than with the mental health of his inmates, as is evidenced by his use of 'care' displaced from the medical to the domestic sphere. As regards 'cure', Neill notes that the word is 'conveniently ambiguous', as it can signify 'charge, care', 'medical treatment' or 'restoration to health'.[27] The meanings of the verbs 'cure' and 'care' that one would expect in such a context happen to be twisted by Alibius. And it is significant that economic terminology ('trade', 'living', 'thrive', 'thrift') should be foregrounded in his speech, symptomatic as it is of his interest in lucrative instrumentalization instead of medical treatment.

## Mistreatment and instrumentalization

*The Changeling* shows hospital staff using infantilizing and whipping as crude means of curing their patients. Both madmen and fools are 'under the whip' (1.2.45), which is also termed 'the wire' (211), quite tellingly, 'poison' (3.3.69), and 'commanding pizzle[s]' (4.3.65). The (counterfeit) fools are clearly infantilized by Lollio, as when he addresses the supposed fool Antonio, saying 'Peace, peace, Tony! You must not cry, child; you must be whipped if you do' (1.2.150–1); 'Once more and you shall go play, Tony' (182); 'No, you must to your book now; you have played sufficiently' (3.3.225–6). As for the madmen, they are safely kept away, relegated to their own ward or 'kennel' (3.3.100), like wild beasts caged up, closely associated as they are with the animal kingdom. Isabella reports that '[s]ometimes they imitate the beasts and birds, / Singing, or howling, braying, barking; all / As their wild fancies prompt 'em' (3.3.213–15), as if to confirm Michel Foucault's idea that '[l]a folie emprunte son visage au masque de la bête'.[28] Isabella's description was in effect echoed and enlarged ten years later in *London and the Countrey Carbonadoed and Quartred into Severall Characters*, Donald Lupton's 1632 book of characters illustrating the habits and manners of Englishmen from the reign of James I, in which Bedlam is visited and depicted as follows:

> It seemes strange that any one should recover here, the cryings, screechings, roarings, brawlings, shakings of chaines, swearings, frettings, chaffings, are so many, so hideous, so great, that they are more able to drive a man that hath his witts, rather out of them, then to helpe one that never had them, or hath lost them, to find them again. [. . . T]hey are all *Heteroclites* from Nature, either having too much Wildnesse, or being defective in judgment.[29]

Lupton questions his contemporaries' ability either to manage or to cure madness, a critique already visible in embryo in Middleton and Rowley's play. The scenes located in Alibius' hospital reveal that, as Foucault observes in *Histoire de la folie à l'âge classique*, 'la folie relève, moins que jamais, de la médecine; elle ne peut pas appartenir davantage au domaine de la correction. Animalité déchaînée, on ne peut la maîtriser que par le *dressage* et *l'abêtissement*'.[30] What may have shocked Middleton and Rowley – and their audiences – was perhaps not so much the way madness was contained rather than cured but the neglect of basic human care and the use of '*discipline* and *brutalizing*', combined with lucrative instrumentalization and exhibition.[31]

With Lollio's help, Alibius plans to answer Vermandero's request and exhibit what he calls a 'mixture of our madmen and our fools' (3.3.277) – echoed by Lupton's '*Heteroclites* from Nature, either having too much Wildnesse, or being defective in judgment' – at the wedding entertainment. The doctor is paid to organize 'an unexpected passage over, / To make a frightful pleasure' (280–1), but he has a plan to get even more money out of his inmates by having them dance extravagantly. He tells Lollio:

> Could we so act it
> To teach it in a wild distracted measure,
> Though out of form and figure, breaking Time's head –
> (It were not matter, 'twould be healed again
> In one age or other, if not in this).
> 'Tis this, Lollio: there's a good reward begun,
> And will beget a bounty be it known.
>
> 3.3.282–8

The verb 'heal', unexpected in such a context, betrays the doctor's cynicism. It is symptomatic of a strategy of postponement and, more significantly, it is misapplied: what might be 'healed' in the future is not the distraction of his patients but the 'distracted measure' of the 'morris' dance (4.3.69). Isabella's ironic reaction articulates a criticism of such practices: 'You've a fine trade on't: / Madmen and fools are a staple commodity' (3.3.296–7). But what matters for Alibius, as he tells his wife, is that '[b]y madmen and by fools [they] both do thrive' (300). He intends, that is, to reduce his inmates to a lucrative and entertaining spectacle. As Carroll puts it, 'the "Bedlam poor" are just another form of popular entertainment, culturally equivalent to various urban curiosities, or to such theatricalized spectacles as bear-baiting or "stage plays"'.[32] At the asylum of Bedlam, Salgádo explains,

> both the harmless and the violent were available for important visitors to amuse themselves with. The general public had to pay for admission. [. . .] The entertainment regularly provided included the beating of the inmates with wire whips and the opportunity to harass those who were chained from a safe distance.[33]

In *The Changeling*, Isabella, locked at home by her jealous husband, resignedly accepts Lollio's offer to entertain her with the actions of his patients: 'Afford me then the pleasure of your bedlam' (3.3.24), she says. Alibius' man produces one of the fools, 'a gentle nidget' (114), for her entertainment. While pretending to reassure her – 'you may play with him, as safely with him as with his bauble' (114–16) – he introduces a bawdy *double entendre* (the 'bauble' refers to both the 'fool's baton' and the 'penis'), suggesting more licentious pleasure.[34] Far from being considered an object of medical attention, deficiency in understanding is reduced to a form of entertainment that transforms it into an object of mockery or a useful satirical vehicle, becoming another form of instrumentalization. 'I'll undertake to wind him up to the wit of constable' (1.2.129–30), says Lollio about one of his newly acquired patients, thus mocking both this fool in particular and constables, who were popularly represented as unintelligent in the manner of Dogberry in Shakespeare's *Much Ado About Nothing*. If Lollio seems to be having fun, there is clearly no 'mirth in madness' (3.3.30) for Isabella, and she casts a critical glance at such practices: 'Alack, alack, 'tis too full of pity / To be laughed at' (48–9). The spectacle of insanity should elicit pity and charity instead of being frivolously presented as another sort of recreation. Middleton and Rowley's play probably reflected the fact that 'the show of Bethlem', as Jackson notes, 'had come under criticism for emphasizing its "theatre" rather than its charity'.[35]

# A satire of charitable practices

Jackson reminds us that '[e]arly modern Europe relied primarily on religion and religious discourse to explain, justify, and manage its charitable practices.'[36] He argues that *The Changeling* is Middleton and Rowley's answer to John Fletcher's *The Pilgrim*, performed a year earlier in 1621, and particularly to the 'valorization of Catholic good works' in that play through the Master of the mental hospital in Segovia, who shows concern and compassion for his inmates. Rowley and Middleton, conversely, expose the mismanagement of Alibius' private hospital, that is, 'the potential for perversion in the holy motivation for charity', the 'corrupt uses that relied on the Catholic notion of caritas'.[37] According to Jackson,

Antonio and Franciscus have come to the madhouse previously as visitors, Middleton and Rowley suggest, masking *cupiditas* for Isabella with *caritas* for the mad. In unmasking these two, the playwrights critique this 'Catholic' charitable logic as a whole.[38]

It is significant in this context that *The Changeling* should include no charitable visitors having a genuine interest in and compassion for Alibius' inmates.

What is Alibius' main preoccupation? That his man Lollio should watch his wife rather than his inmates, for fear she should cuckold him with the 'daily visitants that come to see / [His] brainsick patients' (1.2.52–3). This is why, unaware of the bawdy *double entendre* of his own words, he tells Lollio: 'Here, I do say, must thy employment be: / To watch her treadings, and in my absence / Supply my place' (37–9). In addition to the ambiguous phrase 'Supply my place', Neill points to the double meaning of 'treadings' as 'acts of copulation' and 'place' as 'vulva'.[39] Alibius' insecurity and fantasies turn the asylum into a stage propitious for a farce, whose standard target is the old cuckold. From the start, the stakes are domestic, not medical or charitable; the asylum administration is perverted by the doctor's private obsession, or what Joost Daalder calls his 'paranoia'.[40] Both the institution and its hypocritical visitors are exposed; care and cure are reduced to a convenient cover for sexual opportunities that appear to pervade not only the castle plot but also the hospital plot. Lunatics are exhibited, but what is exposed is the mismanagement and abuse of those who are supposed to be sane.

Beyond the religious implications pointed out by Jackson, the play may reflect what was at issue in Jacobean England, that is, the change from individual to institutionalized charity, the emergence of a new sensibility regarding madness that is no longer religious but social. As Foucault notes, the (mis) management of madness is closely associated with the new apprehension of misery, which 'glisse d'une expérience religieuse qui la sanctifie, à une conception morale qui la condamne. Les grandes maisons d'internement se rencontrent au terme de cette évolution: laïcisation de la charité'.[41] Consequently: 'Si la folie, au XVIIe siècle, est comme *désacralisée*, c'est d'abord parce que la misère a subi cette sorte de déchéance qui la fait percevoir maintenant sur le seul horizon de la morale.'[42] As Walter Kaiser has noted, the 'natural fool' was no longer 'thought to be under the special protection of God' – and thus not only 'tolerated' but possibly 'venerated' – as he used to be in the Middle Ages.[43] Laicized in this way, insanity is morally condemned and treated as a social, even socio-economic, problem: lunatics are to be contained or/and turned into commodities for 'the dramaturgy of the margins'.[44]

# From 'clinical' to human folly

Alibius' hospital is, in fact, a stage for counterfeit lunatics, namely Antonio and Franciscus – and later on Isabella, when she disguises herself as a madwoman to make fun of Antonio and catch him out at his own game. The 'genuine' fools and madmen are relegated to the background: they are mainly *heard*, and when they are *seen*, or rather *caught a glimpse of*, they are located '*above*' (s.d. 3.3.207), in the distance. They are, as Carol Thomas Neely observes, 'less characters than performative fragments', existing only as 'disembodied voices or dumb performers'.[45] *The Changeling*, Neely notes, 'banishes the mad to the very edge of the play-space'.[46] Middleton and Rowley's disclosures about mental disability in the hospital scenes may be mirrored in what Alibius is asked to exhibit for the wedding entertainment: in both cases, it seems that madness is exhibited just long enough to create a spectacular effect, to 'make a frightful pleasure, that is all' (3.3.281). In the end, the lunatics' masque does not take place since the bride, Beatrice-Joanna, is dead, so we have no indication of how the wedding guests would have reacted. But Isabella's earlier reaction at seeing a madman on display – one whose counterfeit nature has not yet been revealed to her – needs no further gloss. Her response – 'Alack, alack, 'tis too full of pity / To be laughed at' (3.3.48–9) – is enough to cue the audience to question the 'theatrical' practice of the asylum. There is no 'pleasure' (24) in the show of madness, and the so-called 'delight' (28) it supposedly creates can be only oxymoronic and 'pitiful' (28). Further in the scene, Isabella says of those patients with genuine mental disability that they 'act their fantasies in any shapes / Suiting their present thoughts' (3.3.210–11). But lunacy is no prerequisite to act in such a way. Isabella's complete cue, ending with 'all / As their wild fancies prompt 'em' (214–15), may read not only as a description of what – depending on how much time is allotted to enacting the preceding stage direction: '*Madmen above, some as birds, others as beasts*' (s.d. 3.3.207) – the audience is barely allowed to see in the hospital but also as a comment on the whole tragedy, in which we see high characters 'suit their present thoughts' and so act 'their wild fancies'. Alibius' private hospital is indeed, as Neill notes, 'the parodic double of Vermandero's castle': 'the wild antics of the madhouse inmates' read as 'figurations of a world given over to vicious insanity'.[47]

In Alibius' hospital, the patients are divided into 'two sorts of people' (1.2.44): the fools and the madmen. According to Lollio, '[t]he one has not wit enough to be knaves, and the other not knavery enough to be fools' (45–7). But if the 'inmates' of Vermandero's castle are taken into account, a third sort can be added: those who have knavery enough to be fools. Susan Neal Mayberry questions the watertightness of reassuring and simplifying categories in the play, pointing to their reversibility:

> The playwrights alternate their tales dramatizing a society's gradual disintegration with scenes depicting the antics of the inmates of an asylum. We are drawn into a nightmare where people who exhibit unconventional but relatively harmless behaviours are deemed insane while those who deliberately lie, deceive, commit adultery and murder but

maintain a conventional appearance are not. The very structure of the drama asks us to question exactly who belongs to the madhouse.[48]

Interestingly, Middleton and Rowley's two plots both encompass the various meanings of the term 'folly'. Quite obviously, two basic meanings – 'madness, insanity, mania (French *folie*)', on the one hand, and 'want of good sense, weakness or derangement of mind', on the other hand – are epitomized by Alibius' madmen and fools. But 'folly' in the sense of 'a foolish action, error, idea, practice; a ridiculous thing, an absurdity' is the lot of all the foolish suitors, ranging from Antonio and Franciscus to Alonzo de Piracquo and Alsemero, without forgetting De Flores' obsession for Beatrice, which points to folly as 'lewdness, wantonness'.

Finally, when the focus is on the main plot, folly comes to signify 'wickedness, evil, mischief, harm'.[49] In this regard, the most evil 'fools' in the play are Beatrice and De Flores, those whom Alsemero aptly calls 'twins of mischief' (5.3.142). Over the whole play we are presented with what Foucault terms 'la danse insensée des vies immorales'.[50] But, as Neill observes, '*The Changeling* repeatedly figures erotic passion as a disease of the mind, compared to whose destructive frenzies the crazy antics of Alibius' lunatics seem almost harmless'.[51] At the end of the play, most of the characters who are not dead seem to learn from their blindness or errors and are apparently ready to 'change' for the best. Yet Alibius' future 'transformation' (5.3.210) concerns only the domestic sphere: 'I see all apparent, wife, and will change now / Into a better husband, and never keep / Scholars that shall be wiser than myself' (213–15). If the doctor comes to realize that he has neglected his wife, it never dawns upon him that he might have neglected his patients too.

Mental disability becomes a remarkable dramatic tool in the hands of Middleton and Rowley. On the surface, it retains the potential to create both farce and spectacular effects and thus be entertaining; more significantly, it questions the abusive practices of 'medical' institutions, such as neglect and cruelty, and it elicits pity, thus inviting both awareness and charity from the Jacobean audience. The playwrights may also have been suggesting that insanity, in spite of its senseless microsyntax (words that cannot be logically arranged with other words in the lunatics' psyches), is part of society's macrosyntax (the set of rules governing the arrangement of sociopolitical elements). For Jackson, the hospital of Bethlehem was 'an authentic, non-representational "theatre" that more fully incorporated madness in the world of reason'.[52] It might be suggested that the other theatre, the representational one, through plays such as *The Changeling*, helped defer, on the level of social consciousness, what Foucault calls 'le grand renfermement'[53] – the Great Confinement.

# Notes

1 Robert Rentoul Reed, *Bedlam on the Jacobean Stage* (Cambridge, MA: Harvard University Press, 1952), 4. The present essay is an enlarged and revised version of 'Madness and Mismanagement in Middleton and Rowley's *The Changeling*', *Theta X – Folly and Politics*, Richard Hillman and Pauline Ruberry-Blanc (eds), online publication, Scène Européenne, Centre d'Études Supérieures de la Renaissance, Tours (http://sceneeuropeenne.univ-tours.fr/theta/theta10) 2013, 139–52. Earlier material has been reproduced with permission.

2 William Shakespeare, *Hamlet* [Q2 text], Ann Thompson and Neil Taylor (eds), revised edition, The Arden Shakespeare, Third Series (London: Bloomsbury Arden Shakespeare, 2016), 4.5.172; *King Lear*, R.A. Foakes (ed.), The Arden Shakespeare, Third Series (London: Bloomsbury Arden Shakespeare, 1997), 4.4.2.

3 Gámini Salgádo, *The Elizabethan Underworld* (Stroud: Sutton Publishing, 1997), 198–9.

4 William C. Carroll, *Fat King, Lean Beggar: Representations of Poverty in the Age of Shakespeare* (Ithaca, NY: Cornell University Press, 1996), 107. The quotation is from William Shakespeare, *Macbeth*, Sandra Clark and Pamela Mason (eds), (London: Bloomsbury Arden Shakespeare, 2015), 5.3.40.

5 Michael Neill, 'Introduction', Thomas Middleton and William Rowley, *The Changeling*, 'Revised Edition', Michael Neill (ed.), New Mermaids (London: Methuen Drama, 2019), xi.
6 Neill, 'Introduction', xi.
7 See Edward Geoffrey O'Donoghue, *The Story of Bethlehem Hospital from Its Foundation in 1247* (New York: Dutton, 1915), 157–60.
8 O'Donoghue, *The Story of Bethlehem Hospital*, 110.
9 Sir Richard Gresham, cited by O'Donoghue, *The Story of Bethlehem Hospital*, 111.
10 O'Donoghue, *The Story of Bethlehem Hospital*, 111.
11 O'Donoghue, *The Story of Bethlehem Hospital*, 128.
12 O'Donoghue, *The Story of Bethlehem Hospital*, 156.
13 William Birken, 'Crooke, Helkiah (1576–1648)', *Oxford Dictionary of National Biography*, published online 23 September 2004. https://doi-org.ezproxy.bu.edu/10.1093/ref:odnb/6775
14 O'Donoghue, *The Story of Bethlehem Hospital*, 158.
15 Patricia Allderidge, 'Management and Mismanagement at Bedlam, 1547–1633', in Charles Webster (ed.), *Health, Medicine, and Mortality in the Sixteenth Century* (Cambridge: Cambridge University Press, 1979), 141–64 (156).
16 Ken Jackson, *Separate Theaters: Bethlem ('Bedlam') Hospital and the Shakespearean Stage* (Newark: University of Delaware Press, 2005), 204.
17 Jackson, *Separate Theaters*, 213.
18 O'Donoghue, *The Story of Bethlehem Hospital*, 160.
19 Birken, 'Crooke, Helkiah', *ODNB*.
20 Neill, *The Changeling*, footnote at 4.3.197–8, 104.
21 O'Donoghue, *The Story of Bethlehem Hospital*, 167.
22 O'Donoghue, *The Story of Bethlehem Hospital*, 168.
23 Piero Camporesi, *Bread of Dreams: Food and Fantasy in Early Modern Europe* [*Il Pane Selvaggio*, 1980], trans. David Gentilcore (Chicago: Chicago University Press, 1989), 125.
24 O'Donoghue, *The Story of Bethlehem Hospital*, 160.

25 O'Donoghue, *The Story of Bethlehem Hospital*, 164.

26 Neill, *The Changeling*, footnote at 'Dramatis Personae', '*names*', 2.

27 Neill, *The Changeling*, footnote 1.2.47, 21.

28 Michel Foucault, *Histoire de la folie à l'âge classique* (Paris: Gallimard, 1972), 197. 'Madness borrowed its face from the mask of the beast', trans. Richard Howard, *Madness and Civilization: A History of Insanity in the Age of Reason* (New York: Vintage Books, 1973), 72. Unfortunately, the published English translation is brutally abridged, so the translation will be mine when necessary (and so identified).

29 Donald Lupton, *London and the Countrey Carbonadoed and Quartred into Severall Characters* (London: Nicholas Okes, 1632), 75–7.

30 Foucault, *Histoire de la folie*, 200: 'madness was less than ever linked to medicine; nor could it be linked to the domain of correction. Unchained animality could be mastered only by *discipline* and *brutalizing*', trans. Richard Howard, *Madness and Civilization*, 75.

31 '*Discipline* and *brutalizing*' as well as instrumentalization and exhibition had already been drastically exposed in Webster's *The Duchess of Malfi*, when Ferdinand is 'resolved / To remove forth the common hospital / All the mad folk' (4.1.123–5) to madden his sister, and when the Doctor attempts to 'buffet his madness out of him' (5.2.26) after Ferdinand has fallen prey to lycanthropy (ed. Leah S. Marcus, Arden Early Modern Drama, 2017). On this topic see Pascale Drouet, 'Madness in *The Duchess of Malfi*', in William C. Carroll and Pascale Drouet (eds), *The Duchess of Malfi: Webster's Tragedy of Blood* (Paris: Belin, 2018), 142–55.

32 Carroll, *Fat King, Lean Beggar*, 100.

33 Salgādo, *The Elizabethan Underworld*, 202.

34 Neill, *The Changeling*, footnote at 3.2.101, 58.

35 Jackson, *Separate Theaters*, 204.

36 Jackson, *Separate Theaters*, 206.

37 Jackson, *Separate Theaters*, 213, 223, 221.

38 Jackson, *Separate Theaters*, 223.

39 Neill, *The Changeling*, footnote at 1.2.37 and 1.2.38, 21.

40 Joost Daalder, 'Folly and Madness in *The Changeling*', *Essays in Criticism*, vol. XXXVIII, January 1988, no. 1, 1–21, here 4.

41 Foucault, *Histoire de la folie*, 84. 'Misery shifts from a religious experience that sanctifies it to a moral conception that condemns it. The great houses of confinement meet at the end of this evolution: the laicization of charity' (my translation).

42 Foucault, *Histoire de la folie*, 89 (Foucault's italics). 'If madness, in the 17th century, seems *desacralized*, it is first of all because misery has undergone this kind of decline which makes it perceived now only on the horizon of morality' (my translation).

43 Walter Kaiser, *Praisers of Folly: Erasmus, Rabelais, Shakespeare* (Cambridge, MA: Harvard University Press, 1963), 6.

44 Steven Mullaney, *The Place of the Stage: Licence, Play, and Power in Renaissance England* (Chicago: The University of Chicago Press, 1995), 31. This 'dramaturgy of the margins' involved not only 'madhouses' but also 'hospitals', 'brothels', 'scaffolds of executions', 'prisons' and 'lazar-houses'.

45 Carol Thomas Neely, '"Distracted Measures": Madness and Theatricality in Middleton', in Suzanne Gossett (ed.), *Thomas Middleton in Context* (Cambridge: Cambridge University Press, 2011), 306–13, here 307, 310.

46 Carol Thomas, Neely, *Distracted Subjects: Madness and Gender in Shakespeare and Early Modern Culture* (Ithaca/New York: Cornell University Press, 2004), 198.

47 Neill, 'Introduction', *The Changeling*, xxvi, xliii.

48 Susan Neal Mayberry, 'Cuckoos and Convention: Madness in Middleton and Rowley's *The Changeling*', *Mid-Hudson Language Studies* 8, 1985, 21–32, here 22.

49 *Oxford English Dictionary Online*, 'folly, *n*.1', 4; 1. a; 1. c.; 3. a.; 2. a.

50 Foucault, *Histoire de la folie*, 180. 'The senseless dance of immoral lives' (my translation).

51 Neill, 'Introduction', *The Changeling*, xxv.

52 Jackson, *Separate Theaters*, 245.

53 Foucault, *Histoire de la folie*, 67.

# 6

# Passions, Affections and Instinct in *The Changeling*

## Jesse M. Lander

Criticism of *The Changeling* has emphasized the play's depiction of a peculiarly modern sexuality. While these readings respond to an obtrusive, indeed inescapable aspect of the play, the deployment of a psychoanalytic or quasi-psychoanalytic frame reads past the play's own highly developed vocabulary of attraction and repulsion.[1] An approach informed by the history of emotions, in contrast, not only recovers the specific early modern understandings of passion, affection and instinct but also reveals the degree to which the play's use of this vocabulary is bound up with developments in both philosophy and theology. Of particular importance for *The Changeling*'s engagement with the passions are a newly fashionable stoicism and a still dominant, but increasingly embattled, Calvinism.[2] An attention to these two discourses suggests that *The Changeling*'s finely calibrated investigation of what we now call emotions operates at some distance from contemporary accounts of desire.

The pioneering scholarship of Gail Kern Paster has led to an outpouring of work on the emotions in early modern culture and drama. Her rehabilitation of humoralism, which had been relegated to gloss notes and treated as quaint Tillyardian trivia, presents it as a ubiquitous framework that is at once strange and familiar. The technical vocabulary of blood, phlegm, choler and black bile remains intransigently antiquated, but the idea of a humoral body that is traversed by outside forces and deeply impacted by its environment, a nexus Paster describes as 'the ecology of the passions', resonates deeply with modern readers who are themselves exposed to the consequences of environmental degradation in its many forms.[3] The appeal of Paster's approach is, in part, its materialism, and *The Changeling*, in her account, 'provides vivid examples of the early modern understanding of emotions as material events – bodily in origin, humoral in nature, and influenced by social and environmental factors inside and outside the body itself'.[4] At the same time, the humoral approach tends to obscure the importance of the soul and of supernatural forces in its rendering of early modern passions. In what follows, I am especially interested in the way that instinct operates in the play alongside passions and affections. The larger argument is that the play's insistence on instinct reveals that the evaluation of early modern emotions is frequently complicated by an entanglement with the supernatural or spiritual world.

The opening of *The Changeling* announces a play that will interrogate human passions and affections. A familiar dynamic presents itself: a lover announces himself in the grip of strong, unalterable passion. After Alsemero's opening soliloquy, describing his newly established love for the as-yet-unnamed Beatrice-Joanna, his companion Jasperino enters and, puzzled by his friend's reluctance to depart, observes:

> Lover are you none; the stoic
> Was found in you long ago – your mother
> Nor best friends, who have set snares of beauty
> (Ay and choice ones too), could never trap you that way.
>
> 1.1.36–9

This identification of Alsemero as a stoic establishes him as intellectually committed to the pursuit of *apatheia* and thus protected from the 'snares of beauty'. Of course, Jasperino describes what Alsemero used to be; as the play's first example of a changeling, he has already abandoned stoicism. By introducing an already absent stoic at the outset, the play signals its interest in contemporary debates over the proper place of the passions and the affections, an interest that extends considerably beyond the typical Elizabethan denunciation of stoicism as an insensate, indeed, inhuman philosophy, a criticism that is registered colloquially by the common pun on stoics as stocks, as in Tranio's 'Let's be no stoics nor no stocks' in *The Taming of the Shrew*.[5] The play's more extensive engagement is signalled not only by the identification of Alsemero as a stoic but by Lollio's joking response to Antonio's attempts to kiss Isabella: 'Have you read Lipsius? He's past *Ars Amandi*; I believe I must put harder questions to him, I perceive that' (3.3.195–7). The invocation of Justus Lipsius, the most prominent proponent of neostoicism at the time, is usually explained as a trivial pun on lips, though some have made the connection between Lipsius' notoriously shifting commitments and Antonio's status as another one of the play's several changelings.[6] The possibility that *The Changeling* presents a more sustained response to Lipsius and his neostoicism has not attracted much attention.[7] Yet, the presence of stoicism in different scenes attributed to Rowley and to Middleton suggests that the integration of the hospital plot and the castle plot is more carefully coordinated than many critics have assumed.

The hospital scenes provide a comic perspective on the passions and affections that complements the tragedy that unfolds in the castle. As Pascale Drouet notes, these scenes involve topical satire that points towards contemporary abuses at the Hospital of Bethelem, but they also raise questions about the moral status of the insane and the history of madness.[8] Commenting on the display of madmen acting as birds and beasts, Isabella observes that they 'act their fantasies in any shapes / Suiting their present thoughts – if sad, they cry; / If mirth be their conceit, they laugh again' (3.3.210–12). The expressive transparency of the lunatics, whose comportment is constantly shifting to reflect new fancies and feelings, figures madness as a radical inability to control oneself. The lovers disguised as madmen are capable of deceit, unlike the truly mad, but by committing themselves to the asylum in pursuit of Isabella they reveal themselves to be controlled by an irrational passion. Isabella, in contrast, 'exercises agency' as Douglas Bruster writes.[9] Importantly, however, her agency does not entail a stoic rejection of the affections: her rebuke of Antonio only accuses him of superficiality and a lack of discernment.

While the precise degree to which the play takes up the question of neostoicism remains open, there is no doubt that *The Changeling*, with its emphasis on what Paster has described as 'mysteriousness of the twinned circuitries of desire and aversion', is deeply interested in the passions and their consequences. What a modern audience sees as sexual obsession, however, looks slightly different when considered in the light of early modern psychologies. As Thomas Dixon has pointed out, the standard pre-modern psychology is deeply informed by theology and is not as uniformly hostile to strong feelings as has sometimes been supposed. The key point is that the discourse in respect of what we now refer to as emotions made a distinction between passions and affections. Passions were seen as bodily, appetitive, involuntary and disruptive; affections, in contrast, were intellectual and voluntary.[10] Dixon deploys this crisp taxonomy in order to describe the history of psychology as a process of secularization and to recover the centrality of the soul as a category of analysis for earlier approaches to the mind. However, the sharp distinction made in the philosophical tradition that draws on Augustine and Aquinas is treated with less precision in much of the early modern writing on the passions and affections. As Erin Sullivan has shown, even Thomas Wright's *The Passions of the Mind* does not consistently mark a distinction between the two terms, though it does tend to differentiate affections ('almost always linked with religious feeling and devotion') from passions (linked to bodily perturbations).[11] Given this semantic range, it is hardly surprising that in early modern literary usage the terms reveal considerable overlap and little consistent differentiation.

A notable, and instructive, exception is *The Changeling*'s source text: John Reynolds' *The Triumphs of God's Revenge* (1621). A collection of providential narratives all demonstrating the inevitable exposure and punishment of murder, Reynolds' account regularly uses 'affection' for benign attachment and 'passion' for transgressive feelings; usually derided for its psychological implausibility and its heavy-handed moralizing, the *Triumphs* reveals a consistent interest in the way its characters speak about their feelings.[12] Beatrice-Joanna, for example, begins a letter to Alsemero, 'As it is not for earth to resist heauen, nor for our wills to contradict Gods prouidence, so I cannot deny, but now acknowledge, that if euer I affected any man, it is your selfe' (S1$^v$). Though Alexandra Walsham faults *The Triumphs of God's Revenge* for its 'salacious and bloodthirsty character' and its inconsistent invocation of fortune and chance, the book does suggest that in a providentially ordered world, passions and affections are not merely voluntary.[13]

Reynolds' interest in affections and passions carries over into the play, and *The Changeling* also exhibits a distinction between the two terms. When Tomazo arrives on the scene, the quality of Beatrice-Joanna's attachment to Alonzo is explicitly discussed and, unlike his brother, Tomazo assesses Beatrice-Joanna's feelings accurately: 'I see small welcome in her eye' (2.1.107). This observation provokes an elaborate rebuttal from Alonzo:

> Fie, you are too severe a censurer
> Of love in all points: there's no bringing on you.
> If lovers should mark everything a fault,
> Affection would be like an ill-set book,
> Whose faults might prove as big as half the volume.
>
> 2.1.108–12

Alonzo's extended book metaphor vindicates 'affection' as a settled disposition toward some good, and his use of it is congruent with the language found in contemporaneous marriage manuals, such as William Whately's *A Bride-bush*, which urges that sex between married couples should be accompanied by 'all demonstrations of heartie affection'.[14] The usage here conforms to *OED* (*n*. 1, I.2.a): 'Favourable or kindly disposition towards a person or thing; fondness, tenderness; goodwill, warmth of attachment. Esp. in early use also more strongly: †love (for another person) (obsolete).' *Affection* as love for another person is distinct from passion and lust though it also carries a sexual sense. Alonzo's defence of loving affection is appealing, despite being mistaken about Beatrice-Joanna. As Tomazo presses his point, he establishes a clear contrast between affection and passion: 'Unsettle your affection with all speed / Wisdom can bring it to; your peace is ruined else' (130–1).[15] Affection, according to Tomazo, is voluntary and subject to the intellect ('wisdom'). He then goes on to describe, in graphic detail, the prospect of sex with a partner whose libidinous attachments are elsewhere:

> She lies but with another in thine arms,
> He the half-father to all thy children
> In the conception – if he get 'em not,
> She helps to get 'em for him in his absence.
>
> 136–9

The general meaning is clear enough: Beatrice's absent lover will haunt the moment of conception. But the idea, common in the early modern period and also relevant later in the play, that female orgasm was necessary for conception makes Tomazo's observation even more pointed.[16]

The passage is further complicated by a significant moment of textual instability. The Oxford edition's 'in his absence' is an emendation of the quarto text, which reads 'in his passions' (D1r).[17] The possibility that something has gone wrong here is difficult to dismiss, but rather than emend 'passions' to 'absence', one might instead make the case that 'his' is a misreading of 'her'.[18] This emendation yields a line that makes good sense in context: whatever pleasure Beatrice achieves in the marital bed ('her passions') will be owing to her ability to imagine that she is, in fact, in the arms of her true love. Whether one accepts the argument for such an emendation or simply reverts to the Quarto reading, emending 'passions' to 'absence' places the emphasis on phantasmal paternity and obscures Tomazo's sharp distinction between lawful affection and transgressive passion. Ultimately, the gender of the possessive matters less than the presence of 'passions'; after all, Tomazo's claim is that Beatrice has forged a passionate attachment to another, unknown man.

Alonzo and Tomazo's consideration of affection and passion echoes the exchange about love between Alsemero and Beatrice-Joanna that opens the play. Their flirtatious banter presents familiar ideas about love, sight and judgement, but things take a strange turn when De Flores appears. Trying to explain her visceral recoil, Beatrice-Joanna invokes the idiosyncrasy of taste:

> Nor can I other reason render you,
> Than his or hers, of some particular thing
> They must abandon as a deadly poison,
> Which to a thousand other tastes were wholesome.

1.1.110–13

As editor Douglas Bruster observes in the *Oxford Middleton*, this claim draws on a familiar proverb: 'One man's meat is another man's poison'.[19] Alsemero seizes the opportunity to descant upon 'a frequent frailty in our nature': 'one distastes / The scent of roses, which to infinites / Most pleasing is' (1.1.116, 118–19). The notion of a peculiar antipathy draws on what Mary Floyd-Wilson describes as a 'hidden logic [. . .] which attributes people's strange behaviors and motives to the hidden sympathies and antipathies that course through the natural world'.[20] Despite his own commitment to the pursuit of nature's secrets, Alsemero here presents a trivializing version of antipathy as mere distaste that concludes by compressing the proverb into a witty paradox: 'There's scarce a thing but is both loved and loathed' (125). What this aphoristic proposition points towards is less a fundamental ambivalence within the human subject, a condition in which love and loathing, attraction and repulsion, are adjacent affects, than the great diversity of responses to a single object.[21] Loathing is, according to Alsemero, merely a personal preference.

According to Alsemero, such idiosyncratic likes and dislikes are not the result of judgement and are not subject to argument. Unlike Alsemero, whose legislative metaphor for the ratification of eyes by his judgement is elaborately witty and worryingly glib (1.1.76–82), Beatrice-Joanna gives sustained attention to the issue. Alone at the start of Act 2, she returns to the subject, 'How wise is Alsemero in his friend! / It is a sign he makes his choice with judgement.' (2.1.6–7). Her insistence on Alsemero's judgement seamlessly turns into an assertion of her own discernment: 'Methinks I love now with the eyes of judgement, / And see the way to merit, clearly see it' (13–14). Beatrice-Joanna here presents her 'intellectual eyesight' (19) as unencumbered by the body and acute. Her confident rationalism, when paired with a claim about the identification and pursuit of merit, would have sounded dangerously delusory to a reformed audience for whom such language would have sounded suspiciously Catholic. Though mistaken about the acuity of her judgement, Beatrice-Joanna engages in a form of self-scrutiny that tries to subject affection to careful assessment.

Beatrice-Joanna attempts here to present her attachment to Alsemero as a rational affection, and yet the immediate appearance of De Flores is a reminder that she is still subject to passions: 'This ominous ill-faced fellow more disturbs me / Than all my other passions' (2.1.53–4). There is a tendency to read this as an admission that Beatrice-Joanna's response to De Flores is from the start sexual; the perturbation of the mind that he provokes joins an unspecified set of 'other passions' that might well include her earlier interest in Alonzo and her current desire for Alsemero. However, in the immediate context it seems plausible to read this claim as marking a distinction between her attachment to Alsemero and her aversion to De Flores. On the one hand, an affectionate attachment that has the apparent ratification of her judgement and, on the other, a passionate aversion that remains disturbing and inexplicable. This scene of self-scrutiny leads, with the entrance of Vermandero, Alonzo and Tomazo, to the consideration of affection discussed above and, despite the clear theoretical distinction between a voluntary and benign affection and an involuntary and disabling passion, the play suggests that a proper understanding of ardent feelings remains elusive.

Of all the play's desiring characters, De Flores is clearest about the compulsive aspect of his attachment. Initially, De Flores presents himself using the language of a Petrarchan lover – 'Must I be enjoined / To follow still whilst she flies from me?' (1.1.101–2) – but things take a darker turn when his attempt to return Beatrice-Joanna's dropped glove is met with utter contempt.[22] Her hyperbolic refusal to touch the glove that he has touched draws attention to the skin, the tactile and the threat of contamination.[23] Left in possession of both gloves, De Flores reflects:

> Now I know she had rather wear my pelt tanned
> In a pair of dancing pumps than I should thrust
> My fingers into her sockets here.
>     [*He thrusts his hand into the glove*]
>                                 I know
> She hates me, yet cannot choose but love her.
>
>                                               1.1.236–9[24]

De Flores is secure in a knowledge that remains inexplicable. His own attachment to Beatrice-Joanna is involuntary and humiliating, and he regards her enmity towards him as equally inexplicable: 'yet / She knows no cause for't but a peevish will' (106–7). The critical response to this mysterious opacity has tended, unsurprisingly, toward demystification. While De Flores' actions are usually passed over as the expression of a familiar male sexual aggression – 'Though I get nothing else, I'll have my will' (1.1.241) – the behaviour of Beatrice-Joanna is understood to be its opposite: the expression of a hidden desire. The play invites interpretation of her loathing, but the critical conversation has tended to overlook an important term for the play's depiction of her aversion: instinct.

The early modern word, *instinct*, carries a range of meanings, not all of which are available in our contemporary understanding of the term. In its earliest English sense, the word is a straightforward borrowing from Latin *instinctus* and means an impulse, instigation or prompting (c. 1412–20). The next sense, first emerging in 1568, is 'Innate impulse; natural or spontaneous tendency or inclination. Formerly applicable to the natural tendencies of inanimate things' (n. 2). Shakespeare is credited with the first instance of a newly specialized sense of the word that appears at the end of the sixteenth century: 'An innate propensity in organized beings (esp. in the lower animals), varying with the species, and manifesting itself in acts which appear to be rational, but are performed without conscious design or intentional adaptation of means to ends. Also, the faculty supposed to be involved in this operation (formerly often regarded as a kind of intuitive knowledge)' (n.3.a). The set of examples that begins with Shakespeare ('Beware instinct, the lion will not touch the true prince, instinct is a great matter. I was now a cowarde on instinct') also includes Darwin: 'The very essence of an instinct is that it is followed independently of reason'.[25] Importantly, for *The Changeling*, early modern instinct combines knowledge and feeling in a way that is at once benign and mysterious.

The shift from a punctual impulse to something durable is captured in the common phrase 'secret instinct of nature' which recurs frequently in Topsell's *History of Four-footed Beasts* (1607) but also makes repeated appearances in Fenton's *Tragical Discourses* (1567) as well as in numerous sermons and theological works. The presence of the phrase in works that are explicitly religious is a reminder that the nature invoked is the orderly creation of God and remains enchanted. 'Secret instinct' is an occult force that moves objects, creatures and humans, and it demonstrates a hidden rationality that operates invisibly in the world. When Tomazo comes seeking his missing brother, he asks the guilt-stricken De Flores, 'Thou canst guess, sirrah / (One honest friend has an instinct of jealousy) / At some foul guilty person?' (4.2.46–8). Ironies soon multiply as 'honest' De Flores protests that he thinks 'none / Worse than myself' (49–50) and quickly departs, leaving Tomazo to remark 'That De Flores has a wondrous honest heart' (58). *Instinct*, for Tomazo, is close to intuition, a direct and immediate apprehension, and yet its proximity to 'guess', suggests that the knowledge it produces remains provisional.

Frustrated in his attempt to identify the murderer of his brother, Tomazo delivers a soliloquy that echoes Hamlet's world weariness, and concludes that

> because
> I am ignorant in whom my wrath should settle,
> I must think all men villains, and the next
> I meet – whoe'er he be – the murderer
> Of my most worthy brother.
>
> 5.2.4–8

The stark irrationality of this plan amplifies the familiar association of wrath with madness, but its twisted logic is made nugatory by the entrance of De Flores, the very person whom the unwitting Tomazo seeks. In another of the play's many examples of inconstancy, Tomazo's evaluation of De Flores is immediately reversed: he now refers to him as 'the fellow that *some* call honest De Flores', apparently forgetting that he had himself only the day before credited De Flores with a 'wondrous honest heart' (4.2.58). Declaring, 'I find a contrariety in nature / Betwixt that face and me' (5.2.13–4), Tomazo strikes De Flores, but before the two begin to duel, De

Flores begs off, remarking in an aside: 'I cannot strike. I see his brother's wounds / Fresh bleeding in his eye, as in a crystal' (32–3). The image invokes two occult operations: the 'Fresh bleeding' refers to the common claim that a murdered body would begin to bleed again in the presence of its murderer, and the reference to seeing 'as in a crystal' invokes the practice of scrying, which involved gazing into water, glass or another reflective surface in order to discern the secrets of the past or future. As they part, De Flores wonders, in an aside, 'Why this from him, that yesterday appeared / So strangely loving to me? / O, but instinct is of a subtler strain; / Guilt must not walk so near his lodge again' (38–41). Tomazo's demonstrative affection from the day before has been displaced by the subtler power of instinct, which operates below or beyond mere appearances.

This episode, coming in the play's penultimate scene, adds instinct to the established vocabulary of passions and affections, and invites reconsideration of one of the play's more memorable occult moments: Beatrice-Joanna's discovery of Alsemero's 'physician's closet'.[26] In addition to the glass vials, containing various liquids, Beatrice finds a manuscript, '"The Book of Experiment, Called *Secrets in Nature*"' (4.1.20, 24–5), that explains how to perform tests for both pregnancy and virginity, both of which cause her alarm. Often considered an embarrassment by critics of the play, Alsemero's laboratory has attracted significant scholarly attention in recent years.[27] Most recently, Mary Floyd-Wilson has presented the episode as an example of normal early modern science, suggesting that the play's 'hidden logic' conforms to the 'occult knowledge' described by early modern natural philosophy.[28] The play's treatment of passions, affections and instinct conforms to the framework of hidden sympathies and antipathies that made natural magic possible. At the same time, the play presents Alsemero's science as deficient, and earlier critics who dismissed the episode as ridiculous were not entirely wrong.

The procedures described in Alsemero's manuscript are notably mechanical. If a dose of a particular substance is given to a pregnant woman, she will sleep for twelve hours straight. If she's not pregnant, she will not sleep for twelve hours. More elaborately, a spoonful of the liquid in glass 'M' given to a virgin will have 'three several effects': she will gape, sneeze and then laugh. These behaviours are caused by occult mechanisms that are regular and inexorable: the response described is involuntary, and the mastery conferred by the book will allow the practitioner to reveal the secrets of nature (here identified with the female body). The accuracy and efficacy of Alsemero's experiments are in fact vindicated by the action of the play, but Beatrice-Joanna is able to turn his occult knowledge to her own advantage by mimicking the necessary response. Alsemero, the quondam stoic and natural philosopher, proves to be doubly vulnerable in the play: susceptible to passionate desire, which he quickly designates legitimate affection, he then attempts to use his science to reveal the truth of Beatrice-Joanna's sexual history only to be deceived once again by appearances.

While the instinct of aversion that moves Tomazo operates according to the same general principles as Alsemero's occult natural philosophy, there are significant differences between them.[29] In the case of instinct, the compelling force that provides a person with a strong apprehension, a felt knowledge that combines the affective and cognitive, remains fundamentally mysterious. Unlike the natural magic practised by Alsemero which only appears wonderful because its occult causes are not known, the inner prompting of instinct may have a supernatural cause. After all, early modern English Protestantism, with its emphasis on moral self-scrutiny, provided reason to think that 'some feelings and affections were divinely inspired'.[30] Critics, who have consistently demonstrated an interest in Middleton's psychological realism, have been less curious about the presence of the supernatural in *The Changeling*. When the supernatural does get discussed, it is usually in connection with soteriology and Calvinist predestination.[31] Less has been made of the ghost that appears first in the dumbshow at the beginning of Act 4 and then again in 5.1.³² Supernatural manifestations on the stage invariably provoke powerful affective responses both from the characters in the play and the audience in the playhouse. Rather than being evidence of naïve sensationalism, these moments establish a deep and complex connection between human feelings and the supernatural. Such occasions invite reflection on the appropriate affective and intellectual response to supernatural phenomena and on the division between the supernatural and the natural.

Frequently viewed as a sticky bit of generic residue, left over from earlier Senecan revenge plays, the ghost of Alonzo features prominently in the dumbshow, but its subsequent appearance on stage is fleeting. This brevity contributes to the ghost's mystery, and like the ghost in *Hamlet* its appearance is designed to provoke disparate reactions. On the one hand, De Flores responds to the ghost with defiance and rationalization: 'I dread thee not; / 'Twas but a mist of conscience. – All's clear again' (60). On the other hand, Beatrice-Joanna is almost overwhelmed by fear and is incapable of even recognizing the ghost. Immediately after De Flores exits, Beatrice-Joanna asks: 'Who's that, De Flores? Bless me! It slides by!' (61).³³ Afterwards, she adds: 'Some ill thing haunts the house; 't has left behind it / A shivering sweat upon me. I'm afraid now'. The ghost is, according to Michael Neill, an emblem of the 'uncanny fatality' that suffuses the play; at the same time, the staging of this moment places an emphasis on Beatrice-Joanna's affective response. Beatrice-Joanna responds to the unidentified entity with fear that is registered by her body – the 'shivering sweat' is presumably her own, but her syntax suggests that it is the physical residue of the ill thing that has just slid past her. The simple declaration, 'I am afraid now', suggests that the fears that preceded the appearance of the ghost have now been radically amplified. The character who had earlier confidently declared, 'So wisdom by degrees works out her freedom' (3.4.13), finds herself in a state of terror. Her shivering continues when Alsemero appears on the scene – 'I prithee, tremble not' (86) – and this involuntary response recalls the conclusion of 3.4 when De Flores remarks, "Las, how the turtle pants! Thou'lt love anon / What thou so fear'st and faint'st to venture on'.[34] Of course, this is not the first time that Beatrice-Joanna trembles in response to De Flores. After he exits in 2.1, she observes: 'I never see this fellow but I think / Of some harm towards me: dangers in my mind still, / I scarce leave trembling of an hour after (2.1.89–91). This description of passion's power to disrupt neatly combines the mental (*think* and *mind*) with the physical (*tremble*) and, despite Alsemero's earlier attempt to diminish the significance of her aversion to De Flores, Beatrice-Joanna here concludes that she must at the next opportunity implore her father to get rid of him.

As the wounded Beatrice-Joanna explains herself to the assembled witnesses, she returns once again to her initial aversion toward De Flores: 'My loathing / Was prophet to the rest, but ne'er believed' (5.3.156–7). Locating the play's preoccupation with passions and affections within an established early modern discourse concerning the emotions reveals that this line is something more than an acknowledgement that one strong feeling led to another. The metaphoric designation of her loathing as prophetic suggests a very different assessment. Investing her aversion with a religious authority, Beatrice-Joanna insists that a failure to credit her instinct was an act of impiety. Though 'ne'er believed' includes an element of self-accusation, the charge also extends to Alsemero (who first trivializes her response) and perhaps to Vermandero, who after all has employed De Flores despite his daughter's determined antipathy. Beatrice-Joanna's retrospective assertion about the importance of giving credit to inner promptings serves as a direct rebuttal to the neostoicism of Justus Lipsius, who had argued that the enemies of constancy are 'the foure principall affections which do greatly disquiet the life of man: Desire and Joy; Feare and Sorrow'.[35] Instead, the play's treatment of passions, affections and instinct suggests a Calvinist position that considers the goal of *apatheia* both impossible (because the Stoic vision of self-control is a prideful illusion) and undesirable (because proper feelings encourage the pursuit of the good and the rejection of the bad). While the play's critique of hyper-rational and individualistic stoicism may strike contemporary readers as plausible, *The Changeling's* identification of supernatural forces operating on human feelings is deeply disconcerting and alien. We may be perplexed by our feelings, but we take comfort in the thought that they are our own. Attending to Rowley and Middleton's account of passions, affections and instinct is a reminder that we have not always felt the same.

# Notes

1. For an extreme example, see Thomas Middleton and William Rowley, *The Changeling*, Joost Daalder (ed.), 2nd ed. (London: A&C Black, 1990), xxvi, 17 n. 223 and elsewhere throughout the critical apparatus. For a sophisticated psychoanalytic reading, see Marjorie Garber, 'The Insincerity of Women', in Valeria Finucci and Regina Schwarz (eds), *Desire in the Renaissance: Psychoanalysis and Literature* (Princeton, NJ: Princeton University Press, 1994), 19–38. For a critique of post-Freudian interpretations in the staging of *The Changeling*, see Roberta Barker and David Nicol, 'Does Beatrice Joanna Have a Subtext?: *The Changeling* on the London Stage', *Early Modern Literary Studies* 10. 1 (May 2004): 3.1–43.

2. The literature on Middleton and Calvinism is extensive. See Margot Heinemann, *Puritanism and the Theatre: Thomas Middleton and Opposition Drama under the Early Stuarts* (Cambridge: Cambridge University Press, 1982); John Stachniewski, 'Calvinist Psychology in Middleton's Tragedies', in R.V. Holdsworth (ed.), *Three Jacobean Revenge Tragedies* (Basingstoke: Macmillan, 1990), 226–46; Lori Anne Ferrell, 'Introduction to *The Two Gates of Salvation* or *The Marriage of the Old and New Testament* or *God's Parliament House*', in Gary Taylor and John Lavagnino (gen. eds), *Thomas Middleton: The Collected Works* (Oxford: Oxford University Press, 2007), 679–82.

3 Gail Kern Paster, 'The Ecology of the Passions in *A Chaste Maid in Cheapside* and *The Changeling*', in Gary Taylor and Trish Thomas Henley (eds), *The Oxford Handbook of Thomas Middleton* (Oxford: Oxford University Press, 2012), 148–63.

4 Paster, 'The Ecology of Passions', 150.

5 William Shakespeare, *The Taming of the Shrew*, ed. Barbara Hodgdon, The Arden Shakespeare, Third Series (London: Bloomsbury Arden Shakespeare, 2010), 1.1.31.

6 Sidney Gottlieb, 'An Allusion to Lipsius in *The Changeling*, III.iii.175–7', *N&Q* 230 (1985): 63–5, and Thomas M. Barr, 'Justus Lipsius and *The Changeling*', *N&Q* 242 (1997): 96–7.

7 The major exception is A.A. Bromham, '"Have You Read Lipsius?": Thomas Middleton and Stoicism', *English Studies* 5 (1996): 401–21. Bromham focuses on *The Old Law* but concludes that 'though none of his other plays engages so fully or directly with stoicism, the recurrence of the theme of constancy in his work suggests Lipsius as a continuing presence' (421).

8 Pascale Drouet, 'Madness and mismanagement in *The Changeling*', in this volume.

9 Douglas Bruster, 'Isabella', in this volume.

10 Thomas Dixon, *From Passions to Emotions: The Creation of a Secular Psychological Category* (Cambridge: Cambridge University Press, 2003), 26–61.

11 Erin Sullivan, 'The Passions of Thomas Wright: Renaissance Emotions across body and soul', in Richard Meek and Erin Sullivan (eds), *The Renaissance of Emotion: Understanding Affect in Shakespeare and his Contemporaries* (Manchester: Manchester University Press, 2015), 25–44, 37.

12 John Reynolds, *The Triumphs of God's Revenege against the crying and execrable Sinne of Murther* (London, 1621). Later Alsemero is described as letting 'passion and affection' blind his judgement; when he and Beatrice are first married, the narrator asks 'who would imagine that any auerse accident could alter the sweetness and tranquillity of their affections, or that the Sunne-shine of their ioyes should so soone be eclipsed, and ouer-taken with a storme? But God is as iust as secret in his decrees' (T2v).

13 Alexandra Walsham, *Providence in Early Modern England* (Oxford: Oxford University Press, 1999), 113.
14 William Whately, *A bride-bush: or, A direction for married persons Plainely describing the duties common to both, and peculiar to each of them* (London: Thomas Man, 1619), D4r.
15 In the source story, Tomazo, having received word that Beatrice is in love with another man, sends a letter to his brother trying to convince him of the folly of continuing his pursuit (S3v).
16 See Jennifer Panek, 'Shame and Pleasure in *The Changeling*', *Renaissance Drama* 42 (2014): 191–215, esp. 201–2.
17 Thomas Middleton and William Rowley, *The changeling as it was acted (with great applause) at the Privat house in Drury-Lane, and Salisbury Court* (London: Humphrey Moseley, 1653), D1r.
18 Regarding the misreading of *her* for *his*, see Gary Taylor, 'Textual and Sexual Criticism: A Crux in *The Comedy of Errors*', *Renaissance Drama*, New Series, 19 (1988): 195–225. Taylor observes: 'In an Elizabethan secretary hand, terminal *s* was often almost impossible to distinguish from *r*, and in contemporary orthography *her* could be spelled with a medial *i*; in such circumstances, a "hir" and a "his" are materially identical, and can only be differentiated by cultural context' (217).
19 In *Plato's Cap*, a mock almanac published in 1604, Middleton refers to 'one man's meat is another man's poison' as an 'old moth-eaten proverb', 200.
20 Mary Floyd-Wilson, *Occult Knowledge, Science and Gender on the Shakespearean Stage* (Cambridge: Cambridge University Press, 2013), 91.
21 Benedict Robinson, 'Disgust *c.* 1600', *English Literary History* 81 (2014), 553–83. Robinson presents an intriguing argument that disgust is, in fact, a response that depends on the adjacency of desire and aversion, and he suggests that in this respect it is peculiarly modern.
22 For an account of the play's language of love service, see Sara Eaton, 'Beatrice-Joanna and the Language of Love in *The Changeling*', *Theatre Journal* 36 (1984): 371–82; Christopher Ricks, 'The Moral and Poetic Structure of *The Changeling*' *Essays in Criticism* 10.3 (1960): 290–306, provides an excellent

account of the word *service*, which 'for Middleton and his audience could mean copulation as well as the duty of a servant' (296).

23 On the implications of this episode, see Patricia Cahill, 'The play of skin in *The Changeling*', *postmedieval: a journal of medieval cultural studies* 3 (2012): 391–406.

24 On the importance of the gloves as prostheses, see Karen Sawyer Marsalek, 'Phanton limbs', in this volume.

25 *OED*, *instinct* n. 1. The Shakespeare quotation is from *Henry IV, Part 1*, ed. David Scott Kastan, The Arden Shakespeare, 3rd series (London: Bloomsbury Arden Shakespeare, 2002), 2.4.262–4.

26 M.C. Bradbook, *Themes and Conventions of Elizabethan Tragedy* (Cambridge: Cambridge University Press, 1980), 206–32, connects the virginity test with the play's '"omens" and other irrational elements' (220).

27 See Marjorie Garber, 'The Insincerity of Women', and Bruce Boehrer, 'Alsemero's Closet: Privacy and Interiority in *The Changeling*', *Journal of English and Germanic Philology* 96 (1997): 349–68.

28 Floyd-Wilson, *Occult Knowledge*, 91.

29 M.C. Bradbrook connects the play's use of omens with the '"magic" effects of Alsemero's chemistry' (216) in Bradbrook, *Themes and Conventions of Elizabethan Tragedy*, 2nd ed. (Cambridge: Cambridge University Press, 1980).

30 Alec Ryrie, *Being Protestant in Reformation Britain* (Oxford: Oxford University Press, 2013), 42.

31 See Stachniewski, 'Calvinist Psychology', 228–9.

32 For an important exception, see Michael Neill, 'Middleton and the supernatural', in Suzanne Gossett (ed.), *Thomas Middleton in Context* (Cambridge: Cambridge University Press, 2011), 295–305.

33 The interrogative mood is another echo of *Hamlet*; as is 'Bless me!' which hearkens back to 'Angels and ministers of grace defend us!' (1.4.39). Also worth pointing out is Beatrice-Joanna's 'O my presaging soul!' (112).

34 On this moment, and the topos of virginal trembling, see Judith Haber, '"I(t) could not choose but follow": Erotic Logic in *The Changeling*', *Representations* 81 (2003): 79–98.
35 John Stradling, *Two Bookes of Constancie. Written in Latine by Justus Lipsius* (London, 1595), C4r.

# PART FOUR

# Disabilities

# 7

# *The Changeling*'s Phantom Limbs[1]

## Karen Sawyer Marsalek

Lying latent in museum storage, the pair of gloves awaits animation (Figure 7.1).[2] The extravagant floral embroidery reminds us that such accessories were often scented, and although no fragrance now remains, the fingers' contours still manifest the hands that once wore them.[3] As these gloves were being handed on over the centuries, a single finger of another 'well made' and 'pale' seventeenth-century glove lay buried in the Southwark soil.[4] Without a photograph or even a sketch in the catalogue of archaeological finds that records it, the haunting fragment nonetheless invites speculation about how it came to be detached. The two artefacts recall two related props from Middleton and Rowley's *The Changeling*: Beatrice-Joanna's gloves – the 'favour come with a mischief' that De Flores retrieves (1.1.235) – and Alonzo's severed finger. Connected through oft-noted phallic imagery, these props are also linked as disembodied limbs, lifeless appendages of insensible skin that somehow remain charged and 'active' on the stage. Together they bring a range of prosthetic functions to the play: the gloves shape De Flores into a supplement for

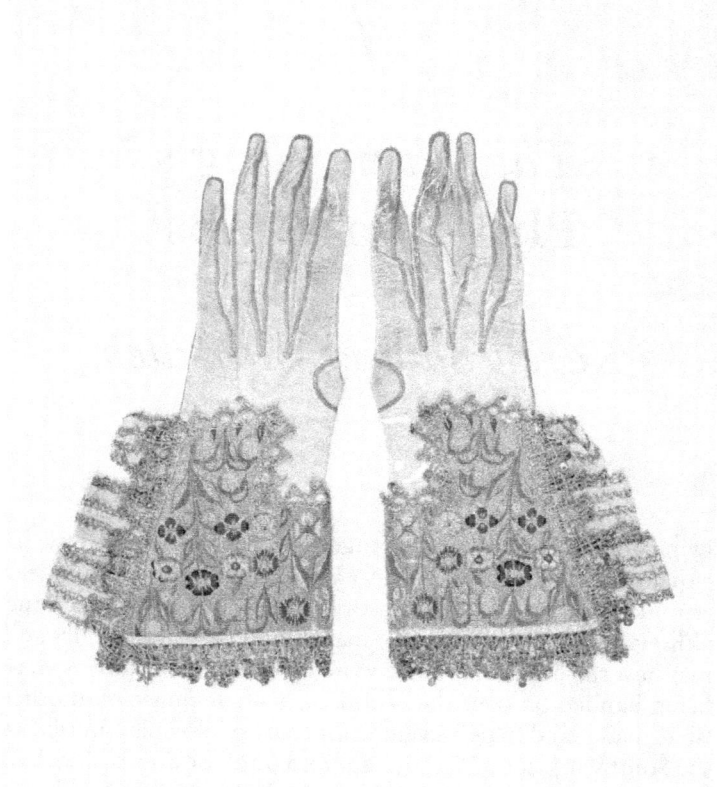

**FIGURE 7.1** *Pair of gloves, early seventeenth century.*

the masculine power that Beatrice-Joanna lacks, while the prop finger and the technology for representing Alonzo's maimed hand partner to demonstrate, rather than mitigate, his loss. The latter set of prostheses produces the able-bodied actor's masquerade of mutilation, a previously unrecognized instance of the 'disability drag' that also structures the hospital plot of *The Changeling*.[5] The system of prosthetic play, developed across the work through gloves' material and symbolic qualities, provides additional perspective on Middleton and Rowley's collaborative authorship.

The prosthetic play is initiated in the very first scene, which marks gloves as a vehicle for De Flores to enact another's will. When Beatrice-Joanna drops one of her pair, signalling her favour to Alsemero, her father directs De Flores to intervene: 'Look, girl: thy glove's fall'n; / Stay, stay. – De Flores, help a little' (1.1.229–30). While Beatrice-Joanna rejects this 'help' at this point in the play, her father's words presage her own later request for De Flores' service as a murderer (2.2). And despite her hostility in this first scene, the discourse and actions surrounding the gloves in 1.1 begin to frame them as proxy hands for Beatrice-Joanna, manual skins that will assist her in obtaining her own desires. Hurling invective at him along with her second glove, she longs for the pair to mutilate the loathed De Flores: 'There, for t'other's sake I part with this. / Take 'em and draw thine own skin off with 'em' (1.1.233–4). These words suggest that she *anticipates* De Flores' will wear the gloves and envisions them inflicting an appropriate punishment.

If Beatrice-Joanna's desired outcome depends on De Flores donning the gloves, then it is worth reconsidering his subsequent lines and action, and their possible effect in seventeenth-century performances. Critics often assume De Flores does put on the gloves easily, if aggressively, while he claims, 'she had rather wear my pelt tanned / In a pair of dancing pumps than I should thrust / My fingers into her sockets here' (1.1.236–8). For example, in the *Oxford Middleton*, editor Douglas Bruster specifies the implied action with the stage direction, '*He thrusts his hand into the glove*' (1.1.238.1); Annabel Patterson's introduction then elides the character's lines with Bruster's editorial intervention, describing 'the famous moment when De Flores picks up Beatrice-Joanna's gloves and visibly "thrust[s his] ... fingers into her sockets"'.[6] Perhaps most bold in this interpretation is Frances Teague, who articulates many choices and possible motivations for those onstage in this moment, and then contrasts them all with 'the one character who is relatively straightforward in his response to the glove. [. . .] Arguing about other meanings for the gloves immediately becomes irrelevant. De Flores knows that the glove represents Beatrice-Joanna's body; he uses the glove to thrust into her sockets until such time as he obtains her body for thrusting.'[7] While it is not hard to recognize the courtier's erotic action as a violation, a disturbing anticipation of De Flores' later sexual triumph, this essay will 'take up the glove' that Teague implicitly throws down so as to argue another reading. For a seventeenth-century glove-wearing audience the gesture could shock in ways not immediately intelligible today.

The material reality of early modern gloves would make De Flores' action unlikely, since women's hands were typically smaller than men's. In her study of surviving leather gloves, archaeologist Annemarieke Willemsen finds 'a clear distinction in sizing between male and female hands' based on the width of a glove and the length of its longest finger.[8] Her findings may explain why the fortunate recipient of a glove would typically display the token in his hatband or belt, rather than wear it.[9] Willemsen notes that these sizing differences can cast doubt on the accepted histories of some artefacts, as in her examples of one pair too small for its traditional association with Sir Walter Raleigh and another too large to have been worn by the purported owner, Queen Elizabeth.[10] Similarly, the historical issue of glove sizing complicates modern assumptions about this moment in the play. Since gloves were meant to be tight-fitting, the spectacle of De Flores putting on Beatrice-Joanna's glove might have resembled the awkward moment in the 1995 O.J. Simpson murder trial, in which the accused celebrity was asked to don bloodstained gloves held as evidence from the crime. His struggle to tug them over his large, football-player's hands elicited the defending attorney's comment, 'if it doesn't fit, you must acquit'.[11]

My point here is not that De Flores *would not* have been able to wear Beatrice-Joanna's gloves but rather that he *should not* have been able to wear them. Yet the lines that imply the action don't suggest any difficulty or black comedy. If such an action were as unusual as I have argued, De Flores' ability to put on the gloves might shock audiences less for its sexual audacity than for its revelation of physical likeness. His gesture of donning her gloves already points (pun intended) to a startling physiological – and ultimately moral – equivalence between the two characters, despite Beatrice-Joanna's revulsion for 'dog-face' De Flores (2.2.146).[12]

Their physical similarity extends beyond hand size to suggest that the skin itself is shared. In her compelling analysis of the materiality of skin in the play, Patricia Cahill proposes, 'the play might even be said to be establishing a kinship – a skin likeness – between [Beatrice-Joanna and De Flores]'.[13] She argues that the glove 'more clearly signifies as Beatrice-Joanna's *skin* than as her body, and hence as something not easily subject to control'; through the multiplicity of two gloves, both with interior and exterior surfaces, and their ability to 'draw' or stretch the skin of De Flores, Beatrice-Joanna initiates a complex tactile connection.[14] Cahill sees this connection as one independent of either character's will, a symptom of skin's own unruliness.[15] Like her, I see the gloves not as mere orifices to be penetrated but rather as shared skins; indeed, I would argue that this sharing goes further than the experience of touch, one skin on another. Beatrice-Joanna's imprecation suggests that her gloves would actually fuse to De Flores' hands through extended wear, so that it is the removal of the gloves that would 'draw off' his skin.[16]

My reading thus follows and extends (or stretches, to use the language of leather) Cahill's argument and considers these gloves as components in a system of prosthetics.[17] The action of putting on these surprisingly well-fitting gloves, I argue, is at least as equally a 'putting on' of Beatrice-Joanna's will. In donning the gloves that she hopes will damage him, he is perversely fulfilling her intention, rather than violating it. As Jay Zysk notes, 'Her defiant *noli me tangere* is not without a parallel and contradictory invitation for physical contact'.[18] While scholars who read the glove as vagina understand this invitation as her subconscious sexual desire for De Flores, I argue instead that the gloves fashion De Flores as another pair of hands, supplying the deficiencies Beatrice-Joanna claims to lack when she later laments, 'Would creation – / [. . .] Had formed me man' (2.2.108–9).[19] Indeed, in imagining his own drawn-off skin, his 'pelt tanned / in a pair of dancing pumps', De Flores already voices a different version of his own prosthetic potential for Beatrice-Joanna. If we follow Will Fisher's attention to the *OED* definition of 'prosthesis', 'an artificial replacement for a part of the body', even shoes can qualify, as they replace 'the calluses that would otherwise form on the bottom of the feet'.[20]

However, prostheses also encode more complex and contradictory fantasies of separation and union. An apt illustration of these qualities is the artificial hand covered with boiled leather depicted in Figure 7.2.[21] Created by French surgeon Ambrosius Paré, it is one of many depicted in his treatise on what he termed 'monsters', figures whose bodily differences might be congenital or acquired. Woodcuts depict his inventions – enamelware eyes, iron arms, ivory teeth – in curious isolation; of twenty-four images, only one shows a prosthesis in contact with the non-standard body using it. In this alienating visual framework, Paré's explanation of the hand's construction and directions for attaching the device call attention to its mechanical, inhuman character. Yet in its surprisingly lifelike appearance and grip on a quill pen, this prosthesis materializes a particular identity of 'writer' for its wearer. As Fisher notes, a prosthesis is simultaneously detachable, even transferable, and integral to self. 'Although prostheses are in a sense objects that can be removed from the body,' he argues, 'they also shape or materialize the body and self in important ways.'[22] In *The Changeling*, these qualities are also present in the gloves. Beatrice-Joanna may remove them from her body (and De Flores may also remove them from his), but as material items gloves retained the shape they developed from the owner's hand. Even hundreds of years later, gloves 'usually still preserve the shape of the hand that

## THE CHANGELING'S PHANTOM LIMBS

D'AIOVSTER CE QVI DEFAVT.  IX.ᶜXVII

*Description du Bras de fer.*

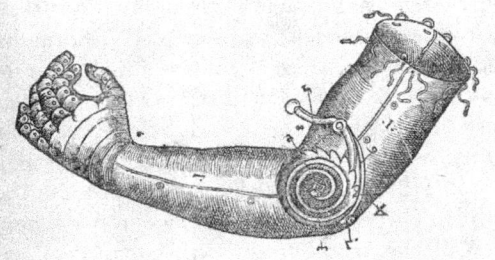

1 Le bracelet de fer pour la forme du bras. 2 L'arbre mis au dedans du grand resort pour le tendre. 3 Le grand resort qui est au coulde, lequel doit estre d'acier trempé, & de trois pieds de longueur ou plus. 4 Le rocquet. 5 La gaschette. 6 Le resort qui poise sur la gaschette, & arreste les dents du rocquet. 7 Le clou à vis pour fermer ce resort. 8 Le tornant de la haulse de l'auant-bras, qui est au dessus du coulde. 9 La trompe du gantelet faict à tornant auec le canon de l'auant-bras qui est à la main: lesquels seruent à faire la main prone & supine: c'est à sçauoir prone vers la terre, & supine vers le Ciel.

*Autre pourtraict*

D'vne main faicte de cuir boullu, ou papier collé, les doigts tenant vne plume pour escrire, à celuy qui auroit eu la main du tout coupee & amputee ( où le malade mettra dedans son moignon le plus auant qu'il pourra) laquelle s'attache à la manche du pourpoint par certains troux que tu vois en la figure.

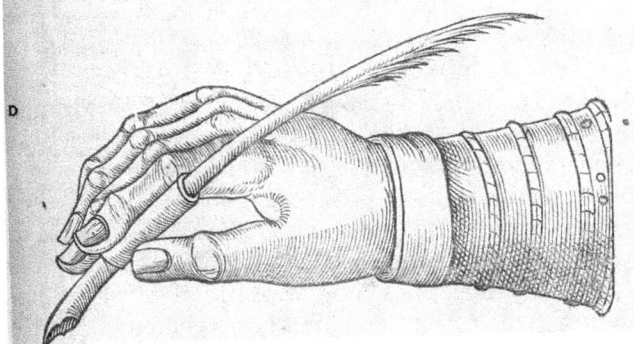

**FIGURE 7.2** *Prosthetic Hand by Ambroise Paré. Illustration from* Les oeuures d'Ambroise Paré . . .: diuisees en vingt huict liures, auec les figures & portraicts, tant de l'anatomie que des instruments de chirurgie, & de plusieurs monstres *(Paris: Buon, 1585), 917.*

wore and used them; the original hand is in some way still sitting "inside the glove"', Willemsen observes.[23] In 1.1, the feminine forms of Beatrice-Joanna's gloves materialize her hands upon De Flores. In 2.2, her limbs gain the masculine strength of his sinews and muscles as he cries, 'Without change to your sex, you have your wishes. / Claim so much man in me' (115–16). The words constitute a kind of prosthetic pledge, as they confirm both her bodily integrity and their physical union.

Beatrice-Joanna sets up her murderous commission with gestures and remarks that further develop cutaneous connections with De Flores. She takes his face in her hands for examination, and as she arouses him with her fingers' touch, he inhales her 'amber' fragrance (2.2.82). His swooning response suggests that the perfume of her gloves lingers on her skin; it journeys from her hands into his body, penetrating his corporeal boundaries. In her tantalizing promise of a healing salve made '[w]ith [her] own hands,' she offers further contact, emphasizing 'Yes, mine own, sir; in a work of cure, I'll / Trust no other' (2.2.84–6). However, the emphasis also reveals her understanding of De Flores' hands as proxies for her own, for she also envisions the deadly plot as a double work of self-cure: 'I shall rid myself / Of two inveterate loathings at one time' (2.2.146). She can use De Flores to 'expel' the 'poison' of Alonzo (2.2.44–7) and then cure herself of the other poison that is De Flores himself by sending him away. After performing as her hands, De Flores, she believes, can be discarded as readily as were the gloves themselves.

Of course, the difficulty of prostheses like these is that they may be reappropriated. If the gloves unite Beatrice-Joanna and De Flores as I have suggested, then his autoerotic actions at the end of 2.2 are also figured as consensual: 'Methinks I feel her in mine arms already, / Her wanton fingers combing out this beard, / And being pleased, praising this bad face' (149–51). In this fantasy of enfolding Beatrice-Joanna's body with his, the phrase 'I feel her in my arms already' also puns on the sensation of her will in his limbs. By the next line, his fingers have become hers. This impression would be particularly potent if De Flores were still wearing the gloves, as Jay Zysk believes he is: 'Locked in his own embrace, stroking his own face with his own hands lodged inside Beatrice-Joanna's gloves, he engages in self-generated foreplay'.[24] In Zysk's reading, informed by post-reformation arguments against relics, De Flores erroneously misreads the relic-gloves as the real hand of the saint. The prosthetic perspective, however, grants the gloved hands a more slippery range of signification – what absence is being remedied at this point? Who is inhabiting the gloves?

I choose the word 'inhabiting' deliberately for its dual references to the clothing item and the wearer's pattern of moral choices. Peter Stallybrass and Ann Rosalind Jones observe this pun in Hamlet's urging of virtue on his mother: 'What we would now describe as an ethical state is imagined by Hamlet as a bodily practice–virtue, like clothing, can be "put on." Repeated wearing acts as an inscription upon the body that can work with or against alternative forms of inscription.'[25] The gloves may work with a ruthless 'habit' already present in De Flores, but he does not express murderous intent until he commits himself to Beatrice-Joanna's service. Alonzo himself recognizes in the courtier a quality De Flores has assumed from another unknown source: 'De Flores, O, De Flores! / Whose malice hast thou put on?' (3.2.15–16). For the audience, the dramatic irony of his question exposes the conspirators' interdependent prosthetic relationship: while Beatrice has put on De Flores' strength, he has put on her malicious will.

Alonzo's severed finger, the 'token' of De Flores' success as Beatrice-Joanna's proxy hands, introduces another kind of prosthesis to the play, one that creates the illusion of mutilation, rather than wholeness. The post-mortem dismemberment takes place onstage after De Flores realizes Alonzo's diamond ring will make a useful trophy:

> It was well found:
> This will approve the work.
> [*He struggles with the ring*]

> What, so fast on?
> Not part in death? I'll take a speedy course then:
> Finger and all shall off. [*He cuts off the finger*]
>
> 3.2.23–6

De Flores' narration of the violence conveys the cutting even if the actors' bodies obscure the hand itself. However, the dismemberment can also be performed through the simple technology of a prop glove. Farah Karim-Cooper posits such a device for hand amputation scenes in the early modern theatre: 'a flesh-colored glove stuffed with straw or sponges' which the actor wore at the end of his sleeve, his real hand hidden inside the sleeve.[26] Similarly, an actor's real finger could be tucked inside the hand of a glove that featured a detachable ringed finger. The technology would establish a material and metatheatrical correspondence present in other artificial limbs on the early modern stage. For instance, Vin Nardizzi has demonstrated how Stump's wooden leg in *A Larum For London* unites the body with the material used to construct the theatre.[27] John Webster achieves a similar effect with wax in *The Duchess of Malfi*; extradiegetically, it is shaped into a prop 'dead man's hand' which the audience accepts as real within the world of the play, but later this hand, as well as the bodies of the Duchess's husband and children are revealed as intradiegetic waxworks (4.1.46–112).[28] In *The Changeling*, the leather gloves of Beatrice-Joanna's costume render De Flores a figurative prosthesis, and the digit that proves his service to her is joined to those gloves through its very extradiegetic materiality.[29]

Even if careful blocking in 3.2 were to obscure the act and evidence of dismemberment, De Flores' presentation of the finger in 3.4 demands a visible prop. As has been widely observed, the metonymic phallic finger and its ring represent Alonzo's murdered body and the marriage Beatrice-Joanna hopes she can now make with Alsemero. De Flores' explanation of the gory gift, 'I could not get the ring without the finger' (29), articulates in internal rhyme the inescapable connection between the ornament and the digit. The finger also further materializes the bond that Beatrice-Joanna has established with De Flores, a bond initiated in the prosthetic gloves. This leathery link informs her allusion when she offers the finger and ring back to De Flores: 'At the stag's fall the keeper has his fees; / 'Tis soon applied: all dead men's fees are yours, sir' (49–50). Several editors have glossed this remark as a reference to customary gift of the stag's pelt to the gamekeeper.[30] In returning the finger, Beatrice-Joanna returns the 'skin' of the hunted quarry, doubly so if that 'finger' is a leather-covered stage prop. However, the hunting connection between this 'fee' and the play's gloves may be even more pointed; one historian has observed a tradition of removing or forfeiting gloves 'at the death of the stag [. . .] if they are not taken off, they are redeemed by money given to the huntsmen and keepers'.[31] Unfortunately, Beatrice-Joanna has already both removed and forfeited her gloves. Her attempt to pay De Flores off with the ring as well as a substantial reward in gold is an effort to reclaim what the gloves represent, to eliminate the bond that has been created through his performance as her hands. But as 'the deed's creature', she cannot escape that connection, and the ringed finger becomes a perverse symbol of their inevitable sexual union in De Flores' dark pun: 'we two engaged so *jointly* / should [not] part and live *asunder*' (3.4.91–2, my emphasis). The unholy 'engagement', obtained through the sundered joints of Alonzo's finger and consummated after this scene, supersedes not only her initial betrothal to Alonzo, but also her subsequent marriage to Alsemero.

Appropriately, the last vision of prosthetic gloves in the play is in the dumb show representing the wedding: '*Beatrice the bride [. . .] in great state, accompanied with Diaphanta, Isabella, and other Gentlewomen; De Flores after all, smiling at the accident. Alonzo's ghost appears to De Flores in the midst of his smile, startles him, showing him the hand whose finger he had cut off*' (4.1.0.9–16). The shorthand stage directions do not specify the characters' costumes, only that this display must convey the elaborateness of the wedding: the '*bride [...] in great state*' and her attendants. Today this direction might encode the visual language of a white dress and coordinated bridesmaids, but for Middleton and Rowley's audiences key symbols of nuptial celebrations were the elegant new gloves worn by the bride and groom and gifts of gloves for all the guests. These gifts 'extended the prosthetic hand of affection. They reached out to pair the guests to the gift-givers and to each other'.[32] The 'bride in great state' *should* thus provide us with a positive frame of reference for gloves in the play.

Yet set against the wedding attire implied in this stage direction is the spectral would-be bridegroom displaying his mutilated hand – or the prop glove concealing the actor's ring finger. If wedding gloves 'extend the prosthetic hand of affection', this theatrical prosthesis does the reverse, signalling Alonzo's desire for revenge. As Catherine Belsey notes, '[t]he most unsettling feature of this episode must be what is *not* there, the missing finger, which has taken on a posthumous life of its own in the course of the play'.[33] A 'phantom limb' twice over, Alonzo's finger seems to point at Beatrice-Joanna and De Flores despite its absence. Incorporeal but insistent, it recalls the 'finger of God' that repeatedly intervenes in the prose source for this plot, John Reynolds' *The Triumphs of God's Revenge*.[34] De Flores does not mutilate Alonzo's corpse in Reynold's story, nor does a ghost appear. However, a hint for these theatrical innovations is present in Beatrice-Joanna's efforts to distance herself from Alonzo's disappearance: she attempts to prevent Alsemero 'from imagining that she had the least shadow, or finger herein' (sig. T2r). On stage, the couple's guilt manifests in Alonzo's four-fingered shade.

Without his material, phallic finger, the ghost of Alonzo is simultaneously threatening and impotent. Like most of the non-standard bodies in Paré's treatise, his display of bodily difference appears to lack a corresponding prosthetic invention. Yet, paradoxically, the glove prosthesis is what *renders* his visible loss. The explanation of prosthesis supplied by David Mitchell and Sharon Snyder is useful here. They explain, 'In a literal sense, a prosthesis seeks to accomplish an illusion. A body deemed lacking, unfunctional, or inappropriately functional needs compensation, and prosthesis helps to effect this end'.[35] The actor's whole and skilled hand – a hand trained to wield a rapier and perform rhetorical gestures – is too 'functional' for the role of Alonzo's ghost and must be disguised.

In this way, the ghost participates in a larger practice of 'disability drag' in the early modern theatre. While scholars have explored this practice in other scenes of *The Changeling*, Alonzo's ghost enlarges its range in the play.[36] This drag takes place on several levels. The play's hospital plot requires able-minded actors to perform mentally ill inmate characters; it also juxtaposes their 'real' disability with three further characters, Isabella, Antonio and Franciscus, who deliberately fake mental illness. In the effortless 'cure' of the play's dissemblers, Lauren Coker-Durso identifies a 'triumphalist' trajectory that implies that real-world disability is also falsified and easily overcome.[37] Surveying the corpus of early modern plays, Lindsey Row-Heyveld has found that characters whose fakery is a plot feature, like Isabella, Antonio and Franciscus, are far more common than characters portrayed as having 'genuine' disabilities. She further notes that 'in replacing real disabled characters with frauds, the ["dissembling disability"] tradition worked to remove even the facsimile of genuinely disabled people from the early modern imagination'.[38] The metatheatrical allure of 'dissembling disability' and its pervasiveness in early modern drama may explain why Alonzo's maimed ghost has been neglected as an instance of disability drag. The character partially resists the triumphalist presentation of disability present in the hospital plot. Yet the metatheatrical web of glove prostheses in the play still underscore his impairment as a temporary condition. The actor will enjoy his whole hand again when the performance is over, unlike the maimed figures in the streets outside the theatre or on the pages of Paré.

In reconsidering the much-discussed props of gloves and dismembered finger, I have sought to unpack their practical implications, to show how they might stage the dis/abled bodies of the characters and help us to re-member the bodies of the early modern players Middleton and Rowley wrote for. The development of prosthetic play over the course of *The Changeling* also aligns with the division of scene labour favoured by David Nicol and other scholars. Like earlier critics, Nicol credits Rowley with the opening and closing scenes and the hospital plot; he also finds Rowley's work in several passages that link the hospital and castle plots.[39] Rowley's contribution, he maintains, is 'more diverse' and 'organizational' than Middleton's.[40] This 'organizational' role might also be seen in his introduction of Beatrice-Joanna's gloves in 1.1, objects that Middleton figuratively 'picks up' through his subsequent scenes featuring the maimed hand and severed finger.

In reconsidering the playwrights' joint authorship, Nicol urges that Rowley 'should not be imagined as merely following Middleton's orders, or executing plans devised entirely by Middleton'.[41] Similarly, I argue that we should understand Beatrice-Joanna's gloves as expressions of her own power and recognize the disability drag that links Alonzo's ghost with the 'real' and 'dissembling' patients in the hospital scenes. An anatomization of *The Changeling*'s phantom limbs thus complements the collaborative practice of the play's authors, a process of both 'handing off' and working 'hand in glove'.

# Notes

1  An earlier version of this essay was presented in the seminar on *The New Changeling* at the Shakespeare Association of America's Annual Meeting in Los Angeles, April 2018. I am grateful to the seminar's organizers, Gordon McMullan and Kelly Stage, and to the other seminar members for their feedback, especially Gregory Schnitzpahn. Thanks also to Rodney and Susan Jagelman of the Glove Collection Trust and Rosemary Harden of the Fashion Museum, Bath for their patient responses to my many queries about items in their collections.

2  Pair of gloves, early seventeenth century, Metropolitan Museum of Art, 28.220.1, 2. Gift of Mrs. Edward S. Harkness, 1928. https://www.metmuseum.org/art/collection/search/222226
3  For the practice of scenting gloves, see Holly Dugan, *The Ephemeral History of Perfume: Scent and Sense in Early Modern England* (Baltimore: Johns Hopkins University Press, 2011), 126–53.
4  Geoff Egan, *Material Culture in London in an Age of Transition: Tudor and Stuart Period Finds c. 1450–c. 1700 from Excavations at Riverside Sites in Southwark* (London: MoLAS, 2006), 31.
5  The term was coined by Tobin Siebers in *Disability Theory*, Corporealities: Discourses of Disability (Ann Arbor: University of Michigan Press, 2008), 114–16; see below for critical application of it to the hospital plot in *The Changeling*.
6  Annabel Patterson, 'Introduction' to *The Changeling*, in Gary Taylor and John Lavagnino (eds), *Thomas Middleton: The Collected Works* (Oxford: Oxford University Press, 2007).
7  Frances Teague, '"What About Our Hands?": A Presentational Image Cluster', *Medieval and Renaissance Drama in England* 16 (2003): 220.
8  Annemarieke Willemsen, 'Taking up the glove: finds, uses and meanings of gloves, mittens and gauntlets in western Europe, c. AD 1300–1700', *Post-Medieval Archaeology* 49 (2015): 13.
9  Peter Stallybrass and Ann Rosalind Jones, 'Fetishizing the Glove in Renaissance Europe', *Critical Inquiry* 28.1 (2001): 124–5.
10  Willemsen, 'Taking up the glove', 13–14.
11  Michael Neill's stage direction, '*Tries to pull the glove onto his hand*,' is the only one I have seen that suggests Beatrice-Joanna's glove is smaller than De Flores' hand (s.d. 1.1.227); see Michael Neill, ed. *The Changeling*, by Thomas Middleton and William Rowley, 4th. edition, New Mermaids (London: Bloomsbury Methuen, 2019), 18.
12  Here I follow Roberta Barker and David Nicol's argument; both characters are driven to possess the object of their desire at all costs, and for Beatrice-Joanna, this person is Alsemero; see 'Does Beatrice-Joanna have a Subtext?: *The Changeling* on the London Stage', *Early Modern Literary Studies: A Journal of Sixteenth-*

*and Seventeenth-Century English Literature* 10. 1 (May 2004) 3.1–43.

13 Patricia Cahill, 'The Play of Skin in *The Changeling*', *postmedieval: a journal of medieval cultural studies* 3.4 (2012): 397.

14 Cahill, 'The Play of Skin', 395.

15 Cahill, 'The Play of Skin', 393–7.

16 See, for example, Michelangelo's experience: 'he took to wearing buskins of dogskin on his legs, next to the skin; he went for months at a time without taking them off, then when he removed the buskins, often his skin came off as well [. . .] constantly for whole months together, so that afterwards, when he sought to take them off, on drawing them off the skin often came away with them', Giorgio Vasari, *The Lives of the Artists*, translated by John Bull (London: Penguin, 1971): 430.

17 Cahill, 'The Play of Skin', 396.

18 Jay Zysk, 'Relics and Unreliable Bodies in *The Changeling*', *English Literary Renaissance* 45.3 (2015): 411.

19 Joost Daalder, 'Folly and Madness in *The Changeling*', *Essays in Criticism* 38.1 (1988): 10–11.

20 *Oxford English Dictionary*, 'prosthesis' n. 2b; Will Fisher, *Materializing Gender in Early Modern English Literature and Culture* (Cambridge: Cambridge University Press, 2006), 29.

21 Ambroise Paré, *Les oeuures d'Ambroise Paré . . .: diuisees en vingt huict liures, auec les figures & portraicts, tant de l'anatomie que des instruments de chirurgie, & de plusieurs monstres : reueuës & augmentees par l'autheur* (Paris: Buon, 1585), 917, *Historical Anatomies on the Web*, National Library of Medicine, National Institute of Health, 24 June 2019. https://www.nlm.nih.gov/exhibition/historicalanatomies/pare_home.html

22 Fisher, *Materializing Gender*, 31

23 Willemsen, 'Taking up the glove', 13.

24 Zysk, 'Relics and Unreliable Bodies', 414.

25 Stallybrass and Jones, 'Festishizing the Glove', 117.

26 Farah Karim-Cooper, *The Hand on the Shakespearean Stage: Gesture, Touch and the Spectacle of Dismemberment* (London: Bloomsbury Arden Shakespeare, 2016), 220.

27 Vin Nardizzi, 'The Wooden Matter of Human Bodies: Prosthesis and Stump in *A Larum for London*', in Jean E. Feerick and Vin Nardizzi (eds), *The Indistinct Human in Renaissance Literature*, (London: Palgrave, 2012), 119–36.

28 John Webster, *The Duchess of Malfi*, ed. Leah Marcus (London: Methuen, 2009).

29 Although he does not discuss *The Changeling*, Anston Bosman also identifies many other ways that metaphors and materiality of leather intersect in Shakespeare's theatre. See 'Shakespeare in Leather', in L. Barkan, B. Cormack and S. Keilen (eds), *The Forms of Renaissance Thought: New Essays in Literature and Culture* (Basingstoke, UK: Palgrave Macmillan, 2009), 225–45.

30 See, for example, Bruster in the *Oxford Middleton*, 1658 n. 41, and Neill, ed. *The Changeling*, 67 n. 39.

31 S. William Beck, *Gloves, Their Annals and Associations: A Chapter of Trade and Social History* (London: Hamilton, Adams, 1883), 498.

32 Stallybrass and Jones, 'Fetishizing the Glove', 119; see also Felicity Heal, *The Power of Gifts: Gift-exchange in Early Modern England* (Oxford: Oxford University Press, 2014), 66–7.

33 Catherine Belsey, 'Beyond Reason: Hamlet and Early Modern Stage Ghosts', in Elisabeth Bronfen and Beate Neumeier (eds), *Gothic Renaissance: A Reassessment* (Manchester: Manchester University Press, 2014), 42–3. Alonzo's finger may also have haunted William Heminge. Around 1632, Heminge, poet, playwright, and son of the King's Man John Heminge, composed a mock-elegy on the posthumous travels of a finger his friend lost in a duel. The finger encounters several literary figures in the underworld, including Middleton, who is lauded for his recent scandalous work, *A Game at Chess*. Although none of Middleton's other plays are mentioned in the poem, *The Changeling* influenced Heminge's later play, *The Fatal Contract*, so he may also have been thinking of it in the poem. See 'The Elegy on Randolph's Finger' in Carol A. Morley (ed.), *The Plays and Poems of William Heminge* (Madison, NJ: Farleigh Dickinson University Press, 2006), 414–40.

34 John Reynolds, *The Triumphs of Gods Revenge against the crying and execrable Sinne of Murther* (London, 1621).

35 David T. Mitchell and Sharon L. Snyder, *Narrative Prosthesis: Disabilities and the Dependencies of Discourse* (Ann Arbor: University of Michigan Press, 2006), 6.

36 See, for example, Lauren G. Coker-Durso, 'Metatheatricality and Disability Drag: Performing Bodily Difference on the Early Modern Stage' (PhD diss., St Louis University, 2014), Lindsey Row-Heyveld, *Dissembling Disability in Early Modern English Drama* (London: Palgrave, 2018), and Katharine Schaap Williams's essay in this volume.

37 Coker-Durso, 'Metatheatricality', 83.

38 Row-Heyveld, *Dissembling Disability*,182.

39 David Nicol, *Middleton & Rowley: Forms of Collaboration in the English Playhouse* (Toronto: University of Toronto Press, 2012), 39; Michael E. Mooney, '"Framing" as Collaborative Technique: Two Middleton-Rowley Plays', *Comparative Drama* 13. 2 (1979): 131–41.

40 Nicol, *Middleton & Rowley*, 39, 31.

41 Nicol, *Middleton & Rowley*, 32.

# 8

# Disability Representation and Theatrical Form in *The Changeling* and *The Nice Valour*

## Katherine Schaap Williams

What does the hospital plot of Thomas Middleton and William Rowley's *The Changeling* accomplish for the play? Alibius and his assistant Lollio claim to 'cure fools and madmen' (4.3.32) in their hospital, and the terms by which they describe their 'brainsick patients' (1.2.53) connote what we might call, in modern terminology, intellectual disability and mental illness. What, then, might this play also teach us about the representation of disability in the early modern English theatre? The hospital plot of *The Changeling* comprises around 760 lines, or nearly half of the lines devoted to the castle plot (around 1,650 lines), in the span of only three scenes. In the first scene, Alibius discloses to Lollio that he is worried about his wife Isabella's fidelity and has decided to confine her to the hospital while he is away; then the men welcome a new patient, the gentleman Antonio, testing his intellectual capacity before they are interrupted by the cries of '*Madmen within*' (s.d. at 1.2.203). In the second scene at the hospital, Isabella protests her restriction and asks Lollio to entertain her with his charges; first Franciscus, the 'last-come lunatic' (3.3.26) enters, and then Antonio, who reveals – as soon as he is alone with Isabella – that he only feigns 'the shape of folly' (133), and seeks to court her in secret; finally, she evades the advances of Lollio, who threatens a sexual assault of his own, before Alibius enters to announce that Vermandero, the 'castle captain' (273), has requested 'a mixture of our madmen and our fools' (277) in a performance to celebrate the marriage of 'Beatrice-Joanna, his fair daughter bride' (275). In the final scene at the hospital – which occurs after Beatrice-Joanna's wedding and feigned virginity test in the castle plot – Isabella learns that Franciscus, too, enacts the 'counterfeit cover of a madman' (4.3.13–14); Isabella dresses up as a madwoman in order to 'fool' (145) Antonio himself; and Lollio pits Antonio and Franciscus against each other as rival suitors of Isabella, instructing each to kill the other after their performance at the wedding. As this summary of events in the hospital suggests, the two plots of *The Changeling* operate in tonal contrast yet echo each other in theme. The first hospital scene proceeds in a comic key that shifts from the play's opening in the hushed solemnity of the church to a zany, send-in-the-clowns mode of slapstick between keeper, assistant and patient. The clandestine threat of sexual violence that the beleaguered Isabella endures, meanwhile, recapitulates problems of constraint and consent that drive the castle plot, and the show to be performed by Alibius' patients at Beatrice-Joanna's wedding – announced in the second scene and rehearsed at the end of the third scene – suggests a future of shared action that is never accomplished.

Despite the textual prominence of these three long scenes, however, one persistent critical answer to the question of what the hospital plot accomplishes for *The Changeling* is: not much. As Annabel Patterson discusses in her introduction to Douglas Bruster's edition of *The Changeling* in the *Oxford Middleton*, the hospital plot was initially attributed to Rowley, and scholars used the authorial collaboration to let Middleton off the hook for its perceived deficiencies: the physical and verbal comedy is 'stupid and tedious, and the treatment of insanity is offensive to the modern reader'.[1] Subsequent critical work argued that disability offers a conceptual link across the play's double plot: the 'madness and folly which are literal in the hospital plot metaphorically indict the behaviour of *all* the castle-plot characters'; and madness operates as an 'ethical undecidability' that helps to produce 'reciprocal exchange of meaning between the two plots'.[2] Another critical answer to the question of why the play needs the hospital plot, therefore, is that feigned disability enables the play to reflect on theatrical plotting, for madness and foolishness expose the irrational desires that drive actions and choices in both plots. A third critical answer, expressed in Carol Thomas Neely's classic argument about madness in early modern drama (to which I will shortly return), is that the hospital plot offers 'self-contained metatheatrical scenes' that meditate on the pleasures of spectacle.[3] The hospital plot's madness and foolishness – or, more precisely, its feigning of madness and foolishness – are a vehicle through which 'the play self-consciously explores the ingredients of theatre' and demonstrates the actor's capacity for imitation and disguise.[4]

These interpretations of the hospital plot as antiquated characterization, motor of plot and metatheatrical mode, however, do not entirely account for what disability does in *The Changeling*. In this essay, I am interested in what makes the hospital plot appear 'tedious', why these scenes take up so much time in performance beyond a summary of what happens in them, and why they have seemed extraneous to readers who skip over them and directors who routinely trim them in productions of the play. Representing foolishness and madness, *The Changeling* does not simply comment on the materials of the theatre; rather, the play turns theatrical materials against the operations of plot, prolonging the time of performance without aiming toward a clear end.

Staging disability, I argue, the play experiments with the temporality of performance and explores a concept of action that is answerable to neither tragic determination nor comic accident. In this generic distinction, I follow Susan Snyder's insight (in the context of Shakespeare's plays) that the tragic dramatic world is 'governed by inevitability' while the comic world presupposes 'evitability', enabling 'opportunistic shifts and realistic accommodations'.[5] For Snyder, the contrast between tragic inevitability and comic evitability is marked by different generic relations to 'time and its value': the pace of comedy may be swift but 'short-term urgencies are played against a dominant expansiveness', while tragedies 'acquire urgency' through 'the sense that time is limited and precious'.[6] Though Middleton and Rowley's hospital plot may appear to offer a comic counterweight to the castle plot's tragedy, it forecloses the possibility of evitability too: while counterfeiting madness and foolishness creates opportunities for Antonio and Franciscus, the madmen and the fools who remain patients have no such access to agency. More broadly, the scenes devoted to signifying madness and foolishness are characterized by theatrical action that refuses both the meaningful urgency of tragic time and the expansive future of comic time. The labours required to show disability – presentational actions of singing, dancing, gesturing, and miming, along with far more speech than is strictly necessary to advance the plot – dilate performance far beyond the script. The hospital plot calls attention to the time of theatrical enactment, disabling the temporal ordering of theatrical form through a generative disability aesthetic.[7]

To explore this disability aesthetic, I turn to *The Nice Valour; Or, The Passionate Madman*, a play now generally regarded as Middleton's, and recently dated to 1622, the same year as *The Changeling*.[8] A tragicomedy, *The Nice Valour* foregrounds the Passionate Lord, identified as 'a passionate madman' (2.1.93, 4.1.2), whose madness is caused by the recurrence of overwhelming bodily passions disordered in temporal sequence and duration.[9] Considering Middleton's own scripting of madness corrects the critical tendency to exempt him from the hospital plot of *The Changeling*, and the sustained representation of madness in *The Nice Valour* offers a vivid example of the dynamics of temporality and action adumbrated in *The Changeling*. In what follows, I begin by considering early modern disability and *The Changeling*'s challenge to theatrical form. In *The Nice Valour*, I consider how the Passionate Lord's madness operates beyond identification: the play employs his madness as a vehicle to disrupt the linear order of plot and frustrate the legibility of theatrical action. Returning to *The Changeling*, I elaborate Middleton and Rowley's scripting of madness as more than a tactic of characterization, a verdictive problem of collaborative authorship, or a powerful metaphor grounded in a patient's literal incapacity. Madness exceeds the dramatic character to become an aesthetic that changes the temporality of theatrical form and enables the play to experiment with performance that is not reducible to plot.

## 'Out of form' and early modern disability

Critics have commonly understood dramatic representations of early modern madness and foolishness as symbols of social disorder in the world of the play, or as uncomfortable historical indices of attitudes towards intellectual disability and mental illness in the past. In Renaissance drama, characters described in stage directions as '*mad*', '*raving*' and '*distracted*' offer particularly memorable set-pieces, from Hieronymo's 'running mad' in *The Spanish Tragedy* to Ophelia's scenes of distraction and Hamlet's 'antic disposition' in *Hamlet* to the show of madmen in *The Duchess of Malfi*, to flag a few plays.[10] Robert Rentoul Reed's early work, *Bedlam on the Jacobean Stage*, situated mad characters as reflections of early modern social conditions, though subsequent critical work by Michael McDonald, Duncan Salkeld and Kenneth Jackson has complicated an easy correlation between 'Bedlam' scenes in drama and the treatment of actual people with mental illnesses and intellectual disabilities in Bethlem Hospital in early modern London.[11] Neely's foundational argument, as I indicated above, demonstrated that theatrical scenes of distraction remain distant from the historical realities of distracted, mad or foolish people. Although Alibius worries about the 'daily visitants that come to see / My brainsick patients' (1.2.52–3), gallants who visit the hospital to 'see the fools and madmen' (59), Neely explores the paucity of evidence for such exhibitions and finds that such references disclose theatrical traditions rather than medical practices.[12] While hospital scenes with 'madmen' allow the theatre to dwell on its own pleasures of spectacle, plays like *The Changeling* ultimately 'withdraw sympathy from the mad, hence rendering unnecessary the charity that supports them'.[13] In Middleton's plays specifically, she argues, staged madness functions as a social release valve, since 'performing theater or watching it performed might curb excess', but the play ultimately turns away from mad people.[14]

The idea that disability offers a resource for dramatic innovation resonates with David Mitchell and Sharon Snyder's influential formulation of disability as a 'narrative prosthesis': disability is a device of characterization that prompts a story about the significance of a physical anomaly, and the plot concludes by curing the disability or removing the disabled character from view.[15] Thus 'a narrative disability establishes the uniqueness of the individual character', and then 'a disability is either left behind or punished for its lack of conformity'.[16] Building on this insight, Lindsey Row-Heyveld has argued that madness, understood as 'volatile, violent, and temporary distraction', and foolishness, which 'described a wide spectrum of longer-term mental impairments', are staples of the 'counterfeit-disability tradition' in early modern drama, which 'enforced suspicion' by teaching audiences to assume that disability is feigned.[17] Thus, critics read the scenes of performed foolishness and madness in *The Changeling*'s hospital plot as a metatheatrical gloss on the early modern theatre's practices of disguise and feigning; a narrative device that prompts a story about what disability can mean; and a useful tool for a character's dissembling, which in turn cements the association between disability and deceit.

*The Changeling*'s hospital plot, indeed, underscores the fact of feigning and leaves the hospital behind in order to conclude. Alibius, Isabella, Antonio and Franciscus appear in the final scene at the castle, and as the tragedy ends with the spectacle of De Flores' and Beatrice-Joanna's deaths and Alsemero's ponderous attempt to reduce the play's awful, thrilling complicities to a moral lesson, the three men from the hospital plot are likewise 'changed' (5.3.197). Alibius promises that he 'will change now / Into a better husband' (213–14); Antonio notes his change 'from a little ass as I was, to a great fool as I am' (204–5); and Franciscus declares that he has been changed 'from a little wit to be stark mad' (208). These reformed characters appear integral to the play's resolution – and, importantly, their foolishness and madness are only metaphorical. Once Franciscus and Antonio are revealed only to be 'counterfeits' (5.2.73) who were faking their conditions, the hospital plot abandons the 'hospital of fools and madmen' (72). Despite *The Changeling*'s glimpses of Alibius' other patients, the play never returns to their curative space as it ends.

If we understand disability solely through the narrative operations of plot or metatheatrical commentary, however, we miss a crucial dimension of the hospital plot's work with those other patients. To be clear, I am not suggesting that *The Changeling* is invested in realistic or authentic representations of disability, for the play emphasizes the difficulty of distinguishing disability and comments on the ease with which disability may be feigned. The opening scene with Antonio, Lollio and Alibius culminates in a joke about 'we three' (1.2.203) that paints all the men as fools, and later, when Lollio confronts Franciscus about his feigned madness, Franciscus exclaims: 'I am discovered to the fool' (4.3.177). The slippage between feigning and being the fool is a feature of the hospital plot, blurring the lines of rationality. Furthermore, when Isabella dons the 'habit of a frantic' (4.3.133), complete with songs, gestures and speech, her performance of a madwoman succeeds to the point that Antonio, failing to recognize her, responds: 'I'll kick thee if again thou touch me, / Thou wild unshapen antic' (130–1). The difficulty of detecting the 'bedlam' (132) figure contests the diagnostic impulse that spectators may bring to the play.

Rather, the brief glimpses of the 'madmen' and 'fools' in the hospital plot foreground theatrical form in enactment. When Alibius envisions the show that his patients will perform at Beatrice-Joanna's wedding revels, he explains that it will be:

> Only an unexpected passage over,
> To make a frightful pleasure, that is all –
> But not the all I aim at. Could we so act it,
> To teach it in a wild distracted measure,
> Though out of form and figure, breaking Time's head –
> (It were no matter, 'twould be healed again
> In one age or other, if not in this).
>
> 3.3.280–6

Alibius describes their performance: his patients will make an 'unexpected passage over', moving through the space in which the guests are gathered, a sight which will grip the audience in a complex affective response of 'frightful pleasure', and then the performance will conclude: 'that is all'. The turn of the next line – 'But not the all I aim at' – therefore arrives as a surprise. Shifting into the register of possibility ('Could we so act it'), Alibius interrupts himself as he speculates on the achievement of such a performance, which he associates with acting, though 'wild distracted measure' also encodes music and dance. His line breaks off at Time's broken head – often glossed as a cuckold joke, with topical relevance to the play's concern with female sexuality – and the speech concludes with a parenthetical reassurance that such a temporal disjuncture will be 'healed' before Alibius turns his attention to the matter of payment.

This brief vision, associated with 'madmen' and 'fools' and elaborated as spectacle and dance in addition to acting, imagines a performance that is 'out of form'. In the editorial note on these confusing lines, Douglas Bruster offers a valiant paraphrase: 'Presenting our show in a wild and distracted measure, even though this would be formless and disordering of Time itself it wouldn't matter, for it would all mend itself sooner or later' (1657). Alibius' lines, Patterson suggests, produce a 'more mysterious relation between the two plots'; she links his language to Hamlet's advice to the players and suggests that as Alibius conjures this vision of performance, its 'strangeness plausibly gives these playwrights an alibi for defining *their* larger purpose'.[18] If this glimpse evokes the play's purposes, however, Alibius' lines suggest that madness offers a generative disruption of theatrical form that severs action from causation. This performance, characterized as 'breaking Time's head', escapes both tragic and comic senses of 'time and its value', to follow Snyder. Rather than being 'formless' (as Bruster glosses) or, conversely, invested in the linear drive of a 'passage over' that moves towards an end, Alibius' fantasy of a show reaches for the limit of a performance that departs from the sequential ordering of plot. In the condition of being 'out of form and figure', to put it in his terms, what comes next does not follow from what came before.

This vision of performance is never fully enacted in *The Changeling*. As Alibius and Lollio discuss their preparations, they worry over the 'madmen's morris' (4.3.68–9) and the 'fooling' (70) of their charges, with imperatives to 'instruct' (70) and 'rehearse the whole measure' (71) in order to 'perfect' (56) their show. The closest that spectators of *The Changeling* come to witnessing a performance from Alibius' charges is the brief rehearsal at the end of Act 4, Scene 3, a single stage direction with a verb that is temporally elastic: '*The Madmen and Fools dance*' (s.d. at 224). Yet this glimpse of performance from the hospital's other patients, a presentational display of dancing that extends the length of a very long scene, gestures to the formal possibilities of an 'out of form' display.

## Temporality and theatrical action

Such an 'out of form' performance characterizes the Passionate Lord in *The Nice Valour*, whose madness makes him the vehicle for performances that reorient the play's preoccupation with bodily comportment and repunctuate the plot's development. The Passionate Lord spends all but the final scene of the tragicomedy subject to madness, in which he 'runs through all the passions of mankind, / And shifts 'em strangely too' (1.1.51–2): his madness is the result of, though not reducible to, swiftly changing passions.[19] Even though he is the Duke's kinsman, the Passionate Lord's privileged status is irrelevant, since even the power of a title cannot 'cut a fit but one poor hour shorter' (1.1.248), and this emphasis on the time of his fit refracts the way his madness reorders the play around the clock of his virtuosic performance. The Passionate Lord mimics words spoken to him, he sings, he demands a masque (and is rewarded with one in the same scene), he beats a man while singing; he is called a 'walking trouble' (2.1.140) and a 'walking song' (3.4.63), epithets that figure his interruptions of the play's other plots. Through extended scenes of song, dance and laughter in every act of the play, the Passionate Lord's madness prolongs a theatrical display that delays linear plot development.

These scenes frustrate the attempt to ascribe meaning to the Passionate Lord's strains, refusing even the possibility of correlating the songs and snippets of verse with the dramatic fiction. The final scene in which he appears while mad is crammed with onomatopoetic registers of bodily response – 'Ha, ha, ha!' (5.1.1, 3, 11, 14, 15, 17, 23, 29, 41, 44, 52, 58, 64, 70) – repeated and evolving into a duet with his jester, Base. His exclamations begin as laughter and continue as song, phonetically hollow diction expressed as a concatenation that erupts from within the Passionate Lord. Even if (at best) we understand such speech effects suggest an interior impulse that will not be communicated as meaning, these scenes of unsignifying bodily presentation calibrate the time of spectacle around presentational effect. The question these scenes provoke is not: what does his madness mean? Or: how might the disordered content of his speech operate as mimetic comment on the world of the play? Instead, his final lengthy performance prompts another question: when will this scene end?

As the Passionate Lord's singing and dancing overtake the play's other plots, his madness also makes it impossible to correlate his actions with reasoned intention, troubling attempts to hold him accountable for his speech and behaviour. The Passionate Lord's madness is legible not simply through rhetorical denotation or appearance (as in the stage direction, '*Enter the Passionate cousin, rudely and carelessly apparelled, unbraced and untrussed*' (s.d. at 3.3.0)) but through the problem of inexplicable action he introduces. At his first entrance in the play, the Lord '*makes a congee or two to nothing*' (s.d. at 1.1.183). This 'nothing' encapsulates the illegibility of his madness, for there is no apparent cause by which to rationalize his actions. When the Lord angers the Soldier by what the Soldier perceives as intentional mimicry (the Soldier protests that the Lord 'speaks still in my person, and derides me' (2.1.80)), the gentleman assures the Soldier, ''Tis rage ill spent upon a passionate madman' (93). It is fruitless to be angry about a madman's insults, the gentleman insists, since his madness means he does not know what he is saying. Incredulous, the Soldier insists that the Lord acts in willed malice: 'A madman call you him? I have found too much reason / Sound in his injury to me to believe him so' (95–6). The Soldier reads conscious provocation in the Passionate Lord's mockery; the Lord appears to have 'reason', understood as a logic of intent, because his insults appear to be designed precisely to anger the Soldier.

Indeed, two acts later the Soldier refuses to 'set off with madness' (4.1.13) the final injury committed by the Passionate Lord, who ordered a group of men to beat up the Soldier, an imperative for which the Passionate Lord insists there was 'never any' cause (5.1.25). The play ends by valorizing the cure of madness, exactly as the critique of disability as a narrative prosthesis might suggest. Raging at the insults he has received, the Soldier stabs the Passionate Lord, and the Passionate Lord is presumed dead after this attack, a conclusion that appears simultaneously to be the rightful consequence of his offensive actions and undeserved retribution for reflexes he could not control. In the final scene of the play, however, the Passionate Lord returns to court 'free from passions' (5.3.157), and the Soldier is praised at having 'wrought that cure which skill could never find' (195). To be sure, *The Nice Valour* concludes by dismissing the Passionate Lord's madness, a resistant kernel of temporal unruliness that will not be disciplined into meaningful action accountable either to tragic inevitability or comic evitability. Yet the Passionate Lord's madness provides *The Nice Valour* with a distinct form of action: one that is not attributable to anything other than reflex, but one that looks as if it might be. His madness allows the play to run out the clock on spectacle, whether that spectacle tries a spectator's patience or an actor's stamina, and to experiment with inexplicable actions that disrupt the ordering logic of plot.

## Measures of acting

If the Passionate Lord offers a template for the lengths to which disordering speech and actions might go, *The Changeling* refracts these problems through theatrical signification. Franciscus' performance of madness is characterized by singing and gestures of intemperate passion: he hails Isabella as 'bright Titania' (3.3.54) in one moment, exaggerates obeisance to Lollio in another ('Get up, Bucephalus kneels' (63)), and 'grows dangerous' (97) before he is banished from the room. Antonio's performance of foolishness includes being tutored in song ('fa, la, la, la, la' (4.3.91)), the form of 'an honour' (95) or bow, and 'a caper' (100) or leap. Devoting time to the tedious repetitions and physical comedy of characters who feign disability, the hospital plot requires and then dwells on the presentational labour of the actor.

This performance of feigned disability is occasionally interrupted, however, by the offstage figures who represent the 'real' patients in Alibius' care. During the first hospital scene, three madmen upend the testing of Antonio's wit with cries, from 'Put's head i'th' pillory; the bread's too little' (1.2.205) and 'Fly, fly, and he catches the swallow' (206), to 'Cat-whore, cat-whore, her parmesant, her parmesant!' (213–14). Such phrases range from the proverbial to the indexical, and they are comprehensible only as fragments or words rather than speech acts, lacking context that would render them meaningful. Though editors gloss such lines with conjectures on their topical relevance, the madmen's speech does not operate along conventions of self-disclosure within the social world of the play or advance the mechanics of plot. The keepers, in fact, invite the audience to hear them as mere noise: Alibius threatens violence to the madmen ('Peace, peace, or the wire comes' (211)) and Lollio identifies their cries as a ritual ('You may hear what time of day it is, / The chimes of Bedlam goes' (209–10)). The sounds of madmen arrive as if by clockwork, but they keep a time that is legible only as form rather than meaningful content.

The cries of the madmen that echo in the first hospital scene serve as a sonic equivalent to their visual signification in a later glimpse of their show. Just before Alibius bursts in with news of the performance, Lollio enters above the stage with '*Madmen above, some as birds, others as beasts*' (s.d. at 3.3.207), as Isabella and the newly-discovered Antonio watch from below. When Antonio inquires 'What are these?' (3.3.208), Isabella explains:

> Yet are they but our schools of lunatics,
> That act their fantasies in any shapes
> Suiting their present thoughts–if sad, they cry;
> If mirth be their conceit, they laugh again.
> Sometimes they imitate the beasts and birds,
> Singing, or howling, braying, barking; all
> As their wild fancies prompt 'em.
>
> 3.3.209–15

This glimpse of mad patients in *The Changeling* presents their acting as mere reflex, orienting their performance to the present rather than to a logic of past cause or future effect. Like the Passionate Lord, the madmen 'act their fantasies' as the instant expression of 'present thoughts', reacting to fleeting passions of sadness or 'mirth'. Their verbal exclamations signify as commotion rather than language, for they 'imitate the beasts and birds' rather than communicating with human rhetoric. The 'lunatics' follow the promptings of their 'wild fantasies', a refusal of reasoned signification that hollows out their actions: these are not representational roles but mere forms.

From one perspective, the display of madmen in the hospital plot appears to be the limit case of acting, a formal reduction to 'shapes' that refuses even the directives of a script. From another perspective, however, the madmen are the commonplace product of the theatre's own practice of doubling: any casting table for *The Changeling* reminds us that the other part the Beatrice-Joanna actor can double is one of the 'madmen'. These figures, taken together, produce a collective that operates in the background of the hospital plot, reusing key actors from the castle plot but rendering them as sheer sound or spectacle. In the castle plot, *The Changeling* repeatedly returns to the fantasy of converting bodily experience into signs for interpretation: the virginity test, for example, registers Alsemero's desire to transform bodily experience into a legible sequence of compulsory physical responses. The hospital plot's vision of performance as temporal disordering, however, contests Alsemero's presumption that he can extract a narrative from another character's past. The madmen offer an all-hands-on-deck approach to character that brings out fantastical individuation through movement and spectacle.

A second implication of *The Changeling*'s hospital plot points to the generative effect of theatrical repetition. When Edmund Gayton, writing in 1654, discusses the early modern theatre's power to compel spectators to imitation, he talks about those who watch the 'representation of strong passions' and find themselves 'weeping' after a tragedy or 'merry' after a comedy.[20]

As Joseph R. Roach reminds us, such passions are crucial to early modern rhetorical theory, which highlighted the actor's 'powers of precisely controlling the instantaneous transitions between passions' as the actor works upon himself and his audience.[21] For Gayton, however, the effect of the actor's passionate performance goes so far that some spectators 'have so courted the Players to re-act the same matters in the Tavernes, that they came home, as able Actors as themselves; so that their Friends and Wives have took them for Tonies or Mad-men'.[22] Gayton lights on 'Tonies and Mad-men', an allusion to the figure of Antonio in *The Changeling* and a gesture to the division between fools and madmen in the hospital plot, in the roles, or 'matters', that spectators ask actors to 're-act' in the tavern.[23] Antonio, indeed, seems to have remained popular; the dramatis personae in the 1653 printed playbook of *The Changeling* identifies Antonio as 'The Changeling' and the title page engraving from a 1672 collection of theatrical drolls entitled *The Wits* (probably by Francis Kirkman) depicts the figure of the 'Changling' among other iconic characters of the early modern stage.[24] Gayton's account of amateur theatre-goers turns the single character from hospital plot into the recognizable, reproducible type: the play's spectators come home as 'able Actors' who inhabit the role's distinctive gestures and recognizable speech to perform it again for their friends and wives. The anecdote highlights the pleasurable imitation of the persona of a changeling or a madman, an imitation that threatens even the distinction between feigning and being. Through the representation of disability, *The Changeling* generates theatrical possibilities, according to snippets of performance rather than throughlines of plot, notable for the time they take and the acting they prompt.

*The Changeling*'s prominence in the canon of non-Shakespearean drama, acclaimed by many critics as Middleton's greatest tragedy, means that the hospital plot's depiction of madness and intellectual disability continues to figure in modern performances. Refusing to subordinate the hospital plot to the castle plot – by way of reading the Passionate Lord's madness – we can challenge the assumptions that prioritize the narrative operations of plot or legibly predictive action as the primary criteria for theatrical form. Though I have focused on madness here, the hospital scenes in *The Changeling* demand that we consider representations of disability that are at once historically specific and uncomfortably persistent in a modern medical regime of the present. The play does not offer an ethical claim that allows us to revalue disability as an identity but a formal claim about an aesthetic that discharges time differently and reorients theatrical action. Staging disability enables the theatre to reflect on the problem of theatrical action and, through a disability aesthetic, *The Changeling* marks performance's present and the virtuosic labour of the actor who repunctuates theatrical temporality.

# Notes

1 Samuel Schoenbaum, *Middleton's Tragedies: A Critical Study* (New York: Columbia University Press, 1955), 147. As David Nicol has shown, scholars have tended to narrate *The Changeling*'s collaboration as the product of Middleton's genius, either by considering Rowley's contributions 'blots on Middleton's more sophisticated style' or by treating the play as having been composed by 'a transcendent singular author' operating under the sign of Middleton. Nicol, *Middleton and Rowley: Forms of Collaboration in the Jacobean Playhouse* (Toronto: University of Toronto Press, 2012), 9, 37.

2 Annabel Patterson, 'Introduction,' to *The Changeling*, in Gary Taylor and John Lavagnino (eds), *Thomas Middleton: The Collected Works* (Oxford: Oxford University Press, 2007), 1633, 1635.

3 Carol Thomas Neely, *Distracted Subjects: Madness and Gender in Shakespeare and Early Modern Culture* (Ithaca: Cornell University Press, 2004), 186.

4 Carol Thomas Neely, '"Distracted Measures": Madness and Theatricality in Middleton', in Suzanne Gossett (ed.), *Thomas*

*Middleton in Context* (Cambridge: University of Cambridge Press, 2011), 311.
5 Susan Snyder, *Shakespeare: A Wayward Journey* (Newark: University of Delaware Press, 2002), 19.
6 Snyder, *Shakespeare*, 19–20.
7 Elsewhere I have explored how the performance of disability operates as a formal aesthetic for the early modern theatre: see Katherine Schaap Williams, *Unfixable Forms: Disability, Performance, and the Early Modern English Theater* (Ithaca, NY: Cornell University Press, 2021).
8 Although the play was initially attributed to Fletcher, Cyrus Hoy's work on authorship suggested it was primarily written by Middleton, with about half of the play going to Middleton and Fletcher; Baldwin Maxwell argued for a date of 1615–16 but Gary Taylor argues convincingly for 1622. See Gary Taylor, 'Thomas Middleton, *The Nice Valour*, and the Court of James I', *The Court Historian* 6.1 (2001): 1–27. On thematic links to James I's court, see also Susan Wiseman, 'Textual Introduction to *The Nice Valour*,' in Taylor and Lavagnino, (eds), *Thomas Middleton*, 1680.
9 Thomas Middleton, *The Nice Valour; or, The Passionate Madman*, introduced and annotated by Susan Wiseman, text edited by Gary Taylor, in Taylor and Lavagnino (eds), *Thomas Middleton*, 1679–1713.
10 Stage directions and play listings are taken from Alan C. Dessen and Leslie Thomson, *A Dictionary of Stage Directions in English Drama, 1580–1642* (Cambridge: Cambridge University Press, 1999), 137–8.
11 See Michael MacDonald, *Mystical Bedlam: Madness, Anxiety, and Healing in Seventeenth Century England* (Cambridge: Cambridge University Press, 1981); Duncan Salkeld, *Madness and Drama in the Age of Shakespeare* (Manchester: Manchester University Press, 1993); and Kenneth S. Jackson, *Separate Theatres: Bethlem ("Bedlam") Hospital and the Shakespearean Stage* (Newark: University of Delaware Press, 2005). See also Pascale Drouet's chapter in this volume.
12 On early modern concepts of intellectual disability, see C.F. Goodey, *A History of Intelligence and 'Intellectual Disability'*:

*The Shaping of Psychology in Early Modern Europe* (Burlington, VT: Ashgate, 2011); on the 'fool' in relation to the clown, see Richard Preiss, *Clowning and Authorship in Early Modern Theatre* (Cambridge: Cambridge University Press, 2014); on fooling and theatrical virtuosity, see Nicole Sheriko, 'Acting Naturally: Imitation, Disability, and the History of Stage Clowning', in *Imitating Difference: Renaissance Entertainment Culture and the Ethics of Popular Form*, PhD diss. (Rutgers University, 2021).

13 Neely, *Distracted Subjects*, 194.
14 Carol Thomas Neely, '"Distracted Measures": Madness and Theatricality in Middleton', 311. Neely identifies three models of madness, including 'tragic madness: prestigious, elevated, characterized by thematically rich and disjointed speech and behavioral excess'; a comic model, in which 'a nominally mad figure [. . .] maddens others to catalyze plot chaos'; and a third model, which Middleton 'pioneers': 'the play-within-play performance by Bedlamites for the sane' (306).
15 David T. Mitchell and Sharon L. Snyder, *Narrative Prosthesis: Disability and the Dependencies of Discourse* (Ann Arbor: University of Michigan Press, 2000).
16 Mitchell and Snyder, *Narrative Prosthesis*, 55, 56.
17 Lindsey Row-Heyveld, *Dissembling Disability in Early Modern English Drama* (Cham: Springer Nature/Palgrave Macmillan, 2018), 21, 45, 43, 41.
18 Patterson, 'Introduction', 1633.
19 The Lord's 'passions' thus reflect the early modern understanding of what Gail Kern Paster calls 'emotions as material events – bodily in origin, humoral in nature, and influenced by social and environmental factors inside and outside the embodied self' ('The Ecology of the Passions in *A Chaste Maid in Cheapside* and *The Changeling*', in Gary Taylor and Trish Thomas Henley (eds), *The Oxford Handbook of Thomas Middleton* (Oxford: Oxford University Press, 2012), 150). In addition to extensive critical work on the passions by Paster and others, see also Jennifer Panek, '*The Nice Valour*'s Anatomy of Shame', *English Literary Renaissance* 48.3 (2018): 339–67.

20 Edmund Gayton, *Pleasant Notes upon Don Quixot* (London: William Hunt, 1654), sig. T1v.

21 Joseph R. Roach, *The Player's Passion: Studies in the Science of Acting* (Ann Arbor: University of Michigan Press, 1993), 42.

22 Gayton, *Pleasant Notes*, sig. T1v–T2r.

23 On 'Tony' in reference to Antonio, see Sara Jayne Steen, *Ambrosia in an Earthen Vessel: Three Centuries of Audience and Reader Response to the Works of Thomas Middleton* (New York: AMS Press, 1993), 6–7, 58–59.

24 Thomas Middleton and William Rowley, *The Changeling* (London: Printed for Humphrey Moseley, 1653), sig. A1v; [Francis Kirkman], *The Wits, or, Sport Upon Sport* (London: Printed by E.C. for F[r]ancis Kirkman, 1672), title page.

# PART FIVE

# Actor and Audience in Jacobean Performance

# 9

# *The Changeling*, The Boy Actor and Female Subjectivity

## Lucy Munro

In her late-Jacobean romance, *Urania*, Mary Wroth refers twice to the boy actors of the professional stage.[1] In Part 1, she describes a man whose emotions are undisturbed by the sight of the queen, his erstwhile lover, wooing another: 'there hee saw her with all passionate ardency, seeke, and sue for the strangers loue, yet he vnmoueable, was no further wrought, then if he had seene a delicate play-boy acte a louing womans part, and knowing him a Boy, lik'd onely his action'.[2] In Part 2, an allusion to a boy actor appears in a longer description of another woman, an 'enchantress' who has bewitched Leonius, the younger brother of Amphilanthus and Urania. The Lady who rules the island of Robollo describes her to Steriamus as

> A woeman dangerous in all kinds, flattering and insinuating aboundantly, winning by matchless intising, and as soone cast of[f], butt with hasard sufficient to the forsaken or forsaker; her traines farr exceeding her love, and as full of

faulshood as of vaine and endles expressions, beeing for her over-acting fashion more like a play-boy dressed gawdely up to shew a fond, loving, woemans part then a great Lady; soe busy, so full of taulke, and in such a sett formallity, with so many framed lookes, fained smiles, and nods, with a deceiptfull downe-cast looke, insteed of purest modesty and bashfullnes (tow rich Juells for her rotten Cabbinett to containe). Som times a little (and that while painfull) silence, as wishing, and with gestures, as longing to bee moved to speake againe, and seeming soe loath as supplications must bee (as itt were) made to heare her toungue once more ring chimes of faulse beeguilings, and intrapping charmes, witt being overwourne by her farr nicer, and more strange, and soe much the more prised, inchanting inventions. Soe as her charming phansies and ther aluring daliings makes true witt a foole in such a schoole, and bace faulenes and luxury the Jalours of her house, and unfortunate prisoners.[3]

In both of these passages, the figure of the boy actor is evoked in the context of emotion, vision and performance. In the first, the queen's ardent wooing of another man no longer moves her former lover because her passion has given him 'new sight ... to see her shame, and his owne together' (sig. I2v). In the second, the 'enchantress' presents a false face to the world. 'Is she beautifull?' asks Steriamus; the Lady replies, 'Noe, truly, Sir ... What she hath, she pais for (and itt is nott good neither)' (160). She is over-dressed, dependent on cosmetics and overly histrionic, yet her 'false beeguilings', 'intrapping charmes' and 'charming phansies' have the power to enthral Leonius.

Wroth's commentaries on the 'play-boy' offer a powerful context for the composition and performance of Thomas Middleton and William Rowley's *The Changeling*, which – like *Urania* – emerged from late-Jacobean literary and theatrical cultures. Written around 1615–20, the first part of *Urania* was published in late summer or autumn 1621; *The Changeling* was licensed for performance by Lady Elizabeth's Men at the

Cockpit playhouse, also known as the Phoenix, on 7 May 1622.[4] The second part of *Urania* was never published, but Wroth appears to have been working on it between 1620 and 1630. Her allusions to boy actors are part of a wider network of theatrical references in *Urania*, and they are perhaps unsurprising given her other interactions with dramatic culture.[5] In 1605, she appeared in Jonson's court entertainment, *The Masque of Blackness*, an experience upon which she reflects in one of the sonnets in her sequence 'Pamphilia to Amphilanthus', published in the first part of *Urania*.[6] Jonson dedicated *The Alchemist* to Wroth, addressed three poems to her and appears to have represented her in his pastoral *The May Lord*.[7] At the same time as Wroth was working on *Urania*, she also composed *Love's Victory*, a pastoral tragicomedy that was probably intended for household performance.

I do not argue here that Wroth exercised a direct influence on *The Changeling*, although it is possible that Middleton and Rowley were familiar with the first part of *Urania*. Instead, I use *Urania* as an intertext that brings to the fore a set of issues that are central to this essay: gendered performance, spectatorship and the techniques through which female subjectivity was constructed on the Jacobean stage. Wroth's work forcibly reminds us not only of the material and histrionic elements that were brought together when a boy actor played a woman on stage, from dress and cosmetics to gestures and facial expressions, but also the contribution of the response of female spectators to the construction of female roles. Moreover, Wroth employs a set of repeated images in her own construction of female subjectivity – eyesight, cabinets and the labyrinth – all of which appear prominently in *The Changeling*.

Questions of surveillance, witnessing, watching and judging feature elsewhere in this collection, connected with gender by Jean E. Howard, with emotion and Calvinism by Jesse Lander and with spectatorship by Jennifer Low. My interest here, in contrast, lies in the potential gap between the female spectator and the female character, to which Wroth's commentary points, and the ways in which her own work illuminates the strategies that Middleton and Rowley take to close that gap. In what follows, I look first at what we can recover about the design of female roles in the play, and their potential impact in performance by boy actors, drawing on documentary evidence about the personnel of Lady Elizabeth's Men in 1622 and the work of Evelyn Tribble, Scott McMillin and John Astington on actor training. I then return to the work of Wroth, reading the female roles of *The Changeling* through the linguistic framework that her writing establishes.

In its treatment of subjectivity in the play, this essay follows the lead of scholars such as John Stachniewski, Ania Loomba, Roberta Barker, David Nicol and Nora Williams. Stachniewski's influential reading of *The Changeling* argues that what resembles psychological depth in Beatrice-Joanna is an effect of Calvinist structures of thought around predestination and salvation; if Beatrice-Joanna has an unconscious, it is because there is a gap between her understanding of herself as elect and her true status as reprobate.[8] In *Gender, Race, Renaissance Drama*, published a year before Stachniewski's essay, Ania Loomba analyses the 'schisms' in female subjectivity presented in plays such as *The Changeling*, arguing that '[t]he contradictions imposed on women are internalised, but then they catalyse an alienation which radically disrupts all notions of social or psychic stability'.[9] More recently, Barker and Nicol critique what they term the 'the Freudian/romantic reading of *The Changeling*', viewing it as 'a *mis*reading in which Beatrice's hatred for De Flores is turned into love, and her misery into lust'.[10] Focusing on the play's performance tradition, Williams points to the ways in which the play's asides both allow characters to articulate hidden thoughts and emotions and complicate its presentation on twentieth- and twenty-first-century stages. She comments that the aside 'plays deliberately in the metatheatrical space between the character, the actor, and the audience', disrupting naturalistic conventions that often depend on the very erasure of this 'space'.[11] The object of my enquiry here is thus the 'subjectivity effect' (to adapt Joel Fineman's term) that is created when Middleton and Rowley embed the performances of boy actors – themselves dependent on an established set of internal structures, gestural conventions and material aids such as costume and cosmetics – within a network of images that spectators might associate with female agency and desire.[12] Created by two male dramatists, and performed by an all-male cast, *The Changeling* nonetheless offers a complex mediation between the creative expression of women such as Wroth, the desires of female spectators, and the conventions that underpinned the creation of what looks to us like dramatic character.

## *The Changeling* and gendered performance

I want to offer two conjectures about the potential casting of *The Changeling* in May 1622, both of which have implications for how we understand its female roles. The first is that Andrew Cane – a notable comic actor who also trained boys for the stage and is linked with Lady Elizabeth's Men in a list drawn up in 1622 – would have been well cast as Lollio if he was available to the company, and that the role may have been designed for him.[13] Cane's only recorded role is that of the '*humorous gallant*' Trimalchio in Shakerley Marmion's *Holland's Leaguer*, performed by Prince Charles's Men in 1631. Trimalchio is the largest role in that play, and he appears in more scenes than any other character; as John H. Astington points out, the role also appears to have been intended to give him substantial stage-time with the boy actors who were apprenticed to him.[14] A pamphlet published in 1641, *The Stage Players Complaint*, written as a dialogue between a fictionalized Cane and another Caroline stage clown, Timothy Read, also gives a flavour of Cane's fast-talking stage persona, a quality that also marks out Trimalchio in *Holland's Leaguer*. Read tells Cane, 'You incuse me of my nimble feet; but I thinke your tongue runnes a little faster, and you contend as much to out-strip facetious *Mercury* in your tongue, as lame *Vulcan* in my feete'.[15]

Like Trimalchio, Lollio is voluble and highly articulate. Moreover, as David Nicol points out in his essay in this volume, his 'devious, and vicious personality' gives the impression that he was 'created for an actor with a quite different stage persona' from that of the play's co-author, William Rowley, who specialized in 'guileless plain-speakers'.[16] Playing Lollio would also enable Cane to supervise the performance of the boy actor playing Isabella, who may have been one of his apprentices. We know that Cane entered a new apprentice, Thomas Staynoe, in the books of the Goldsmiths' company, of which he was a member, on 20 July 1621.[17] The cast of *Holland's Leaguer* featured a later apprentice of Cane, Arthur Saville, in the demanding role of Quartilla, which he took on within four months of beginning his apprenticeship. Astington suggests that Saville 'had been carefully chosen', and the same may have been true of Staynoe if he played Isabella in May 1622.[18]

My second conjecture is that the role of De Flores may have been designed for Elliard Swanston, who appears alongside Cane in the 1622 list. Swanston was a rising star – by 1624 he had joined the King's Men, becoming one of that company's leading actors. He was remembered in the Restoration as 'a brave roaring Fellow' who 'would make the stage shake again' if he were to be resurrected and brought back to the stage, but his known roles – which include Othello, Richard III and the title-roles in Chapman's *Bussy D'Ambois* and Beaumont and Fletcher's *Philaster* – suggest that he was capable of a greater range and subtlety than the image of a 'brave roaring Fellow' alone conveys.[19] Not only Richard III but also two smaller roles in 1620s plays by Philip Massinger – Domitian's spy, Aretinus, in *The Roman Actor* (1626) and the sleazy courtier Ricardo in *The Picture* (1629) – argue that he could manage ambivalent, villainous characters with ease.[20] If this identification is correct, it suggests that the boy playing Beatrice-Joanna was required to be more independent of his master than the boy playing Isabella, a supposition that is supported by a closer analysis of the play's female roles.

Internal structures within the text of *The Changeling* suggest that its female roles were tailored to actors with varying degrees of experience or aptitude, and that the techniques that we often associate with the theatrical presentation of subjectivity, such as the aside, were carefully managed. The roles of Diaphanta and Isabella include a number of the 'scaffolding' structures identified by Evelyn Tribble in the plays of Christopher Marlowe, which include moments at which characters played by boy actors are 'shepherded' onto the stage by other characters, 'attentional devices' in which they are addressed directly, repetitions or echoes of cue lines, and the 'alternation of relatively restricted, highly scaffolded scenes with more voluble and demanding scenes'.[21] These roles are also 'restricted' in the sense outlined by Scott McMillin, who argues that roles for boy actors might be designed to interact with a limited number of other characters, meaning that some sequences could be rehearsed one-on-one and in larger cast scenes a boy actor could listen for his cues from a small set of his fellow performers.[22]

The cues for Diaphanta's lines, entrances and exits are spoken by only two characters, Jasperino (1.1), and Beatrice-Joanna (2.2, 4.1 and 5.1). The most demanding of her scenes is 4.1, which requires her to speak in aside, sing and display a series of symptoms when she drinks the liquid 'M', proffered by Beatrice-Joanna. The actor's performance is still, however, supported by the text. Two of Diaphanta's short lines, 'Is't possible?' and 'Are you in earnest?' (75, 79), could be transposed without doing violence to sense or metre, and she sometimes repeats elements of Beatrice-Joanna's lines, replying to her mistress's comment, 'You're too quick, I fear, to be a maid', with 'How? Not a maid?' (95–6) and to 'You dare put your honesty / Upon an easy trial?' with 'Easy? Anything!' (100–1). Her responses to the liquid are closely tracked in the dialogue; Beatrice-Joanna watches as she gapes or yawns, and then comments,

>                                there's the first symptom,
> And what haste it makes to fall into the second –
>     (*Diaphanta sneezes*)
> There by this time! Most admirable secret!
> On the contrary, it stirs not me a whit,
> Which most concerns it.
> DIAPHANTA
>   Ha, ha, ha!
> BEATRICE (*aside*)
>                 Just in all things and in order
> As if 'twere circumscribed.
>
>                                                   4.1.109–15

The text incorporates pauses during which Beatrice-Joanna watches for the first and third symptoms, and she directly cues the second. Moreover, even in the small Cockpit/Phoenix playhouse, where a greater number of spectators could see actors' facial expressions clearly than in a large, outdoor playhouse, it would not matter too much if Diaphanta's gaping, sneezing and laughing were not precisely on cue because they are managed through Beatrice-Joanna's dialogue.

The role of Isabella would have been more testing for an apprentice actor, but it nonetheless includes a number of scaffolding techniques. The demanding sequence in 3.3, in which Isabella is assailed by Antonio and Lollio, includes long speeches and a short soliloquy (230–5), but some of its lines are also structured to support the boy actor. For example, Isabella's comment about the 'madmen', cued by offstage singing, could easily be dropped if the boy actor forgot his line:

> MADMAN (*singing, within*)
>             Bounce! Bounce!
>             He falls! he falls!
> ISABELLA
>   Hark you, your scholars in the upper room
>   Are out of order.

LOLLIO
*(shouting offstage)* Must I come amongst you there?
3.3.122–7

Similarly, Isabella's lines in her dialogue with Antonio are repetitive and could be swapped without doing too much damage to the meaning or the metre: 'You are a fine fool indeed. [. . .] You're a parlous fool. [. . .] A forward fool too!' (136, 142, 147). Her responses to Lollio's assault are structured similarly – 'How now? [. . .] What's the matter? [. . .] You bold slave, you' (237, 240, 243) – and the fact that these lines are in prose means that scansion is not an issue. Against this backdrop, the sequence in 4.3 in which she adopts the guise of a madwoman and humiliates Antonio functions as a set-piece in which the boy actor is given an opportunity to demonstrate his developing prowess.

Beatrice-Joanna is by some distance the most demanding of female roles in *The Changeling*. She is given some support from structures within the text – for instance, when she enters in 5.3, she echoes Alsemero's cue lines:

BEATRICE
Alsemero!
ALSEMERO
How do you?
BEATRICE    How do I?
Alas! How do you? You look not well.
ALSEMERO
You read me well enough. I am not well.
BEATRICE
Not well, sir? Is't in my power to better you?
5.3.14–17

However, these structured moments appear in the midst of a number of far more demanding sequences. Beatrice-Joanna is as likely to initiate an exchange as to speak in response to direct address, and she cues Diaphanta in three scenes, enacting a miniature scaffolding structure in which she takes the role of the 'master'. At the start of Act 5, she enters alone and speaks an eleven-line soliloquy in which she is required to perform in tandem with the striking clock (5.1.1–11); this double-act is resumed later in the scene, when she holds the stage during the sequence in which the offstage De Flores sets fire to Diaphanta's chamber (5.1.61–71).

In three scenes – 2.1, 2.2 and 3.4 – Beatrice-Joanna and De Flores enact duologues in which many of their lines are spoken in aside; such exchanges require the actors not only to modify their tone and direction of address but also to manage their own non-verbal performance while the other actor is speaking their aside. In 2.1, for instance, De Flores speaks one aside of twenty-five lines (2.1.26–51) and another of twelve lines (2.1.78–89), during which time the actor playing Beatrice-Joanna receives no support from the text. The boy actor is also required to enact non-verbal performances that trigger lines from other characters, such as Alsemero's 'You seemed displeased, lady, on the sudden' (1.1.108) and Tomazo's comments to Alonzo: 'I see small welcome in her eye' and 'did you mark the dullness of her parting now?' (2.1.107, 125) These aspects of the ways in which the roles of Beatrice-Joanna and De Flores are constructed may reflect early modern assumptions about what constituted good acting. In a commentary on Richard Burbage, Richard Flecknoe praises his ability to sustain his role when he was not speaking, writing that 'when he held his peace [...] he was an excellent Actor still, never falling in his Part when he had done speaking; but with his looks and gesture, maintaining it still unto the heighth'.[23] In early performances of *The Changeling*, a performance by Cane as Lollio or Swanston as De Flores would have supported and been supported in turn by the work of the apprentice boy actors, whether they were speaking or silent.

## *The Changeling* and gendered subjectivity

The techniques that made the role of Beatrice-Joanna challenging for a trainee actor also supported him creating a credible impression of female subjectivity on stage. Some of these effects, such as the facial expressions that act as cues for commentaries from the men on stage, could be bolstered by other aspects of stage presentation. If the boy actor playing Beatrice-Joanna wore white or lustrous make-up, as it is likely that he did, his cosmeticized face would have been easier to 'read' on the small Cockpit/Phoenix stage. However, the use of cosmetics would have connected his performance with broader discourses of status and race in *The Changeling*. The play's representation of gendered subjectivity and agency is grounded in its language of fairness and blackness, initially associated with Beatrice-Joanna and the 'foul' De Flores respectively, the racialization of which is reinforced by the narrative's setting in southern Spain.[24] If the play presented a cosmeticized Beatrice-Joanna, it would have drawn on what Farah Karim-Cooper terms '[t]he paradox of cosmetic whiteness', in which 'whiteness symbolized a virtuous and superior racial ideal' but '[p]retending to embody the ideal complexion seems to have been considered almost as bad as, if not worse than not having white skin at all'.[25] Furthermore, when Alsemero suspects Beatrice-Joanna's sexual relationship with De Flores, he comments, 'The black mask / That so continually was worn upon't / Condemns the face for ugly ere't be seen' (5.3.3–5), referring not only to the masks that high-status European women wore to preserve their white complexions but also one of the technologies, besides cosmetics, through which blackness was presented on early modern stages.[26]

It is striking, in this context, that the next play licensed for Lady Elizabeth's Men after *The Changeling*, on 10 May 1622, was entitled *The Black Lady*.[27] The actor who played Beatrice-Joanna is likely also to have played the protagonist of *The Black Lady*; when these two plays were performed in repertory together spectators would have been forcibly reminded of the material, gestural and linguistic conventions that underpinned the gendered and raced performance of female subjectivity. Moreover, both plays may also be connected with the 'embodied technique[s] of racialization' that Noémie Ndiaye identifies in plays performed by Lady Elizabeth's Men in the period between 1623 and 1625, such as *The Spanish Gypsy*, *The Martyred Soldier* and *The Bondman*.[28]

Beatrice-Joanna's 'black mask', an image that brings together performance technologies and the inner life of the character, is one of the subjectivity effects of *The Changeling*. Middleton and Rowley embed it within a series of images that Wroth uses to add depth to the female characters of her sonnets and prose fiction. Two appear in the description of the 'enchantress', quoted at the start of this essay, when Wroth describes her 'deceiptfull downe-cast looke, instead of purest modesty and bashfullnes (tow rich Juells for her rotten Cabbinett to containe)'. Literal and metaphorical cabinets recur in *Urania* as vehicles in which women's secrets are hidden, circulated and imagined. In Part 1, the narrator comments that Pamphilia 'could bee in greatest assemblies as priuate with her owne thoughts, as if in her Cabinet' (sig. 3C3r) and Urania's friend Liana likens her own barely contained emotions to 'a Cabinet so fild with treasure, as though not it selfe, yet the lock or hinges cannot containe it, but breake open' (sig. 2E2r). Similarly, the enchantress's 'deceiptfull downe-cast looke' is reflected in the repeated references to the eyes, and their capacity to deceive, in 'Pamphilia to Amphilanthus'. In Sonnet 5, Wroth asks, 'Can winning eyes proue to the heart a sting?', while Sonnet 34 describes the need for lover to manage her own gestures: 'Take heed mine eyes, how you your looks doe cast, / Lest they betray my hearts most secret thought [. . .] Catch you alwatching [*sic*] eyes ere they be past, / Or take yours fix't' (sigs 4A1v, 4C1v). A third key image is that of the labyrinth, which animates the

'Crown of Sonnets Dedicated to Love'. The first sonnet opens with the lines,

> In this strange Labyrinth how shall I turne,
> Wayes are on all sides, while the way I misse:
> If to the right hand, there in loue I burne,
> Let mee goe forward, therein danger is.
>
> If to the left, suspicion hinders blisse:
>
> sig. 4E2v

The last sonnet, as the form requires, returns to the same image in its final lines: 'So though in love I fervently do burn, / In this strange labyrinth how shall I turn?' (sig. 4F1r). The corona sonnets thus enact the stifling contortions of the labyrinth itself, in which there is no true progress but only repetition and regression.

All of these images appear in *The Changeling*, structuring and supporting its subjectivity effects. Like Wroth, Middleton and Rowley play on the literal and figurative capacity of the cabinet to conceal women's secrets. Beatrice-Joanna's discovery of Alsemero's cabinet enables her to enact the role of the virginal bride despite her concealed sexual experience, and it also recalls Alsemero's earlier description of Diaphanta, 'These women are the ladies' cabinets; / Things of most precious trust are locked into 'em' (2.2.6–7). Middleton and Rowley similarly make use of the eyesight and the gaze, their extensive use of asides mirroring Wroth's use of first- and third-person narrators. In the hospital plot, Alibius tasks Lollio with watching Isabella, commenting with apparently unconscious sexual innuendo, 'Here, I do say, must thy employment be: / To watch her treadings, and in my absence / Supply my place' (1.2.37–9). Isabella is more aware than Beatrice-Joanna of the extent to which she is subjected to scrutiny by 'watchful bankers' (3.3.231), but the latter consistently returns to the image of the eye when discussing her desires and the ability to transcend obstacles placed in their way. For example, when she is brought the news of Alonzo's death, Beatrice-Joanna's response connects the eyes not only with emotion but the ways in which it was performed on stage: 'My joys start at mine eyes; our sweet'st delights / Are evermore born weeping' (3.4.25–6). Because she is so ready to connect her emotional state with her eyesight, the fact that she characterises De Flores as a 'basilisk' (1.1.115) suggests his power to unsettle her; Alsemero unconsciously reworks this image when he suspects the sexual relationship between the pair, imagining Beatrice-Joanna herself as having 'eyes that could shoot fire into kings' breasts' (4.2.107).

The image of the labyrinth similarly connects the two plots. Isabella describes the hospital in ways that evoke the classical labyrinth in which the Minotaur was kept prisoner, asking Lollio at the start of 3.3 'Whence have you commission / To fetter the doors against me?' (1–2) and referring to it as a 'cage' and a 'pinfold' (3, 7). The image is crystalized, however, in the following scene, in which Beatrice-Joanna attempts to pay off De Flores for murdering Alonzo and De Flores attempts to take – and, at length, brutally succeeds in taking – his payment in the form of sex. Half-way through the exchange between them, she comments in aside, 'I'm in a labyrinth! / What will content him?' (73–4). Like Isabella, Beatrice-Joanna is in a labyrinth shaped by the desires of men; the difference is that she has not noticed it before. The sexual contours of this labyrinth are made yet more clear in 4.3, the scene that points most directly to the difference between Isabella and Beatrice-Joanna: where Beatrice Joanna makes use of the servant De Flores to do away with her unwanted fiancé, hoping to leave the way clear for Alsemero, Isabella instead makes use of the servant Lollio – like De Flores a sexual predator who is waiting for her to slip – to neutralize Antonio, Alsemero's structural equivalent, and remain faithful to her husband. Thus, while Beatrice-Joanna finds herself trapped in a 'labyrinth' of De Flores' desire, Isabella instead controls the image, alluding directly to Dedalus's labyrinth when she takes on the guise of a madwoman. Making its sexual undertones explicit, she pretends to take Antonio for Icarus, crying, 'Stand up, thou son of Cretan Dedalus, / And let us tread the lower labyrinth; / I'll bring thee to the clue' (4.3.113–15). Like the play's images of cabinets and eyes, the image of the labyrinth lends the female characters of the play a multi-layered quality, in which allusion combines with gesture and performed emotion to present a compelling impression of complex subjectivity.

Although Middleton and Rowley could not have been familiar with Wroth's commentary on the boy actor in Part 2 of *Urania*, and they may not have read Part 1 either, their use of the images of labyrinth and cabinet mounts a challenge to female spectators. Wroth describes in Part 1 a female spectator for whom the 'action' of a boy player is pleasing but emotionally uninvolving, and in Part 2 a woman whose calculated emotional performance is likened to an 'over-acting' boy. Middleton and Rowley forestall both of these criticisms by writing female roles with internal structures that support their boy actors in the performance of emotion and by surrounding these roles with images that evoke the representation of female subjectivity elsewhere in their culture. In doing so, they create a series of subjectivity effects, moments at which their female characters are granted additional depth and complexity. They also give the apprentices who played Beatrice-Joanna and Isabella the ammunition to take on charismatic leading actors like Elliard Swanston or Andrew Cane and to hold the stage in their own right.

# Notes

1  Earlier commentaries on these allusions include Michael Shapiro, 'Lady Mary Wroth Describes a "Boy Actress"', *Medieval and Renaissance Drama in England* 4 (1989): 187–94; Roberta Barker, '"Not One Thing Exactly": Gender, Performance and Critical Debates Over the Early Modern Boy-Actress', *Literature Compass* 6.2 (2009): 460–81.

2  *The Countesse of Mountgomeries Urania* (London, 1621), sig. I2v.

3 *The Second Part of the Countess of Montgomeries Urania*, ed. Josephine A. Roberts, completed by Suzanne Gossett and Janel Mueller (Tempe, AZ: Renaissance English Text Society, 1999), 159–60.

4 N.W. Bawcutt, *The Control and Censorship of Caroline Drama: The Records of Sir Henry Herbert, Master of the Revels 1623–73* (Oxford: Clarendon Press, 1996), 136.

5 See, for instance, *Countesse of Mountgomeries Urania*, sigs I2r, K1r, 2B4v, 2R4r–v, 2Vr–v, 2X4r, 3A4r, 3C1r, 3O1v, 4F3v; *Second Part of the Countess of Montgomery's Urania*, 105, 127, 234.

6 Sonnet 22, in *Countesse of Mountgomeries Urania*, 4B2v.

7 Ben Jonson, 'To the Lady, Most Deserving her Name and Blood: Mary, Lady Wroth', in David Bevington, Martin Butler and Ian Donaldson (gen. eds), *The Cambridge Edition of the Works of Ben Jonson* (henceforth *CBJ*), (Cambridge: Cambridge University Press, 2012), 4: 557; *Epigrams*, 103 and 105, in *CBJ*, 5: 170, 171; *Underwood*, 28, in *CBJ*, 142. On *The May Lord* see *CBJ*, 5: 343–5.

8 John Stachniewski, 'Calvinist Psychology in Middleton's Tragedies', in R.V. Holdsworth (ed.), *Three Jacobean Revenge Tragedies* (Basingstoke: Macmillan, 1990), 226–47.

9 Ania Loomba, *Gender, Race, Renaissance Drama* (Manchester: Manchester University Press, 1989), 96, 102.

10 Roberta Barker and David Nicol, 'Does Beatrice-Joanna Have a Subtext?: *The Changeling* on the London Stage', *Early Modern Literary Studies* 10.1 (May 2004): 3.1–43 (30).

11 Nora Williams, '"Cannot I keep that secret?": Editing and Performing Asides in *The Changeling*', *Shakespeare Bulletin* 34 (2016): 29–45 (31).

12 See Joel Fineman, *Shakespeare's Perjured Eye: The Invention of Poetic Subjectivity in the Sonnets* (Berkeley: University of California Press, 1986); *The Subjectivity Effect in Western Literary Tradition: Essays Towards the Release of Shakespeare's Will* (Cambridge, MA: MIT Press, 1991). My approach differs here from the classic account of keywords in *The Changeling*, Christopher Ricks' 'The Moral and Poetic Structure of *The Changeling*', *Essays in Criticism* 10 (1960): 290–306, in two important respects: (1) I am interested specifically in images that

are used to present female subjectivity; and (2) the images that I trace cut across both of the play's plots.

13 On the composition of Lady Elizabeth's Men in 1622, see Bawcutt, *Control and Censorship*, 136; John Tucker Murray, *English Dramatic Companies, 1558–1642*, 2 vols (London: Constable, 1910), 1: 215–16; Gerald Eades Bentley, *The Jacobean and Caroline Stage*, 7 vols (Oxford: Clarendon Press, 1941–68), 1: 184.

14 John H. Astington, *Actors and Acting in Shakespeare's Time* (Cambridge: Cambridge University Press, 2010), 149.

15 *The Stage-Players Complaint. In a Pleasant Dialogue Between Cane of the Fortune, and Reed of the Friers* (London, 1641), sig. A2r.

16 For more on the perception of Rowley as an actor and the parts he might have played, see David Nicol, 'A secret within the castle: William Rowley and *The Changeling*' in this volume.

17 See John H. Astington, 'The Career of Andrew Cane, Citizen, Goldsmith, and Player', *Medieval and Renaissance Drama in England* 16 (2003), 130–44 (132–3); David Kathman, 'Grocers, Goldsmiths, and Drapers: Freemen and Apprentices in the Elizabethan Theater', *Shakespeare Quarterly* 55 (2004): 1–49 (22).

18 Astington, *Actors*, 156.

19 Thomas Shadwell, *The Virtuoso* (London, 1676), 14. On Swanston's roles see Astington, *Actors*, 159; Lucy Munro, *Shakespeare in the Theatre: The King's Men* (London: Bloomsbury Arden Shakespeare), 10, 19–21, 32.

20 Although Swanston played Richard III later in his career, the connections that Mark Hutchings draws between the two plays in arguing for Shakespeare's influence on Middleton and Rowley also point to the strengths that an individual actor might bring to the performance of Richard and De Flores. See '*Richard III* and *The Changeling*', *Notes and Queries* 52 (2005): 229–30.

21 Evelyn Tribble, 'Marlowe's Boy Actors', *Shakespeare Bulletin* 27 (2009): 5–17 (11).

22 Scott McMillin, 'The Sharer and his Boy: Rehearsing Shakespeare's Women', in *From Script to Stage in Early Modern England*, eds, Peter Holland and Stephen Orgel (London: Palgrave, 2004), 231–45 (235).

23 Richard Flecknoe, *Love's Kingdom: A Pastoral Trage-comedy* [...] *With a Short Treatise of the English Stage* (London, 1664), G5v–6r.

24 On Beatrice-Joanna as 'the figure of the heretical, easternised, and hence changeable woman', see Clare McManus, '"Constant Changelings", Theatrical Form, and Migration: Stage Travel in the Early 1620s', in Claire Jowitt and David McInnis (eds), *Travel and Drama in Early Modern England: The Journeying Play* (Cambridge: Cambridge University Press, 2018), 207–29 (220). On race in the play, see also Lara Bovilsky, *Barbarous Play: Race on the English Renaissance Stage* (Minneapolis and London: University of Minnesota Press, 2008), 137–58; on *The Changeling* and Spain, again see David Nicol's essay on the spectre of Spanish threat: 'A secret within the castle: William Rowley and *The Changeling*' in this volume.

25 Farah Karim-Cooper, 'Staging the Black and White Binary in the Early Modern Theatre', in Ayanna Thompson (ed.), *The Cambridge Companion to Shakespeare and Race* (Cambridge: Cambridge University Press, 2021), 17–29 (23).

26 On the use of black fabric in racial impersonation, see Ian Smith, 'Othello's Black Handkerchief', *Shakespeare Quarterly* 64 (2013): 1–25.

27 Bawcutt, *Control and Censorship*, 137.

28 Noémie Ndiaye, '"Come Aloft, Jack-little-ape!": Race and Dance in *The Spanish Gypsy*', *English Literary Renaissance* 51 (2021): 121–51.

# 10

# Witnessing at the Phoenix

# Early Modern Audiences at *The Changeling*

## *Jennifer A. Low*

Marjorie Garber once used the phrase 'the burden of witness' to describe the spectator's experience of watching a tragedy when the audience is privy to information that the characters are not.[1] This essay is concerned with the theatrical audience's experience of the burden of witness in a more specifically juridical sense, in the context of the substantial body of scholarship on literature and the law. Middleton and Rowley's *The Changeling* engages the spectator in issues of witnessing and judgement long before its final scene mocks the concept of the bed of justice. Beyond the mimetic frame, the watching and evaluating enacted by the characters is mirrored by the playgoers in the auditorium. While the characters act as well as watch, the spectators merely watch – but watching is not doing nothing. This chapter shows how Middleton and Rowley induce the watcher to engage in a variety of juridical positions including witness and jury member through staging elements and use of the conventions of 'gallows confessions' in Beatrice's final speech. While the sight of the wounded Beatrice being carried forward by De Flores may initially seem to function like a judgement tale created by Middleton and Rowley to provide spectators with moral guidance or as a moment in an instance of gallows literature intended to serve didactic and normative purposes, Beatrice's speech draws upon the conventions of gallows confessions for a different purpose: to challenge the spectator to recognize the complexities of her situation and examine it from several viewpoints.[2] This spectatorial position harks back to the role of jurors and witnesses in medieval trials who provided information about the character of the defendants rather than evidential narratives of facts under dispute.

Middleton's techniques induce watchers to slip from one form of engagement to another, in part because the meaning of the words 'witness' and 'testimony' was overdetermined. 'Witness' conveys two divergent ideas in its several *Oxford English Dictionary* definitions.[3] The first idea focuses on *what* is seen. According to these definitions, witness testimony provides evidence of objective fact; the witness is a mere conductor of factual information. In England during the early modern period, witnesses were called into court to provide the judge and jury with information gained through the senses, offering 'attestation of a fact, event or statement; testimony, evidence' (definition 2a). The *OED*'s fourth definition is related: a witness is 'one who gives evidence in relation to matters of fact under inquiry'.

But the term witness can also emphasize the person who witnesses as the noter and re-teller of events or the conveyor of memories, often of marvellous and astonishing occurrences. Here, the significance of the information is outstanding, and the personhood of the witness is emphasized. In such cases, the witness provides veracity in guarantee of the unusual or the miraculous. The testimony of such witnesses changes future iterations of the evidence from rumour or legend to verifiably sourced information, and their presence offers future generations some guarantee of a story's truth. This meaning is implied in OED definition 2c: 'applied to the inward testimony of the conscience (after 2 Corinthians 1:12)'. In fact, a witness could be called to observe a specific event for just this purpose, as is suggested by definition 5, which describes a witness as one 'who is called on, selected, or appointed to be present at a transaction, so as to be able to testify to its having taken place'. In any case, a witness is 'one who is or was present and is able to testify from personal observation' (OED, definition 6). Witnessing may be linked to Christian testifying: a witness can be 'one who testifies for Christ or for the Christian faith, esp. by death; a martyr'. The definition of the word's verb form also stresses the need for the personal element to provide verification: 'to experience by personal observation; to be present as an observer at; to see with one's own eyes' (definition 4).[4] The use of the word may thus emphasize the personal element of the observation rather than the evidence provided, or a juridical context.

It would be simplistic to characterize the *seeing* aspect of witnessing as passive and the watching and testifying element as active, though these emphases carry into different aspects of the court system. In Tudor times, witnesses in a court of law respond to the clerk's call 'for anyone to give evidence against the prisoner.'[5] However, as Lorna Hutson explains, jurors of the thirteenth through the fifteenth centuries 'originated as sworn inquests of members of the community whose "verdict" or truth-saying was based on local knowledge and memory, and not on the oral presentation of evidential narratives of facts under dispute during a trial'.[6] In other words, they served as what we now call character witnesses and were not expected to provide eye-witness evidence. Andrea Frisch points out that in Merovingian France, 'witnesses' more often swore to an accused person's character than to what they actually saw, and she suggests on that basis that 'the medieval witness is taken to have neither a subjective nor an objective perspective, but an *intersubjective* point of view', which she describes as 'overtly dialogic'.[7] As she asserts, 'the figure of the modern epistemic witness has more in common with the medieval judge than with the medieval witness. The distinction between the juridical verdict reached via testimony, on the one hand, and that based on the judge's own perceptions, on the other, is a central one throughout the Middle Ages.'[8]

Frisch's point gets to the heart of my argument: when we ignore the overdetermined meaning of the word, we may unintentionally conflate the legal witness with the judge or with watchers at an execution. Such a conflation may derive from historical change: as Thomas Green explains, from the medieval to the early modern period, legal procedure evolved 'from a trial dominated by the self-informing jury to a trial based mainly on evidence produced by the prosecution [that] not only transformed the relationship between judge and jury but gave greater opportunity for judicial instruction and enhanced the growth of the substantive law'.[9] The jury's personal judgement gained more authority, and the judge addressed the jury more directly. During the sixteenth and seventeenth centuries, the roles of witness, jury member and judge were still becoming what they are today.[10] The slippage that remains today in the definitions of these roles shows where the conflation of legal and moral judgement occurred.

In modern terms a legal witness should not assess the information he or she recounts; interpretation is not a desirable or even an acceptable part of testimony. But a watcher who attends an execution hopes to witness a conversion experience or an entertaining punishment, or to hear a memorable confession, judging not merely guilt/innocence but also sincerity/falsity – the effectiveness of a performance of the self. The pre-execution speech should be recognized as a speech-act intended to present the condemned in a more favourable light. The skill with which the soon-to-be-executed person conveys the force of his or her personality provides the watchers with the satisfaction of whatever desire brought them to observe the event, whether they desire endorsement of their religious views, an entertaining spectacle, a testament to religious truth or simply the chance to see a grisly punishment.[11] Regardless of what motivates the watchers, the execution confession remains performative.

While spectatorial judgement is neither authoritative nor official, the ritual nature of performance evokes the context of the theatre of judgement or the public execution.[12] In describing the experience of becoming part of a crowd, Elias Canetti details the community's experience of its role in public executions:

> forms of public execution are connected with the old practice of collective killing. The real executioner is the crowd gathered round the scaffold. [...] The tribunal pronouncing judgement – normally in front of a limited number of people only – stands for the multitude which later attends the institution. The sentence of death, which sounds abstract and unreal when pronounced in the name of justice, becomes real when it is carried out in the presence of the crowd. [...] [R]epentance in the face of death, which priests do their utmost to bring about in malefactors and infidels, has another significance besides the professed purpose of soul-saving. It transfuses the emotional state of the baiting crowd with premonitions of a future festal crowd.[13]

Canetti suggests that witnessing an execution in an assembly is in itself a vestige of the crowd's bygone role as collective executioner. With this experience of witnessing, the crowd commits to the tribunal's sentence as its own, and in watching they pass their own judgement and endorse the punishment, the pronouncement of which they experience emotionally as theirs. This Girardian account of the crowd's role in the ritual of execution harks back to a period considerably before the codification of English common law. When we consider Canetti's point in a historical context, we see that in his account the crowd's experience manifests aspects of all the official juridical roles combined (though by the early modern period these roles were separated and enacted by different figures). When characters onstage actively watch the actions of others, they are assessing and judging, perhaps becoming more judge than witness while appearing only to watch and listen. The silent observers in *The Changeling* reflect the watchers in the auditorium: both respond to characters who engage in private acts on a stage. This reflection can make the audience recognize that they themselves similarly observe and judge. Such a response was all the more likely because watching scenes of judgement and punishment was a pastime in early modern England, and the opportunity to watch brought with it the opportunity to assess and to judge. As Meg F. Pearson points out, 'Witnessing and testimony, whether used in an explicitly legal setting or not, are inextricably entwined with conceptions of judgment and an awareness of how watching matters'.[14]

Another element that engages watchers of a spectacle in active witnessing is the development of a sense of unity – a sense of themselves as part of a group. This feeling often develops from a sense of shared experience or grows out of physical factors. Canetti notes, '[a]s soon as a man has surrendered himself to the crowd, he ceases to fear its touch [. . .] The more fiercely people press together, the more certain they feel that they do not fear each other'.[15] Canetti suggests that the crowd seeks to act in concert, to make its mark on its environment as a way of signifying its unity.[16] Gatherings form in response to preparation for a public event; whether it was a coronation, execution, demonstration of acts of skill or a theatrical performance, these events were not only novel but memorable.

Pearson suggests that '[p]laywrights were arguably using "drama to create an alternative framework of judgment"; the language of witnessing participates in the same discourse'.[17] In *The Changeling*, Middleton and Rowley evoke these responses throughout the dramatic action in part because of the thematic emphasis on surveillance.[18] The plot, coupled with the design of the theatre, forced spectators to be aware of both the other playgoers and the onstage watchers who demonstrate the impossibility of achieving privacy in this world of intimates. Instances of watching, stalking, keeping an eye out, scrutinizing and simply observing are numerous, and tropes of scrutiny recur in the dialogue. Beatrice tells Alsemero she is already engaged by saying, 'Our eyes are sentinels unto our judgements' (1.1.72). De Flores speaks of his insistent desire to put himself in Beatrice's way: 'Some twenty times a day – nay, not so little – / Do I force errands, frame ways and excuses / To come into her sight' (2.1.29–31). Tomazo urges Alonzo to look more closely at how Beatrice responds to him, saying, 'In troth I see small welcome in her eye' (2.1.107).

Realizing this discourse of visuality, the denouement of Beatrice and De Flores' death in *The Changeling* is witnessed by almost all the surviving named characters (most of them men). They offer a range of responses from Vermandero's incredulity – 'An host of enemies entered my citadel / Could not amaze like this. Joanna! Beatrice-Joanna!' – to the egotistically rueful admissions of foolishness from Antonio and Franciscus (5.3.147–8, 204–9). These assessments of Beatrice and De Flores offer possible models for engagement from the spectators: Vermandero presents an emotional response, while his men manifest self-examination and reflection. Tomazo de Piracquo makes it clear that the sight of the pair has brought him closure:

> Sir, I am satisfied; my injuries
> Lie dead before me. I can exact no more
> Unless my soul were loose, and could o'ertake
> Those black fugitives that are fled from thence,
> To take a second vengeance; but there are wraths
> Deeper than mine, 'tis to be feared, about 'em.
>
> 5.3.190–5

His words allude to divine justice, implying his own role is as plaintiff seeking justice for his murdered brother. Justice has been wrought by their deaths and will recur in his imagination as eternal punishment.

But the spectator's position is moved towards judgement, the purposeful inquiry of the jury member, by Beatrice's language in her final speech. As Jean Howard points out elsewhere in this volume, what exactly happens in the closet is not quite clear, and the audience needs the clarification provided by the final words of De Flores and, most especially, Beatrice.[19] As I show, many common elements of the execution speeches made by figures condemned to death during the Tudor and Stuart reigns recur in Beatrice's words.[20] These elements were likely to have evoked the same response from watchers as they had at actual executions. Starting initially in a witness position with a sense of one's importance as a witness, the spectator must have shifted towards judgement as Beatrice's complex language entreated assessment and her repentance called forth sympathy and fellow-feeling – or, inversely, self-righteous repudiation of her apparent justifications.

The broadest and perhaps most compelling element of pre-execution speeches that appear in Beatrice's final words is the acknowledgement of the crowd and the treatment of them as a cohesive group of witnesses. Like Beatrice, Lady Jane Grey addressed her onlookers as she prepared for death: 'And now, good people, while I am alive, I pray you assist me with your prayers"[21] Similarly, Archbishop Cranmer addressed the crowd at his execution:

> Every man, good people, desireth at the time of his death to give some good exhortation that others may remember the same before their death, and be the better thereby: so I beseech God grant me grace, that I may speak something at this my departing, whereby God may be glorified, and you edified.[22]

Both Grey and Cranmer were aware of their audience and sought to sway the group not merely to sympathize with them but also to play a part. The role they assigned to those assembled would influence their watchers to share their point of view. To achieve that same end, George Sprot, a minor figure in the Gowrie conspiracy, promised that as he died he would give his watchers some token in proof that he had spoken only the truth, and accounts say that '[b]efore his last breath, when he had hung a pretty space, he lift up his hands a good height, and clapped them together aloud, three several times, to the great wonder and admiration of all the beholders'.[23]

Like these historical figures, Beatrice is close to death, a circumstance that brings urgency to her words when she gives witness to her truth. Her words similarly evoke a tribunal of judgement when she emerges from the 'closet' and addresses those around her. She initially addresses her father but widens her audience after the first five lines to the assembled company who stand in disbelief, watching her and De Flores. Her address to the assembly assumes that they are a community, and addressing them as such promotes that sense among them.

Verbal self-abasement in preparation for the scaffold or the block recurred frequently; repentance was also commonly expressed. Many state that their execution is just; Sir Thomas Wyatt (leader of Wyatt's conspiracy and son of the poet) acknowledged his punishment 'to be a just plague for my sins', whereas Christopher Norton, one of the Northern rebels who attempted to depose Elizabeth and place Mary, Queen of Scots, on England's throne, stated of himself '[t]hat he had worthily deserved that death, and therefore besought God, and all men to forgive him'.[24] Beatrice characterizes herself as a kind of waste, disposable, and deserving of being thrown away:

> O come not near me, sir. I shall defile you.
> I am that of your blood was taken from you
> For your better health. Look no more upon't,
> But cast it to the ground regardlessly;
> Let the common sewer take it from distinction.
>
> 5.3.149–53

Her repentance is clear: within the image of 'your blood [. . .] taken from you / For your better health' is the sense of the uncleanness of bodily excretions (perhaps with a reference to women's menses) and an evocation of the family as a microcosm of the body politic. Beatrice scapegoats herself, characterizing herself as an unwholesome element that must be cast out for the better health of the body.

The image of blood is often used in these confessional speeches: Beatrice's use of the metaphor characterizes the noble family she belongs to as a holy thing that can be defiled and herself as a mere by-product, an unworthy detritus to be combined, once in the common sewer, with similar waste from innumerable anonymous households. At his execution, Thomas Cromwell, Earl of Essex used the image differently, characterizing Christ's blood as a scouring agent: 'Let thy blood cleanse and wash away the spots and foulness of my sins [. . .] Let the merits of thy passion and blood-shedding be satisfaction for my sins'.[25] Both Lady Jane Grey and the Duke of Suffolk, her father, stated their faith that they would be saved by Jesus's blood. There is a sense of blood's holiness, its power as a symbolic element, which Middleton and Rowley reinforce even with Beatrice's words, which invert the trope by reducing blood to its purely medical character, thereby deconsecrating it.[26]

After warning her father that contact with her will defile him, Beatrice goes on to explain what brought her to this point:

Beneath the stars, upon yon meteor
Ever hung my fate, 'mongst things corruptible;
I ne'er could pluck it from him; my loathing
Was prophet to the rest, but ne'er believed.
Mine honour fell with him, and now my life.

5.3.154–8

Beatrice regrets not only her actions but also the harm she has done to her father and her husband. Her honour, which 'fell with him [De Flores]' is not merely her individual honour (or chastity) but her family's honour, which her actions have besmirched, a term that contains the idea of an unclean substance smeared over some clean, bright surface. The image also evokes ideas of pollution and cleansing, and it describes her punishment (a mortal wound) as justified. In characterizing her death as a way of cleansing the family body, she expresses her willingness to accept this punishment.

Beatrice's concern for her family's honour is not commonly expressed prior to executions, but it is not unheard of. Chidiock Tichbourne, a member of the Babington plot, asked the watchers for sympathy because he had ruined his family's name: 'My dear countrymen, my sorrows may be your joy, yet mix your smiles with tears, and pity my case; I am descended from an house, from 200 years before the Conquest, never stained till this my misfortune'.[27] Tichbourne suggests that his ancient lineage should inspire sympathy for him for the shame that he has brought upon the Tichbournes. Like Beatrice, he ascribes responsibility for the assassination to an associate (in his case, Babington) whom he loved too much:

> Let me be a warning to all young gentlemen, especially *Generosis adolescentulis*. I had a friend, and a dear friend, of whom I made no small account, whose friendship hath brought me to this [. . .] [T]he regard of my friend caused me to be a man in whom the old proverb was verified, 'I was silent, and so consented'.[28]

When Beatrice characterizes De Flores as a meteor, an aspect of fate, she subtly deflects some of the blame for her loss of honour. She puts some responsibility on the man who has fascinated, repulsed and finally coerced her, as well as on fate itself.

Many people facing execution in early modern England expressed regret that they had been too attached to 'things corruptible'. Lady Jane Grey's words were typical: 'when I did know the word of God, I neglected the same, loved myself and the world, and therefore this plague and punishment is happily and worthily happened unto me for my sins: and yet I thank God of his goodness, that he hath thus given me a time and respite to repent'.[29] Cranmer, going to his death, expresses concern for those who 'so much dote upon the love of this false world'.[30] Though Beatrice never references God or Jesus Christ, her statement 'Ever hung my fate, 'mongst things corruptible' suggests that she repents her pursuit of worldly pleasures and what Donne calls 'dull sublunary lovers' love'. She concludes by making it clear that Alsemero was never polluted by congress with her and that their marriage could be annulled on the grounds of non-consummation, cleansing his family reputation from her association with him. The confession lays the ground for her dying request for forgiveness: 'Forgive me, Alsemero, all forgive: / 'Tis time to die when 'tis a shame to live' (5.3.178–9). Although these words are addressed to her husband, they are also enacted as stage performance; the playgoers are witness to it. While ostensibly directed to Alsemero, the request is something Middleton sets up for playgoers to assess. Does her dying reference to Lucrece win over their judgement or does her heinous behaviour render such requests inadmissible? Witnesses of her death, onstage and off, are implicitly urged to judge the legitimacy of this request for forgiveness. Like the Duke of Suffolk, who 'desired all men to forgive him, saying that the queen had forgiven him', and Sir Christopher Blunt, one of Essex's followers who confessed his guilt and stated, 'wherefore renouncing all justification or extenuation of my offence, I wholly cast myself at her majesty's mercy', Beatrice is simultaneously confessing, requesting forgiveness and performing for a crowd.[31] She may be seeking forgiveness from her husband, but she is also hoping to achieve a *coup de théâtre* worthy of Richard III in persuading her listeners to judge her sympathetically.

Beatrice must also, to some extent, be seeking an appropriate vehicle for expressing feelings that she knows are taboo in her society. Throughout the play she has never found a satisfactory register of discourse with which to express her feelings about De Flores. Her unwontedly open expressions of loathing at the start of the play seem inappropriately harsh and direct, and her explanation of them to Alsemero seems coy and implausible:

"tis my infirmity. / Nor can I other reason render you' (1.1.109–10). When De Flores makes it plain that he expects sex in return for killing Alonzo, Beatrice is almost speechless–and entirely unable to render an effective dissuasion: 'Why, 'tis impossible thou canst be so wicked [. . .] [t]o make his death the murderer of my honour!' (3.4.123–5). The servant's challenge to her status–'Look but into your conscience; read me there. / 'Tis a true book, you'll find me there your equal' – undoes her entirely (3.4.135–6). After having mastered her in argument, De Flores easily forces her into his bed. But when he hatches a plan to preserve her reputation despite Diaphanta's dilatory return from Alsemero's bed, Beatrice's terms for him adumbrate reference to his social status with the Petrarchan trope of the adoring lover: 'How heartily he serves me! His face loathes one, / But look upon his care, who would not love him? / The east is not more beauteous than his service' (5.1.69–71). As her feelings alter, she seems to search for a discourse independent of hegemonic Christian morality. She moves from Petrarchan discourse to the language of utility, describing him as 'a wondrous *necessary* man' (5.1.92, italics mine).

With Alsemero's discovery of her illicit liaison and De Flores' stabbing of her, Beatrice's language shifts again. Facing imminent death, Beatrice finds the register she needs in traditional confessional discourse. Her final words settle firmly in that register, and she structures her last speech using the framework of the aristocratic codes that have shaped so much of her life. In resorting to this easily recognized discourse, she takes the traditional route of the penitent Magdalen, an element common to other Jacobean plays such as Webster's *The Duchess of Malfi*. Beatrice's last-minute reversion to a socially endorsed model of female self-abnegation seems to be a concession to dramatic expectation, rendering her more acceptable by her willingness to be framed by conventional ideas of lustful women.

These resonances, like many others, seem to create what Annabel Patterson calls 'ethical undecidability, an experience much attested to in the seventeenth century, and almost endemic today'.³² Jay Zysk suggests that playgoers may initially have perceived the sight of Beatrice Joanna in De Flores' arms as a pièta.³³ But would they have taken the image as cynical parody, gratuitous blasphemy or an appeal to gentler judgement? Playwrights often used signs to suggest an alignment between legal precedents and God's judgement: as Subha Mukherji comments in discussing the dreams described in *A Warning for Fair Women*, theatrical signs are 'systematically mobilised to construct a semiotic that at once indicates providential operation and serves a legal agenda'.³⁴ Bearing Patterson's term in mind, I enquire whether Beatrice's self-condemnation would have recalled Lucrece, who dies because it is 'a shame to live', Mary Magdalen, who expiates her sinful life in penitence, or that more trivial example of inchastity whom Beatrice earlier alludes to, Frances Howard?³⁵

Alsemero initially attempts to suggest that Beatrice's death justly punishes her while clearing the accounts of her family, aligning what he expects would be the legal judgement with that of God. He tells Beatrice's father that '[j]ustice hath so right / The guilty hit, that innocence is quit / By proclamation, and may joy again' (5.3.185–7). His words here pave the way for his proposal to substitute himself for Vermandero's unsatisfactory daughter:

> Sir, you have yet a son's duty living;
> Please you accept it. Let that your sorrow
> As it goes from your eye, go from your heart;
> Man and his sorrow at the grave must part.
>
> 5.3.216–19

The familial connection, which would forward his mercantile aspirations, would also further Vermandero's foiled dynastic hopes and wipe away the blotch on his escutcheon that Beatrice's actions have created. Beatrice's final words seem to be intended as groundwork for convincing her father not to dismiss her entirely. Despite willingly scapegoating herself for the sake of family honour, her last words request forgiveness;

she does not wish to be consigned to oblivion. But Alsemero draws back from his initial stance when he concludes the play with a Puck-like address, urging the audience,

> Your only smiles have power to cause re-live
> The dead again, or in their rooms to give
> Brother a new brother, father a child:
> If these appear, all griefs are reconciled.
>
> Epilogue 5–8

He tasks the audience with bringing the dead to life again, through memory. Shifting to meta-theatrical discourse, he admits that the play cannot replace Alonzo or substitute Alsemero for Beatrice within the mimetic framework. Instead, the conclusion must be diffused as the playgoers exit, carrying the characters within their recollection. In this final moment, then, recollection, dependent on witnessing, is characterized as more important and more powerful than judging. These last words privilege witnessing over judgement, as if Middleton and Rowley are saying that the audience's sight of Beatrice's actions through the entire play may bring a more significant conclusion to the play than the indeterminate, overdetermined judgements that would result simply from their response to Beatrice's final words. Committing the characters to memory, serving as witness to their phantasmic existence, is more important than rendering judgement on the justness of their deaths.[36]

# Notes

1  Marjorie Garber, '"Vassal Actors": The Role of the Audience in Shakespearean Tragedy', *Renaissance Drama* 9 (1978): 80.

2  For a discussion of judgement tales, see Subha Mukherji, *Law and Representation in Early Modern Drama* (Cambridge: Cambridge University Press, 2006), 109; for a historical account of speeches made prior to execution by criminals in early

modern England, see J.A. Sharpe, '"Last Dying Speeches": Religion, Ideology, and Public Execution in Seventeenth-Century England', *Past & Present* 107 (May 1985): 144–67.

3 The *OED* definitions that follow refer to entries following the headward 'witness, n.' *Oxford English Dictionary Online*, March 2021, Oxford University Press (accessed 29 April 2021).

4 For the verb form, see: 'witness, v.' *Oxford English Dictionary Online*, March 2021, Oxford University Press (accessed 29 April 2021).

5 J.H. Baker, *An Introduction to English Legal History* (London: Butterworths, 1990), 581.

6 Lorna Hutson, *The Invention of Suspicion: Law and Mimesis in Shakespeare and Renaissance Drama* (Oxford: Oxford University Press, 2007), 32; see also John G. Bellamy, *The Tudor Law of Treason* (Toronto: University of Toronto Press, 1979), 154, with reference to trial by witness under statute 34 in the Henrician period.

7 Andrea Frisch, *The Invention of the Eyewitness: Witnessing and Testimony in Early Modern France* (Chapel Hill: University of North Carolina Press, 2004), 24–6 and 32.

8 Frisch, *The Invention of the Eyewitness*, 34.

9 Thomas Green, *Verdict According to Conscience: Perspectives on the English Trial Jury, 1200–1800* (Chicago, IL: University of Chicago, 1985), 119.

10 Lorna Hutson carefully details how deeply involved the English jury became during the sixteenth century in gathering evidence on which to base their final decision. See Hutson, 'Rethinking the "Spectacle of the Scaffold": Juridical Epistemologies and English Revenge Tragedy', *Representations* 89, no. 1 (2005): 30–58, especially 38–44.

11 See Bellamy, *The Tudor Law of Treason*, 136, 195 and 206.

12 Sharpe in '"Last Dying Speeches"' describes public executions as 'carried out in a context of ceremony and ritual', 146.

13 Elias Canetti, *Crowds and Power*, trans. Carol Stewart (New York: Farrar, Straus, 1984), 50–1.

14 Meg F. Pearson, 'Audience as Witness in *Edward II*', in Jennifer A. Low and Nova Myhill (eds), *Imagining the Audience in Early Modern Drama, 1558–1642* (New York: Palgrave, 2011), 94.

15 Canetti, *Crowds and Power*, 15, 16.
16 Canetti, *Crowds and Power*, 16, 17.
17 Pearson, 'Audience as Witness', 94, quoting Mukherji, 4.
18 Maurizio Calbi discusses surveillance and the gaze in *The Changeling* in *Approximate Bodies: Gender and Power in Early Modern Drama and Anatomy* (London: Routledge, 2005), 38–42 and 52–3.
19 For a further discussion of the uncertainty of the action in Beatrice's closet, see Jean E. Howard, 'Space, gender and the rules of movement in *The Changeling*', in this volume.
20 Sharpe describes these executions as 'spectacular event[s]' often accompanied by speeches from the condemned that manifested startling consistencies; see Sharpe, '"Last Dying Speeches"', 150. I suggest here that they are more complex than he observed.
21 T.B. Howell (ed.), *Cobbett's Complete Collection of State Trials and Proceedings for High Treason and Other Crimes and Misdemeanors, from the Earliest Period to the Present Time* (London: R. Bagshaw, 1809), I: 729.
22 Howell, *Cobbett*, I: 818–9.
23 Howell, *Cobbett*, II: 707–8.
24 Howell, *Cobbett*, I: 861 and 1084.
25 Howell, *Cobbett*, I: 438.
26 In the words of Jay Zysk, Beatrice 'turn[s] the spiritual power of the relic into the deceptive power of the anti-relic' (409). For an alternate reading of this scene, see Zysk, 422–4 in his excellent article 'Relics and Unreliable Bodies in *The Changeling*', *ELR* 45, no. 3 (2015): 400–24. See also Calbi's reading of Middleton's medical metaphor of bloodletting: Calbi, *Approximate Bodies*, 32–4.
27 Howell, *Cobbett*, I: 1157.
28 Howell, *Cobbett*, I: 1157.
29 Howell, *Cobbett*, I: 728–9.
30 Howell, *Cobbett*, I: 819.
31 Howell, *Cobbett*, I: 764 and 1437.
32 See Annabel Patterson's 'Introduction' to *The Changeling* in Gary Taylor and John Lavagnino (gen. eds), *Thomas Middleton*,

*The Collected Works* (Oxford: Oxford University Press, 2007), 1635.

33 Zysk, 'Relics and Unreliable Bodies,' 422.
34 Mukherji, *Law and Representation*, 112.
35 Patterson efficiently summarizes the connection to Frances Howard and the Howard/Carr involvement in Thomas Overbury's poisoning in her 'Introduction', 1633–4.
36 I am grateful for the thoughtful comments and support of Dianne E. Berg, Dan Kinney, Nova Myhill and Mark Scroggins, whose engagement with this work helped strengthen and deepen my analysis.

# PART SIX

# Rape and the Female Body in Contemporary Performance

# 11

# 'What Would a Foreign Woman Be?' Sexual Borderlands, Hospitality, and 'Forgetting Parentage' in *The Changeling* on Film

*Courtney Lehmann*

> You're no more now;
> You must forget your parentage to me.
>
> 3.4.138–9

Thomas Middleton and William Rowley's 1622 play, *The Changeling*, in many ways anticipates Derrida's late work on the entanglements between hospitality, patriarchal succession and 'the foreigner question'.[1] But I would argue that the play – especially in its late twentieth- and early twenty-first century afterlives on screen – is more concerned with Derrida's more cavalier provocation: 'What would a foreign woman be?' Posed in the conditional mood, this question implies that 'a foreign woman' cannot even be named, so she cannot 'be'. A similar ontological precarity inheres in Middleton and Rowley's lead character, Beatrice-Joanna, who has too many names. An allegorical combination of Dante's earthly saint, Beatríce, and a Spanish variation on the generic English name 'Joan' (referring to a common drab or whore), Beatrice-Joanna's identity is weaponized as the embodiment of the 'virgin'/'whore' paradigm in a play wherein rape serves a structural function. I will argue that the extreme sexual violence depicted in *The Changeling* renders Beatrice-Joanna 'a foreign woman' in her own body, consigning her to inhabit a 'borderland' which, in Gloria Anzaldúa's terms, is 'a vague and undetermined place created by the emotional residue of an unnatural boundary'.[2] While recognizing the racially-coded and culturally specific context of 'the borderlands' as 'la frontera' (contested along the US/Mexico border), I wish to explore how borderland ontologies may be applied to the similarly perilous geographies inhabited by female rape survivors. Having said that, it is critical to acknowledge the fact that women of colour are far more vulnerable to sexual predation and violence than white women.

Disconcertingly, none of the films with which this essay is concerned – Marcus Thompson's *Middleton's Changeling* (1998), Jay Stern's *The Changeling* (2006) and Sarah Harding's spinoff *Compulsion* (2008) – genuinely interrogate Middleton and Rowley's representation of Beatrice-Joanna as the virgin-turned-whore who is complicit in her own serial sexual assault.[3] In Thompson's adaptation, Beatrice-Joanna is depicted as a whore even before she is raped; in the director's fantasy, she is the woman who 'asks for it'. Stern, by contrast, leans heavily on compulsory virginity, anchoring the film in the eyes of a young girl who serves as a silent Chorus, perhaps a representation of Beatrice-Joanna as a child. Ultimately, Thompson and Stern's films prove to be two sides of the same coin, overplaying one or the other side of the virgin-whore borderland. But what happens when Beatrice-Joanna's story is replayed through the gaze of a female director? In Sarah

Harding's spinoff *Compulsion*, the Beatrice-Joanna figure, Anjika, is a non-virgin who seems to control her own border-crossings. Unlike the other two film adaptations examined here, *Compulsion* is a star vehicle, with leading roles played by Ray Winstone of *Sexy Beast* (J. Glazer 2000) fame and Parminder Nagra, who starred in *Bend It Like Beckham* (G. Chadha 2002) and in the critically-acclaimed television series *ER* (1994–2009). Though created as a feature film, *Compulsion* premiered in the prime-time slot on ITV, the UK's largest broadcaster in commercial television and has since been successful in the DVD and streaming market. Nevertheless, despite its 'liberal' auspices, *Compulsion* is the only adaptation of *The Changeling* in which female sexuality is explicitly criminalized. Whereas Thompson's adaptation minimizes the hospital plot with its foregrounding of insanity, actual or acted, both Stern's and Harding's films jettison it altogether; nevertheless, all three films represent the collective madness of a world wherein, in Judith Butler's terms, 'what is female' is 'what is injurable'.[4]

## The pornotropic gaze: Marcus Thompson's *Middleton's The Changeling*

> You must see my castle
> And her best entertainment ere we part;
> I shall think myself unkindly used else.
>
> 1.1.205–7

Shot on location in a seventeenth-century fortress in Alicante, Thompson's adaptation of *The Changeling* begins in classical heritage film style. Establishing shots of the fortress are intercut with the mission bell that swings violently into the spectator's space, propelled by the enormous cross that bears down upon it. When the bell comes to a rest, the cross above it dissolves into a window pane of the castle – a room with a view in, but not a way out, for Beatrice-Joanna is both her father's 'castle' and the source of its perverse 'entertainment'. In fact, in Thompson's film, Beatrice-Joanna exists to be 'unkindly used' indeed as her body becomes a trope for sexual spectacle well before the inaugural rape scene. For example, the director repeatedly cuts away from the narrative to insert a series of interpolated shots that capture Beatrice-Joanna lying naked on her back in a dusty horse ring, thrusting her pelvis upward convulsively while the horses, literally studs, saunter around her in the barn. The message is clear: her imminent 'no' already means 'yes'. Moreover, by representing Beatrice-Joanna's literally unbridled lust through wildly different film genres – including the heritage film, the slasher subgenre of the horror film, Italian neo-realism, *film noir* and the Western – Thompson reveals his own desire to control Beatrice-Joanna's body by situating it as a locus of violent experimentation upon which to cut his teeth as a filmmaker.

'What does sexuality mean', Saidiya Hartman questions, 'when rape is a normative mode of its deployment?'[5] In *Middleton's The Changeling*, rape, fuelled by the pathological assumption of female complicity, is the only 'normative' expression of sexuality. Although Thompson shows Beatrice-Joanna being raped by De Flores throughout the film – and at least three of their encounters are profoundly non-consensual – the first and the last rape scenes make this movie a true horror film. The first time that De Flores rapes Beatrice-Joanna, she is forced onto her back on top of the bleeding trunk that contains Piracquo's corpse. Referencing the iconic shower scene from Hitchcock's *Psycho* (1960) and the slasher subgenre, Thompson inserts flashbacks to a shadow profile of De Flores' rhythmic stabs into Piracquo's chest, which are paired with his savage penetration of Beatrice-Joanna as her virgin blood mingles promiscuously with her dead suitor's still-bleeding body. Inexplicably, in the middle of the rape Thompson abruptly switches to black-and-white footage that shows Beatrice-Joanna wandering the border of her father's property in what appears to be the aftermath of a war. A poorly executed nod to Italian Neorealism, a cinematic movement that used black-and-white film stock to expose the devastated landscapes of post-Second World War Italy, this interpolated scene is yet another ruse. Not only does Thompson imply that Beatrice-Joanna is engaged in a civil war with herself, aimlessly wandering the sexual borderland between virgin and whore, but also, and more insidiously, the director's appropriation of Neorealist motifs conditions the viewer to interpret the return to his rape fantasy as though it were documentary 'truth'.

Immediately, Thompson barrages the audience with visions of Beatrice-Joanna's bestial desires, as De Flores's cruel assault is punctuated periodically by cuts to her degenerate pleasure atop a horse, arching her back as she rides an orgasm. Here the director visually elides the difference between 'whore' and 'horse' in a pornographic image of Beatrice-Joanna's literally unbridled lust. By representing her as a sexual animal, Thompson eroticizes Beatrice-Joanna's body as chattel – a seventeenth-century British vision of women-as-property that bleeds into the long history of slavery. In the context of American slavery, Hortense Spillers' concept of 'pornotroping' is especially instructive, for it refers to the spectacularization of the body-in-pain in an era in which black women and men were legally codified as mules, horses and other beasts of burden – considered to be both insensitive to pain and sexually insatiable.[6] Pornotroping, like rape, is predicated on the vicious reduction of captive human bodies into undifferentiated 'flesh', or what Spillers refers to as 'that zero degree of social conceptualization' that invites dramatic wounding, torture and death.[7] Although Beatrice-Joanna is not racially coded in Thompson's adaptation, she is depicted as her own beast of burden, subject to visual torture and rendered mute by the filmmaker. Indeed, Thompson goes so far as to eliminate all of her confessions of affection for De Flores, inserting instead an unintelligible voiceover comprising heavy panting and musky groans anchored to an off-screen female voice. A staple of *film noir*, voiceover, as Joan Copjec explains, is invariably linked to a dead narrator. And in a sense, Beatrice-Joanna is already dead as a 'ruined' woman, for the breathy moans that spell her imagined pleasure in rape 'bear the burden' of 'a living death, a kind of inexhaustible suffering'.[8] Adding insult to injury, Thompson forces Beatrice-Joanna to carry out his dirty work by becoming her own *femme fatale*.

Throughout his work on hospitality, Derrida equates the foreigner with the potential for parricide, arguing that the true 'foreigner' becomes 'a parricide only when he is in some sense within the family'.[9] In *The Changeling*, however, Beatrice-Joanna is the real parricide who operates 'from within the family', for her death marks the end of Vermandero's aristocratic line. Marcus Thompson's film takes this suggestion one step further by shaming Beatrice-Joanna into sadomasochistic atonement for her sins, reinforcing the notion that only the sacrifice of female flesh – not unlike a ritual *satí* – will ensure the integrity of patrilineal succession. In a final, gruesome interpolation, the director provides Beatrice-Joanna with an escape route only to provide *himself* with one last opportunity to flex his cinematic repertoire. As Beatrice-Joanna attempts to flee the fortress and her destiny, dashing away in a horse-drawn carriage, De Flores pulls a stunt right out of the Western by jumping onto the fleeing vehicle from on high, killing the driver, and proceeding into the carriage. Once inside, he rapes Beatrice-Joanna while stabbing her in the abdomen until she 'willingly' impales herself on his dagger. De Flores then drags her by the hair toward her father's feet, where Vermandero exclaims: 'An host of enemies entered my citadel / Could not amaze like this. Joanna! Beatrice-Joanna!' (5.3.147–8). Vermandero's shocking renaming of his daughter as 'Joanna' already frames her as the author of the crime – indeed, as the whore who has forgotten her place and her parentage. And although Vermandero attempts retroactively to instate her full-name by crying 'Beatrice-Joanna!', his frenzied efforts to make her flesh signify in his terms cannot restore the hyphen or the hymen that separates her virgin 'beauty' from being 'changed to ugly whoredom' (5.3.198–9). Hence, in a last-ditch effort to spare her father from shame, Beatrice-Joanna renders herself 'a foreign woman' by exiling herself from his blood: 'O come not near me, sir, *I shall defile you.* / I am that of your blood was taken from you / For your better health' (5.3.149–51, emphasis mine). As early as 1400, the verb 'to defile' was associated with the rape of maidens and, in 1586, 'defile' became a word associated with men who were dishonoured or defeated in battles with other men. In Middleton and Rowley's play and in Marcus Thompson's film, the daughter who threatens to defile or to rape the father is both a foreigner and a parricide – and very much from 'within the family'.

## The puritanical gaze: Jay Stern's *The Changeling*

Quite unlike Marcus Thompson's pornotropic approach to *The Changeling*, Jay Stern's low-budget indie adaptation is infused with an aura of Puritan austerity and visual sermonizing. The opposite of Thompson's invented scenes of Beatrice-Joanna in the throes of ecstasy, Stern's interpolations emerge from the silent perspective of the young girl, whose structural role in the film effectively replaces the function of rape in Middleton and Rowley's play. Playing the part of border patrol in policing the chastity of his own adaptation, the director thus attempts to split Beatrice-Joanna into two characters, girl and woman, 'virgin' and 'whore', but despite Stern's effort to convert *The Changeling* into a medieval morality film, his adaptation implies from the very beginning that their fates are intertwined.

Opening with an image of Beatrice-Joanna looking out of a window, the camera cuts away to a young girl outside, who gathers her petticoats and climbs up a green slope of grass with her back to us (later we will learn that the girl is headed towards the forest). The reaction shot back to Beatrice-Joanna shows her still gazing, with her view rendered semi-opaque by the floor-to-ceiling lace curtains. Resembling a giant wedding veil (which, in turn, historically represents an intact hymen), the lace almost threatens to envelop her as she stares outwards at the natural world that the young girl inhabits throughout the film. In fact, we never see the girl indoors, much less at home with parents. In contrast to the freedom associated with this unlikely Choral figure, the introduction of Beatrice-Joanna through a frame-within-a-frame establishes an aura of entrapment – a theme that is echoed in her stifling white floor-length skirt and a matching white, high-collared, Victorian blouse. The girl, by contrast, wears bright colours; her beautiful pink, full-length skirt and magenta jacket are complemented by her radiant, rosy cheeks – a twisted acknowledgment, perhaps, that she has yet to be 'deflowered' as a girl on the verge of adolescence. Either way, in Stern's film, the fetishization of virginity creates a suffocating milieu within which, as Katherine Schwarz argues, 'femininity plays on a particularly constricted stage, its embodiment in in sexual virtue imposing claustrophobic limits with explosive potential'.[10]

In his evangelical vision of *The Changeling*, Stern's persistent effort to separate 'Beatrice' from 'Joanna', virgin from whore, is literally written in stone on the façade of Vermandero's fortress. By far the most disturbing establishing shots in the entire film, a series of malformed, decaying gargoyles lunge at the viewer in rapid succession; the lone exception is an infant cherubim who appears to be clinging to a portico for life. At last the camera settles on two Latin inscriptions, '*PATHRS*' [sic] (fatherland) and '*VIRTUTIBUS*' (virtue), words that spell the real limits of Beatrice-Joanna's 'agency' in Stern's film, for the father is the keeper of her land – her body – while the director replaces Vermandero as protector of the anonymous girl's virginity or 'virtue'. As the walls of the citadel make clear, to violate this boundary is to become a monster.

Provocatively, Stern literalizes this sexual borderland in the form of the menacing forest, the wilderness that the young girl encounters every time she walks up the grassy slope. But she soon learns that there is no hospitality in the woods, for in the midst of Beatrice-Joanna's and De Flores' forbidden first tryst, the camera cuts away to the girl as she stumbles upon a macabre sexual object: Piracquo's severed, ring-adorned finger. Whereas Beatrice-Joanna is pictured slouched in the safety of her window seat, her naked body casually draped in white bed linens in an oddly innocent vision of the 'morning after' her first sexual encounter with De Flores, the girl's point of view shows her trapped in the woods, horrified and silenced, framed with briars and branches covering her mouth.

Unlike Thompson, Stern does not silence Beatrice-Joanna's professions of affection for De Flores; instead, he retains her words and represents their sexual encounters as consensual from the start. The burning question is certainly: why *The Changeling*? This question becomes more urgent when the director converts Middleton and Rowley's Jacobean revenge tragedy into a Shakespearean love story, as the forbidden lovers De Flores and Beatrice-Joanna commit double-suicide at the end of Stern's film. But before this culminating gesture, Beatrice-Joanna – seemingly impervious to the pack of angry men who gather around her for the kill after De Flores stabs himself – becomes a kind of parricide, estranging herself from her father by rebuking him for his 'hospitality' in forcing her to circulate between strangers whom she doesn't love. Hence, after cradling De Flores' face in her hands and kissing him, Beatrice-Joanna delivers her final lines without remorse; wresting the knife from De Flores' chest, she kills herself to become 'a foreign woman', collapsing on his bleeding bosom in a radical gesture of re-patriation in death.

But where does this leave the girl? In his whitewashed cautionary tale, Stern, like Thompson, seizes an alarming amount of creative control in policing the female body. In fact, the director seems to 'forget the parentage' of the girl intentionally, isolating the anonymous child from interacting with any of the other characters. In so doing, he mimics formally the ways in which coercive control operates in real social relationships, as if the camera itself could forestall the onset of her adolescence. In her famous lecture on American girls, suffragette and abolitionist Elizabeth Cady Stanton once proclaimed that 'I would have girls regard themselves not as adjectives, but as nouns', but in Stern's crucible, the girl serves a mere ornamental function, remaining mute from beginning to end.[11] Nevertheless, we have to wonder what she learns from her silent act of witnessing. Seemingly incidentally, the film closes with a striking visual quotation of the ambiguous ending of Polanski's *Macbeth* (1971) when – like the young Donalbain disappearing into the witches' lair – the girl climbs up the grassy hill yet again, petticoats in hand, headed straight for the woods.

## Madonna or whore? Sarah Harding's *Compulsion*

Referring to her interest in directing *Compulsion* as a spinoff of *The Changeling*, Sarah Harding recalled that, having read Middleton and Rowley's play in school, she was 'fascinated by Beatrice-Joanna's metamorphosis from Madonna to whore, enthralled by the sexual charge between her and De Flores and disturbed by the ambivalence of my response to these two liars and murderers'.[12] One has to wonder what explains the ongoing appeal of – and rhetorical trafficking in – the virgin-whore construct. Why does this sexualized 'changeling' identity, which is applied to women but never to men, remain so persistent in the twenty-first-century imagination? Harding's film, coupled with Joshua St Johnson's screenplay, offers a refreshingly complex response.

Although the Beatrice-Joanna character in *Compulsion* has only one name, Anjika, her dual or 'changeling' nature is suggested by the men who lay claim to her: her father, Mr Indrani, calls her 'Anji' and her college boyfriend, Alex (eventually her fiancé), nicknames her 'Angel'. Both presume that she is an angel, but Anjika's father, Mr Indrani, also presumes that she is a virgin. Early in the film, when Anjika rejects the idea of an arranged marriage, he interrogates her: 'Have you disgraced yourself?' She replies, politely, 'no, Papa'. But when she asks why Jayman, her dashingly handsome, drug-dealing, womanizing brother gets to go out and she doesn't, her father is visibly outraged and shouts: 'Because you are *my daughter*!' Leaning in to the possessive, Mr Indrani assumes that it is not only her hand, but also her virginity, that is his to give away.

The film begins with Mr Indrani's hospitality on full display throughout his palatial home, where the guests are celebrating Anjika's recent graduation from Cambridge. Meanwhile, the *cause celébre* remains upstairs in her room, applying thick make-up –reluctantly, robotically – as a means of delaying her entrance to the gala. Each time that Anjika is shown applying make-up in the film, a plot twist is signalled; its structural role is yet another demonstration of the ways in which 'femininity', recalling Katherine Schwartz's words, 'plays on a particularly constricted stage'. In fact, unbeknownst to her, Anjika's father has a surprise in store for her at the party: he has arranged for her to marry Hardik, the son of his new business partner in the hotel industry, at a time when Mr Indrani is angling to get out of the tobacco industry. (Behind his back, Anjika describes her father's fortune as built upon 'giving mouth cancer to teenagers in India'.) In this strict Brahmin household, Anjika is trapped within the crosshairs of caste, culture and corporate interests – and monetized by her own father.

Following the pattern of *The Changeling*, Don Flowers, the family chauffeur, solves Anjika's problem in exchange for sex. During the 'seduction' scene in the hotel room, Anjika's body is frozen as Flowers touches her hair. When his hands wander elsewhere, she stares blankly away from the camera with tears pouring down her cheeks. We are not privy to any more of the night's happenings; instead, Harding moves straight into the 'morning after' shot, which begins with a freeze on an image of Anjika's head on the hotel pillow from an upside-down camera angle. Rotating 180-degrees, Anjika is restored to a right face-up position as Harding literalizes the notion that her world has been turned upside down, dizzying the viewer in the process. Consent is not implied anywhere in this scene. At best, it is transactional sex: 'it's a deal', as Flowers describes it; but at worst, it *is* rape. For producer Steve Matthews, however, *Compulsion* is less complicated; it is about 'the sexual awakening of a young girl. [. . .] Her affair with Flowers is the first real thing that happens to her' – stated as though her Cambridge graduation doesn't count as a 'real thing'.[13] The director, too, participates in this logic when she suggests that Anjika's long shower – a reflex among victims of sexual assault – reflects 'a puzzling new sensuality [that] takes over' when Anjika 'realize[s] that she was savouring the previous night'.[14] In the eyes of this viewer, there are no signs of pleasure or sensuality in the shower scene – only feelings of agony, self-doubt and shame that are particularly evident when, in a profile shot with low key lighting, Anjika pounds her fists on the shower wall and hunches over in a posture of defeat.

Adding another layer of complexity to *Compulsion*, Anjika, unlike the other Beatrice-Joanna characters examined here, does not have white privilege. Though presumably born in the UK, Anjika *is* 'a foreign woman' not only in the sense that she is the daughter of Indian immigrants but also because she is visually marked as a woman of colour. Whereas Mr Indrani tries to purchase white privilege with regular visits to his white, blonde mistress, Flowers trolls the streets lined with prostitutes in search of South Asian women, forcing one of them to wear Anjika's discarded gloves as a prelude to purchased sex. At one point, Anjika ceases to recognize herself as anything other than the extension of these men, complaining to Flowers: 'all my life I've been a slave to my father; now I'm a slave to you'. Flowers parries her suggestion and replies: 'No. You've always done exactly what you want. You're a slave to your passions'. In what is both a power play and a bait-and-switch operation, Flowers deflects his own criminal desires onto Anjika and gaslights her by pathologizing the very behaviour that benefits him. As Saidiya Hartman argues, where the 'engendering of race' is at stake, violence isn't always overt, for it can operate surreptitiously within 'different economies of restraint and by way of divergent methods of sexual control'.[15] Indeed, Flowers' one gift to Anjika is a beautiful silver cuff bracelet with elegant latticework, resembling a cage. Although designed to cling to the wrist without a locking mechanism, the cuff, coupled with the casual repetition of the word 'slave' three times in their two-sentence conversation, makes it clear that Anjika's brown flesh is captive to a more insidious, accretive colonising process whereby the 'passions' that are ascribed to her are not, in fact, her own. Instead, they are pre-commodified and extracted by the men in her life – whether for the purposes of her father's corporate empire, Flowers' sexual fascination with her 'exotic' qualities as an Indian woman or Alex's burgeoning green energy business (which her father invests in as a kind of dowry). In the end, Anjika's status as a woman is defined only in terms of 'a patriarchalized female gender', which, as Hortense Spillers concludes, 'from one point of view, is the only female gender there is'.[16]

Yet in *Compulsion*, the cuff simultaneously implies that Anjika is growing increasingly attached to Flowers – for better and for worse. In fact, with the exception of the first and the last sex scenes, Harding goes out of her way to represent the relationship between Flowers and Anjika as one of mutual attraction and commitment. To create this impression formally, Harding visually quotes from Bertolucci's *Last Tango in Paris* (1972), wherein an abundance of 2-shots in the lovemaking scenes 'avoid the voyeurism of pornography and make [the lovers] both mutual agents'.[17] This concept is powerfully rendered by Harding's return to the shot of Anjika's head on a hotel room pillow – only this time, Flowers shares the same pillow; briefly turning their faces towards each other, the two lovers exchange a sideways smile. When they return to the car, Anjika opens the door for herself, refusing to let Flowers do it, as if it were suddenly beneath him. On the way home, he suggests that they 'just run away' to Dungeness, and she actually seems to ponder the possibility by replying simply: 'Sounds nice'.

Complicating her formal homage to the love story featured in *Last Tango in Paris*, Harding reveals in an essay composed after *Compulsion* aired that the film's main shooting location, the Indrani mansion, was formerly owned by Stanley Kubrick, a director responsible for what is widely considered to be the cruellest, most spectacularly violent rape scene in the history of cinema in *A Clockwork Orange* (1971). Wanted or not, Harding found the association eerily fitting, claiming that shooting *Compulsion* there seemed to give 'the ultraviolence' in her film 'some sort of blessing'.[18] This ultraviolence begins when Hardik, recently released from prison after Flowers framed him as a drug dealer, recognizes that he has been played and that Anjika and Flowers are having an affair. Pushing his way into the Indrani mansion, he starts physically and verbally abusing Anjika; however, it is when he calls her a 'whore' that Flowers steps in and swiftly breaks his neck. Although both Flowers and Anjika are visibly shaken by the event, it is Anjika's behaviour that becomes increasingly disturbing and disaffected around Alex, her friends and her family – so much so that her own mother accuses her of violating the Indrani family's hospitality: 'It's like a stranger's moved in', she tells Anjika. Whether she can no longer live with the notion that she is exchangeable property or she genuinely devolves into a sociopath, Anjika is bent on further indulging her increasingly criminal 'compulsions'. Christening the murder with sex, Anjika muses: 'so many fuss about your loss of virginity. It's supposed to change you', but it's 'just like mascara – an empty ritual'. Then, seemingly out of character, she admits to Flowers that she doesn't feel guilty in the least about killing Hardik, stating flatly: 'I just want to get away with it'.

In many ways, the last ten minutes of *Compulsion* are more problematic than both Thompson's and Stern's adaptations combined, for in the conclusion of Harding's film, female desire is not only pathologized – it is expressly criminalized. Carefully applying her make-up, Anjika readies herself for her role as the *femme fatale* who not only survives her own crime but also her own film, calmly concealing a butcher knife under the pillow in Flowers's bed. When he discovers it, Anjika tells Flowers that, to protect her from shame and discovery, she must frame him for rape. When he tries to get Anjika to admit that she loves him, she becomes unbearably cruel, telling Flowers that she would never run away with him to his 'trailer park in Dungeness' and that he is 'a fat, ugly, old man'. This phenomenon, as Anne Dufourmantelle argues, marks the point at which hospitality involutes into 'an impossible, illicit geography of proximity', an 'unbearable orb of intimacy that melts into hate'.[19] A former commando who answers the call of duty to the end, Flowers not only provides Anjika with the alibi she needs but also goes a step further. Violently thrusting into her as she repeatedly screams 'no!', Flowers guides her hand towards the knife, clasping her grip in his, and offers her the satisfaction of stabbing him each time he forcibly penetrates her. When he is about to expire from his wounds, Anjika, shockingly, snatches the knife from his hands and stabs him fiercely twice more in the abdomen. In her reflections on the finished film, Harding explains that Anjika's final plunge of the knife was originally planned as a stab in the back, but such an ending would be redundant with Anjika's actions towards all those who have cared for her throughout the film. Instead, Flowers is subject to a worser fate: he has to watch her finish him off – twice. The conclusion of *Compulsion* clearly positions Flowers as a martyr for her love, the hero whose self-sacrifice preserves Anjika's honour and permits her to live free of all implication. Yet this narrative arc prompts us to forget that he raped Anjika – twice.

In the coda to the film's bloody ending, a flash cut to a small wedding shows Alex and Anjika being showered in flower petals as they head toward the car we associate with Flowers, only this time they are greeted by a younger, more attractive chauffeur. Unlike her counterpart in Middleton and Rowley's play, Anjika is the exception to all the rules in Harding's film. She lives to marry Alex; she is not a parricide, for her father is reborn by his investment in Alex's struggling clean energy business; and she quite literally gets away with murder. Curiously, though, when she embraces her mother, the camera moves in more tightly to reveal that, for the first time, Anjika is wearing her cuff bracelet. It is significant that this accessory is shown only through a lingering embrace with Anjika's mother, for they are now truly kindred spirits in ambiguously satisfying marriages that shore up patrilineal succession and further naturalize a patriarchy that 'shackle[s] [...] in the name of protection'.[20] And 'protection', as Saidiya Hartman argues, '[i]s an exemplary form of dissemblance, for it savagely truncates the dimensions of existence' for women in order 'to ensure their "decency"' in 'sexual and racial terms'.[21] As the camera tracks the couple entering the car previously driven by Flowers, Anjika stares back at her mother through the darkened glass as if she were looking out from a hearse, perhaps grieving the loss of her maiden name and mother's tongue. Somehow, they both know that the cuff is not the key to the house; it's the lock on the door.

## Conclusion: the key to the house?

In her essay 'The key to the house', Patricia Seed explores the ritualized practices of exiled peoples who keep the keys to the houses from which their ancestors were violently expelled centuries ago. This act of memory and mourning is performed by positioning the key above the doorway of their 'new' and indelibly foreign homes.[22] If I have laboured a reply to Derrida's abandoned query – 'What is a foreigner? What would a foreign woman be?' – then it is because there is a violence in the question that an answer would dignify. 'A foreign woman', understood in this context as a survivor of sexual violence, can never truly go home any more than she can become 'indigenous' again. Instead, she is consigned to a borderland where, not unlike Beatrice-Joanna, 'she has this fear / that she has no names / that she has many names / that she doesn't know her names'.²³ In what language, then, do we – so many different 'foreign women' – speak about our violated homes? As Norma Alarcón observes, 'there are those among us who long for "lost origins", as well as those who feel a profound kinship with the "lost"'.²⁴ But in the search for a liveable future, the 'most relevant point in the present is to understand how a pivotal indigenous portion of the mestiza past may represent a collective female experience' and, in so doing, be 'refocused for feminist change'.²⁵ Recognizing that although there *are* differences, *there is no separation between violences*, perhaps we might begin by resituating the organizing discourses of sexual identity, race and gender in a borderland where feminist practice is engaged in 'the meeting of other vital human needs and calls for full democracy to begin from there'.²⁶ Recalling that *The Changeling* was partly inspired by Hispanophobia – based on James I's proposed marriage of his son Charles to the Spanish Infanta, which was perceived as a serious threat to the succession of the Protestant faith – perhaps this democratic experiment might begin by disrupting the codes of 'hospitality' exercised at the US/Mexico border, where one of the most powerful nations in the world has 'forgotten the parentage' of more than 600 children – a full four years after they were forcibly separated from their families.²⁷ They cry for (m)others who have no names.

# Notes

1 See Jacques Derrida's dialogue with Anne Dufourmantelle in *Of Hospitality* (Jacques Derrida and Anna Dufourmantelle, *Of Hospitality: Anne Dufourmantelle Invites Jacques Derrida to Respond* (Stanford, CA: Stanford University Press, 2000), where Derrida devotes the first chapter to 'The Foreigner Question', 2–73. At the end of this dialogue, he asks: 'So the question returns. What is a foreigner? What would a foreign woman be?', 73.

2 Gloria Anzaldúa, *Borderlands/La Frontera: The New Mestiza*, 4th edition (San Francisco: Aunt Lute Books, 2012), 25.

3  Sarah Harding, *Compulsion* (2008, UK: ITV, Size 9 Productions), TV movie; Marcus Thompson, *Middleton's Changeling* (1998, UK: High Time Pictures Productions and United International Pictures (UIP)), Film; and Jay Stern, *The Changeling* (2006, New York, New York: Now and Then Productions), film.

4  Judith Butler, *Precarious Life: The Powers of Mourning and Violence* (London: Verso, 2006), xviii.

5  Saidiya Hartman, *Scenes of Subjection: Terror, Slavery, and Self-Making in Nineteenth-Century America* (New York: Oxford University Press, 1997), 85.

6  See Hortense Spillers, 'Mama's Baby, Papa's Maybe: An American Grammar Book', in *Black, White, and in Color: Essays on American Literature and Culture* (Chicago, IL: University of Chicago Press, 2003), 206.

7  Spillers, 'Mama's Baby, Papa's Maybe', 206.

8  Joan Copjec, 'The Phenomenal Nonphenomenal: Private Space in *Film Noir*', in Joan Copjec (ed.), *Shades of Noir: A Reader* (London: Verso, 1993), 185.

9  Derrida, 7.

10  Katherine Schwarz, 'The Wrong Question: Thinking through Virginity', *Differences: A Journal of Feminist Cultural Studies* 33.2 (2002): 6.

11  See Elizabeth Cady Stanton's quote from her speech, 'Our Girls', in Joan Jacobs Brumberg's *The Body Project: A History of American Girls* (New York: Random House, 1998), xxxii.

12  Sarah Harding, '*Compulsion*: A View from the Director's Chair', *Shakespeare Bulletin*, 29.4 (Winter 2011): 605.

13  Serena Davies, 'Interview: Ray Winstone and Parminder Nagra on Compulsion', *Telegraph*, 28 April 2009, https://www.telegraph.co.uk/culture/tvandradio/5236191/Interview-Ray-Winstone-and-Parminder-Nagra-on-Compulsion.html (accessed 30 April 2021).

14  Harding, '*Compulsion*: A View', 611.

15  Hartman, *Scenes of Subjection*, 84.

16  Spillers, 'Mama's Baby, Papa's Maybe', 216.

17  Harding, '*Compulsion*: A View', 609.

18  Harding, '*Compulsion*: A View', 608.
19  Anna Dufourmantelle, *Of Hospitality*, 2, 4.
20  Anzaldúa, *Borderlands/La Frontera*, 42–3.
21  Norma Alarcón, 'Chicana Feminism: In the Tracks of "The" Native Woman', in Caren Kaplan, Norma Alarcón and Minoo Moallem (eds), *Between Woman and Nation: Nationalisms, Transnationals, and the State* (Durham, NC: Duke University Press, 1999), 69.
22  Patricia Seed, 'The Key to the House', in Hamid Naficy (ed.), *Home, Exile, Homeland: Film Media, and the Politics of Place* (New York: Routledge, 1999), 86.
23  Anzaldúa, *Borderlands/La Frontera*, 65.
24  Norma Alarcón, 'Chicana Feminism: In the Tracks of "The" Native Woman', in Caren Kaplan, Norma Alarcón and Minoo Moallem (eds), *Between Woman and Nation: Nationalisms, Transnationals, and the State* (Durham, NC: Duke University Press, 1999), 66.
25  Alarcón, 'Chicana Feminism', 67.
26  Rosemary Hennessy, *Profit and Pleasure: Sexual Identities in Late Capitalism* (New York: Routledge, 2000), 231–2.
27  In May 2018, the US Government, under then President Donald Trump, pursued a 'zero tolerance' policy for any adult person caught crossing into the US without valid entry, allowing no exceptions for those seeking asylum or traveling with minor children. As a direct result of this policy, as many as 3,000 migrant children were separated from a parent or parents (see Congressional Research Service, Report R45266, 'The Trump Administration's "Zero Tolerance" Immigration Enforcement Policy', version 7, 20 July 2018, https://crsreports.congress.gov/product/pdf/R/R45266/7 ). A report by the US Department of Health and Human Services General Inspector in 2019 revealed that a pilot programme pursuing a similar policy of prosecution had been in effect in El Paso, TX, as early as 2017 and that as many as 5,500 migrant children were actually separated from their parents from 2017–18. In October of 2020, an American Civil Liberties Union (ACLU) Lawsuit against the US Government revealed that 545 migrant children had not been reunited with their parents, sixty of whom had been under the

age of five when separated (see Caitlin Dickerson, 'Parents of 545 Children Separated at the Border Cannot Be Found', *The New York Times*, 21 October 2020 (updated 15 March 2021), US edition, https://www.nytimes.com/2020/10/21/us/migrant-children-separated.html). In December of 2020, an update to the lawsuit by the ACLU revealed that as many as 628 children still in the US had yet to be reunited with their unreachable parents, more than half of whom had been deported to Mexico, Guatemala, El Salvador or Honduras (Daniel Gonzalez, '628 parents of separated children are still missing. Here's why immigrant advocates can't find them', *USA Today*, *Arizona Republic*, 11 December 2020, https://www.usatoday.com/story/news/nation/2020/12/11/immigrant-advocates-cant-locate-parents-separated-border-children/3896940001/).

# 12

# Feminist Staging in Brave Spirits' *Changeling*

## *Charlene V. Smith and Musa Gurnis*

In the Fall of 2018, the Washington DC company Brave Spirits Theatre (BST) presented a feminist production of *The Changeling*.[1] Below, we – Charlene V. Smith, the play's director and artistic director of BST, and Musa Gurnis, the actress who played De Flores – discuss our rehearsal process and staging choices. We hope to offer some transportable strategies for feminist performances not only of *The Changeling* but which will also be applicable to other early modern plays. Our *Changeling* repudiated the common theatrical interpretation of the play as a dark romance between Beatrice-Joanna and De Flores; instead, we recognized De Flores as a coercive rapist. Exhaustive historicized paraphrase of the playtext was the foundation of our work, and our central approach was to underscore the negative portrayal of toxic masculinity that is already in the script.[2] Our task was to expose the damage of rape culture without reinflicting it. Towards that end, we worked not only with the text but also at times against it and outside it. We challenged expressions of rape culture where they appear in the dialogue with our staging choices, and we imagined women's survival beyond the limitations of the 400-year-old script. Rather than cut problematic text we ironized it and answered the written, victim-blaming epilogue with a visual epi-epilogue that offered survivors on stage and in the audience healing from the play's trauma.

Our production was premised on a reading of the De Flores and Beatrice-Joanna plot as coercive rape. This interpretation, advanced by Roberta Barker and David Nicol in a 2004 landmark essay and developed by other scholars such as Kim Solga, has been widely ignored in contemporary performances which, as Nora J. Williams and Sarah Dustagheer document, largely continue to treat the play as a twisted but consensual romance.[3] Our theatrical intervention was rooted in the text. We accepted the given circumstances of the plot: a woman is blackmailed into sex she does not want. We embraced the basic dramatic convention of early modern theatre in which characters speaking straight to the audience are saying what they think, and therefore we credited Beatrice-Joanna's repeated declarations that she hates and fears De Flores. The playtext invites a feminist performance: it presents De Flores' misogyny as villainy and provides an incisive portrayal of the power dynamics of coercive rape as well as its psychological aftermath for survivors.

The present moment is an inevitable intertext for all performances of early modern plays. Our rehearsal period overlapped with a month of Senate confirmation hearings that ended with the lifetime appointment of Brett Kavanaugh to the United States Supreme Court, in spite of the fact that he had been accused of sexual assault by three women. We listened to the hearings on our way into rehearsal and integrated into our staging many of the haunting details from Dr Christine Blasey Ford's brave public testimony of her attack by Kavanaugh. We participated with thousands of others in mass protests; we witnessed survivors sharing their trauma and watched as survivors begging for justice were arrested on the steps of the Supreme Court. This raw time heightened our awareness of our responsibility to our audiences to show sexual violence without compounding trauma, leading us both to adopt Brechtian alienation techniques that provided a safe distance from which to examine the wounds of sexual violence, as well as to offer an ending with reparative emotional balm.

In BST's production, decisions about the representation of sexual violence towards women were made collectively by a creative team in which the majority of the artists were women, many of us survivors ourselves. In the US, women make up the overwhelming majority (90 per cent) of adult rape victims, with one in six experiencing an assault, according to the organization RAINN (Rape, Abuse and Incest National Network).[4] For cis men who are survivors, as well as for transgender and gender-nonconforming people (nearly half of whom are sexually assaulted during their lifetime), part of the trauma of rape is a cultural narrative of forced feminization.[5] Our own varied experiences of misogyny gave us a kind of 'skilled vision' for reading the dynamics of coercive rape in the script.[6] The false assumption underlying many contemporary productions is that because De Flores does not physically attack Beatrice-Joanna, it is not rape. In contrast, we understood that, as RAINN explains, 'force doesn't always refer to physical pressure. Perpetrators may use emotional coercion, psychological force, or manipulation to coerce a victim into non-consensual sex'.[7] Our *Changeling* foregrounded the emotional and mental manipulation that often accompanies acts of sexual violence. Rejecting the 'anachronistically Freudian, textually unsupported, and anti-feminist' reading of Beatrice-Joanna's repeated expressions of hatred for De Flores as suppressed, subconscious desire allowed us to answer the urgent call of the #MeToo movement to 'believe women'.[8] Watching Dr Ford's account of Brett Kavanaugh's attack be discredited and dismissed in the US Senate brought home to us that, as Nora J. Williams writes: 'Dismantling this interpretation of the play [as a romance rather than a rape in spite of everything Beatrice-Joanna tells us] is not just good scholarship – it's an urgent feminist issue'.[9]

## De Flores the incel

Contemporary performances of early modern plays require acts of cultural translation. We helped our audiences understand the danger of De Flores' toxic Petrarchanism by delivering it through line readings and gestures that evoked its modern equivalent: incel resentment. 'Incels' or 'involuntary celibates' are members of a predominantly but not exclusively white, heterosexual, men's online community active primarily in North America but also in Europe, New Zealand and Australia. These internet forums are characterized by resentment, misogyny and sexual entitlement; incels 'routinely argue that violence against women is justified because women deny unattractive men their "right to sex"'.[10] These online fantasies have real world consequences. Incels have been linked to multiple mass murders; Scott Beierle killed two women and injured four more when he opened fire on a yoga studio in Tallahassee, Florida, during the run of our play.[11]

De Flores shares with modern incels a deep resentment, a belief that he is entitled to money and women that have been unfairly denied him. Like Elliot Rodgers, the self-proclaimed 'supreme gentleman' who murdered six women in retribution for ignoring him, De Flores justifies his aggressive claim on Beatrice-Joanna's attention and affection by insisting: 'I tumbled into the world a gentleman' (2.1.49).[12] De Flores fixates on being sexually rejected by a higher status woman, Beatrice-Joanna (in incel terms, a 'Stacy'), for a higher status man, Alsemero (a 'Chad'), because he is unattractive and lower status. Just as incels self-identify with an elaborate taxonomy of perceived male physical defects, De Flores harps on his own appearance: 'I must confess my face is bad enough'; 'these foul chops'; 'this bad face' (2.1.37, 85; 2.2.152). He refers to Beatrice-Joanna's virginity repeatedly as his 'recompense', a term that in the period signified not simply payment for a service but compensation for an injury or retribution for a wrong.[13]

I, Musa, played a De Flores who spat out clichéd Petrarchan complaints – 'I live in pain now: that shooting eye / Will burn my heart to cinders' (3.4.155-56) – with the bitterness of men who vent online about 'bitches who put nice guys in the friendzone'.[14] My word-for-word paraphrase of De Flores' lines reads like an incel manifesto. I did this preparatory work as I was instructed at the Royal Academy of Dramatic Art and translated his dialogue into the most explicit contemporary terms possible: most of it is too obscene to quote. To follow his incel logic across connected language into a visual metaphor for rape: 'My hard fate has thrust me out to servitude' and in compensation 'I should thrust / My fingers into her sockets' (2.1.47; 1.1.237–8). My De Flores stuffed the holes of Beatrice-Joanna's contemptuously dropped glove with an invasive upward claw. This forced penetration of a courtly lady's token was a *gestus*, a physicalization of a cultural attitude, that articulated a distinctively incel combination of social resentment and misogynist violence. My De Flores illustrated his complaint to the audience that he is rejected while an even uglier man with money freely 'plucks sweets' (2.1.46) with a graphic hand gesture that recalled the claw thrust up into the lady's glove. Suiting this action to these words also linked the line to its Trump-era equivalent fantasy of sexual entitlement, the free reign over women's bodies that incels believe is given to rich and powerful men but unjustly denied them: 'When you're a star [. . .] you can do anything [. . .] grab them by the pussy'.[15] I carried this gestural thread into 3.4 to underscore the creepiness of incels' fixation with female virginity and promiscuity; on De Flores' assurance 'That thy virginity were perfect in thee' (3.4.120), I stretched out his hand toward Beatrice-Joanna with a single suggestive finger insinuating upward as if into her to test her hymen. I played his horrifying revelations of his crimes and violent death with the affect of a mass shooter exultant in the wreckage of a final act of domination.

While this conception of De Flores as an incel helped me draw out the social resentment, sexual entitlement and violent misogyny that pervade his lines, the point of this characterization was not so much to target a specific subculture as to foreground an extreme example of the sexism that surrounds us in everyday life. I also modelled many of De Flores' vocal inflections and mannerisms on the newly appointed US Supreme Court Justice, accused sexual predator Brett Kavanaugh. Imitating his public explosion of rage denying Dr Ford's allegations of attempted rape during his confirmation hearing (a frat boy meltdown memorably parodied by Matt Damon on *Saturday Night Live*), I punctuated some of De Flores' more resentful lines with a self-righteous and animalistic 'Kavanaugh sniff'. After the assault, my De Flores watched Beatrice-Joanna's wedding from the side with a nasty smirk, drinking a beer. At that time, this simple prop recalled Kavanaugh's dismissive defence – 'I like beer' – against Dr Ford's account of him 'drunkenly laughing' during the assault.[16] While dying, De Flores gloats over raping Beatrice-Joanna: 'It was so sweet to me / That I have drunk up all, left none behind / For any man to pledge me' (5.2.169–71). To give this subsequent metaphoric language a more graphic point of reference, I had De Flores swagger out of the wedding, having raped the bride, knocking back the last drops of his beer.

To help create a production that enlisted audience members as sympathetic witnesses to Beatrice-Joanna it was crucial for me to present De Flores in a way that substantiated her fear of him, not as the petulant whim, or 'peevish will' (1.1.107), that he takes it for but rather as the recognition of a real danger. I had to play a De Flores who motivated Beatrice-Joanna's many expressions of distress at his relentless, invasive attention; e.g., 'I never see this fellow but I think / Of some harm towards me. Danger's in my mind still; / I scarce leave trembling of an hour after' (2.1.90–2). I interpreted De Flores' decision to 'vex her still' as stalking (1.1.240). Like many actors, I made lists of everything each character says about mine (and vice versa) for playable information about De Flores' demeanour and relationships. The first time Beatrice-Joanna describes De Flores, she calls him a 'basilisk' (1.1.115): an animal that kills by staring. I took this as implied direction and kept De Flores' eyes on her body almost constantly whenever they were onstage together; even as a corpse I kept his empty eyes open and unblinking, locked on her, to physicalize his dying threat to stalk her after death. Inspired by the early modern concept of extramissive vision that underpins the descriptions of his gaze, I treated his roving eyes as if they carried the power of touch, a way for him to molest her from across the room. I made him enjoy her distress the way I have seen men laugh at my own indignation or fear after they have catcalled me on the street.

While I was preparing the role, a male actor told me that I needed to 'find the rapist in [my]self'.[17] This unsolicited, unhelpful and infelicitously phrased advice was not necessary as I had already met De Flores many times in the men who have harassed me, stalked me, abused me and assaulted me. I did not need to search the darkest corners of my psyche for his inner thoughts because De Flores' most degrading, violent, misogynist lines could all be paraphrased as things I have heard men say aloud. Other actors gave me the standard advice 'not to judge the character', warning that to play him 'unsympathetically' would lead to an evil caricature. However, the purpose of my performance was not to humanize De Flores but rather (as one reviewer described it) 'to dissect a rapist'; that is, to show him accurately – both as he appears in the text and in the world – without mitigating or excusing his behaviour.[18] To revise the old French adage, I wanted the audience to understand all so they would forgive nothing.

The challenge for me was to make De Flores compelling without making him sympathetic, highly watchable but completely unlikable. We avoided a heavy 'ugly makeup' for De Flores because we thought it would be ableist to use his face (as the script does) as an index of his depravity.[19] Instead, make-up designer Briana Manente gave De Flores a burn mark on his cheek to resonate with the fire he sets, which suggested a backstory that fed into De Flores' sense of injury. Rather than treat his appearance as a hardship to elicit audience sympathy, whenever De Flores was wounded by an insult about his face I tried to show how quickly that pain soured into resentment and rage. For much of the play De Flores (like Iago or Richard III) has an intimate relationship with the audience created by frequent direct address. Charlene blocked my track so that I often entered from the house, sharing the audience's space and visual perspective on the scene, casually coming up through the risers while commenting on the action we had all just watched together, leaning on seats, teasing people, cracking dirty jokes, conspiratorial. My goal was to make the audience increasingly uncomfortable with the complicity De Flores solicits. I often began a series of sexist jokes lightly to initiate a laugh, so that on the hard misogynist punch line I could make that laugh die. Steven Mullaney describes this dissonance between a character's emotion and an audience's response as 'affective irony'; or to use Brecht's formulation: 'I laugh when they weep; I weep when they laugh.'[20] In 3.4, my De Flores kept turning and checking in with the audience, expecting confirmation that Beatrice-Joanna owed him sex. I thought of Dr Christine Blasey Ford's description of Kavanaugh's 'uproarious laughter' during her assault; my De Flores invited everyone watching to share a laugh at Beatrice-Joanna's expense. Actors often give nicknames to segments of a scene to clarify dramatic storytelling, and I titled one such acting 'beat' in 3.4: 'Can you believe this dumb bitch?' In the mutual visibility of the small theatre, I could see on the faces of audience members how that earlier shallow cosiness with a rapist curdled and froze.

The alienation effect of having a cis woman play a male rapist created a safe distance from which audiences could examine the dynamics of coercive rape. This allowed me to land his degrading dirty jokes and voice his violent daydreams while critiquing rather than simply repeating a cultural script so familiar it too often feels inevitable. Much as early modern cross-gender casting seems to have functioned as a largely invisible convention until specific language calls attention to it, so too in our production it was not merely the difference between my cis woman's body and De Flores' imagined cis male body that created dissonance for the audience, but rather the contradiction of hearing the character's virulently misogynist litany of sexist clichés spoken by a female-bodied and female-identifying actor. We kept my secondary sex characteristics visible through the costume without attempting a seamless appearance of masculinity (no binding, short hair, fake beard or deep voice), so that my feminine body beneath would be a reminder of the real-world targets of his violence. This double vision produced a Brechtian *verfremdungseffekt*; we made the familiar sexism of a victimizer sound strange, jarring, no longer possible to accept as the state of the world, by speaking his words through the mouth of someone who might be his victim. My female body, as well as the critical insight and latent rage I brought to the role as a rape survivor, put De Flores' misogynist vitriol in conspicuous quotation marks.

# Non-realistic staging as a feminist strategy

Staging abuse casually or gratuitously can damage those watching who have experienced trauma or face the threat of violence in their everyday life. As discussed further below, we used non-realistic makeup, costume and puppetry in 3.4 to show the emotional impact of rape instead of re-enacting a physical assault. Puppetry also gave us a non-realistic mode of staging the 'madmen' and 'fools' in the hospital without having able-bodied actors 'crip up' by feigning a disability (as the characters Antonio and Franciscus themselves do in order to gain access to Isabella). Rather than imitating a specific or general pretended physical or mental disability, Antonio and Franciscus wore puppets as their mad/foolish disguises. This device was our solution to the representational challenge Williams describes of giving 'the audience permission to laugh at [the] antics of Antonio and Franciscus, without mocking genuine disability'.[21] In our staging, these puppets consisted of brightly dressed, miniature bodies dangling below the actors' own heads.

Non-naturalistic staging offered not only strategies for protecting the emotional well-being of our audiences, but also techniques for showing the psychological complexity of women's negotiations of a misogynist world. While scholars including Douglas Bruster in this volume rightfully celebrate Isabella's wit and agency, the danger of grounding a performance in this reading is that it can imply that there is a right way for women to successfully handle unwanted advances from men (effectively making Isabella the 'good' foil to a 'bad' Beatrice-Joanna).[22] Puppetry allowed us to keep Isabella's virtuosic performance of 'correct' femininity visible as a performance. The puppet for Isabella represented the male gaze version of her, the woman the men of the story wanted to see, as well as the mask she had to perform in order to remain safe.

The gap between the actor and the puppet created a space in performance to dramatize the code switching that women use in their daily lives to navigate a world of sexual danger. As puppet designer Genna Beth Davidson describes her work:

> We gave the actress playing Isabella a puppet version of her character in order to draw attention to and give visual language to her experience and navigation of the sexual harassment she endures. The puppet Isabella, who I designed as a stereotypical Western ideal of feminine beauty (she wore a corset, had panniers to emphasize the hips, luscious, colorful features and floral motifs throughout her costuming) is an object on which male attention is placed and their sexual desire enacted. The men do not see the true woman behind the puppet. This technique also raises awareness about the defensive tactics women take to navigate an oppressive system. When any person's body is under threat, sexual or otherwise, separating oneself from the body is protective. The actress playing Isabella could act out her disgust behind the puppet-shield and give voice to an experience of having to endure unwanted advances, kisses,

flirtations and being pressed against and touched constantly. The double vision that this style of puppetry provided allowed us to place attention on sexual harassment without threatening anyone's safety.[23]

The Isabella puppet enabled us to juxtapose the objectified male fantasy of Isabella against the full person.

Our feminist commitment to collaboration allowed Adrianne Knapp, the actress playing Isabella, to develop the opportunities for staging objectification and double-consciousness that Genna Beth had designed into her puppet. Adrienne created a performance moment that dramatized women's struggle for control over their bodies in a world where they have been socialized to placate men:

> I suggested that the actor playing Antonio literally remove my puppet from me, and rather comically, I chased him around the stage trying to 'get myself' back. I felt it would be a good comedic counterpoint to Beatrice's scene with De Flores when she also becomes a puppet and no longer herself. We were women who lost the ownership of our space and our bodies, grasping desperately in vain to get it back.[24]

This 'keep away' blocking was repeated when Lollio imitates Antonio's unwanted advances. Puppetry provided a link between the castle plot and the hospital plot, articulating the threat to women's agency that exists in both storylines.

# Consensual choreography for coercive rape

As the director responsible for staging the final moments of 3.4, I, Charlene, had to consider not only audience safety but also the safety of the artists during rehearsal and performance.

Despite the constraints of a small budget, I prioritized the hiring of intimacy choreographer Emily Sucher to ensure the precision and consistency of physical contact between the actors. As they explain: 'This specificity was crucial for clear storytelling [. . .] and our performers' safety. A consent-based choreography process frees actors to rely on the depth of their character work without fear of accidentally harming their scene partner or themselves.'[25] Emily and I blocked multiple instances in which male characters (Jasperino, Antonio, Franciscus, Lollio and De Flores) land non-consensual kisses on female characters (Diaphanta, Isabella, and Beatrice-Joanna) in the play with repeated, slightly stylized choreography.[26] I wanted these conspicuous echoed moments to locate De Flores' pursuit of Beatrice-Joanna in a world pervaded by unwanted touch.

Under my direction, aided by fight director Casey Kaleba who not only choreographs combat but also fine-tunes movement in scenes of psychological aggression, De Flores dominated 3.4 not by force but by wearing Beatrice-Joanna down. For De Flores, this conversation is over before it begins: he knows he already has her. Musa made him enjoy closing in on his victim knowing she has no escape. Danielle Scott's increasingly desperate Beatrice-Joanna struggled to open the visible 'Exit' doors in the theatre. Their long, gruelling exchange left her trapped on a platform, on her knees, exhausted from pleading. As she looked out at the audience, De Flores' hand reached from behind and covered her mouth at 'Let this silence thee' (3.4.162), making contact on the word 'silence'. This was one of only a few moments of direct physical contact between them. It recalled Dr Ford's terrifying description of Brett Kavanaugh covering her mouth to silence her during the attempted rape.[27] Genna Beth worked with costume designer Madeline Belknap to create a version of Beatrice-Joanna's dress that could be removed and manipulated as a puppet or prop by other actors. At the end of 3.4, De Flores peeled away this outer dress from Beatrice-Joanna (who wore underneath a nearly identical full coverage slip). Then, as one reviewer described it, 'in a viscerally disturbing gesture, De Flores thrust his arm into the sleeve to mime his violation of her'.[28] He delivered the remaining lines to the empty puppet-dress, shushing it as he carried it offstage, leaving behind a traumatized Beatrice-Joanna.

I allowed the actors agency in deciding how to stage the rape, giving them a greater sense of control and gaining from their creative insight on the scene. It was important to Danielle Scott, the actress playing Beatrice-Joanna:

> to create a believable violent sequence of events in 3.4 without creating trauma for the audience and myself. I brought up the idea of using paint or a type of makeup that could be imprinted on my body to represent where Beatrice-Joanna had been violated by De Flores. From this idea, make-up designer Briana Manente brought in Mehron charred ash powder. We all made the decision that we wanted to have handprints on the arms and the legs and one handprint over the mouth. Musa, as De Flores, left the first handprint. As De Flores exited with the puppet dress, I was left on stage to put the handprints on my own body as if De Flores was actually putting hands on my body. During rehearsal, Charlene asked if I would like to wash the ash off at a certain moment, but I decided that I wanted to keep the handprints on through the rest of the show. My thought process was that the lasting handprints would reflect the way Beatrice sees herself after being raped by De Flores. I wanted to bring to light the after-effects of the assault and how they still shape Beatrice's actions and the way she interacts with other characters.[29]

The handprints created a visual representation of lingering trauma and Beatrice-Joanna's internalised shame.

Puppetry also offered a means of representing the dissociation that many survivors experience during an assault, often described as an out-of-body experience.[30] In my blocking, the puppet-dress returned as the bride that Beatrice-Joanna watches enter in the dumb show of her own wedding procession, partially rejoining her puppet-self at the altar to say her vows like a ventriloquist. As Genna Beth describes the effect of this device:

> The use of Beatrice-Joanna's empty dress as a puppet was a visual representation of a full-blown dissociative experience for that character. The experience of rape often results in the complete loss of connection to one's body. Again this is a tactic of survival we were depicting albeit different than that of Isabella's experience. Beatrice-Joanna has no control; the dress floated around as she stood outside of the action after the rape. And again here, placing the violating act on the object (a dress) instead of a person created a safer distance for all to witness the heinous crime. Additionally clothing that was removed during a rape often becomes a charged object significant to the victim as a reminder of the event.[31]

In both the case of Isabella (whose performance of femininity and double consciousness was embodied through a puppet), and Beatrice-Joanna (whose dissociation from her body was symbolized by the removal of her puppet-dress), these non-naturalistic devices afforded powerful techniques for representing experiences of rape and sexual harassment without realistic staging that risks (re)traumatizing performers and audience members.

# Feminist revision: working against and outside the text

Many of our collective, feminist performance and production choices built on dynamics already present in the script; however, as the director, I, Charlene bore ultimate responsibility for confronting and critiquing the problematic ending of the play in which Beatrice-Joanna is blamed both for the murder of Piracquo and for her own assault. Alsemero calls her 'deformed' and 'a whore' (5.3.77; 31). De Flores tells her she is 'the deed's creature' (3.4.140) and a 'whore in [her] affection' (3.4.140, 145). Beatrice-Joanna takes the verbal abuse to heart; 'Oh come not near me, sir,' she says to her father, 'I shall defile you' (5.3.151). She kills herself, telling Alsemero, ''Tis time to die, when 'tis a shame to live' (5.3.179). In the world of the play, Beatrice-Joanna's shame necessitates her death. Alsemero moralizes after Beatrice-Joanna's death, 'Justice hath so right / The guilty hit, that innocence is quit / By proclamation and may joy again' (5.3.185–7). For my production to simply recreate these opinions would not only be offensive, it would risk perpetuating these harms.

In contrast to the play as written, which closes with an epilogue reaffirming male bonds over a raped woman's corpse, my staging of the ending focused instead on Beatrice-Joanna's experience.[32] In many productions, the blocking of the double-suicide of Beatrice-Joanna and De Flores reinforces the idea that they were united in death or that they belonged together. Instead of Beatrice-Joanna and De Flores dying in each other's arms, my staging separated them in the playing space both vertically and horizontally. Their final entrance was out of the trapdoor on an upstage platform, Alsemero's 'closet' where he locks them together to enable a final assault. Once released, Beatrice-Joanna, in pain and bleeding, stumbled off and away from De Flores. He then threw her his knife: 'Make haste Joanna, by that token to thee' (5.3.175). Moving centre stage and clasping Alsemero's hands around the knife, Beatrice swiftly guided him to stab her, physicalizing his culpability in her death. Her wound stained Alsemero's hands who passed that bloody handshake to Vermandero and Tomazo as they affirmed their male bonds over her corpse. The final stage picture of the play's scripted text left Beatrice-Joanna dead centre stage, still marked by her attackers' handprints from the assault, her dress unlaced at the back revealing slashes on her skin (De Flores' recent possessive carving), surrounded by three men with blood on their hands.

The whole company was highly conscious of the emotional state in which we left our audiences in the final moments of our play. The script ends with a raped woman killing herself from shame. As the director, I was faced with a creative challenge: how could I stage this plot point without condoning it? Instead of eliminating the original victim-blaming ending, I answered it with a dumb show that restored agency to Beatrice-Joanna and offered healing to actors and audiences. As Alsemero spoke his final lines, 'Man and his sorrow at the grave must part' (5.3.219), Jasmine Thompson's cover of the REM song 'Everybody Hurts' began playing. Adrianne Knapp entered as Isabella, but for the first time without her puppet, carrying bowls of water and washcloths. As the song played, Danielle invited the rest of the cast to gather around her. Existing in a liminal space between characters and actors, the ensemble participated in a communal washing of Danielle's body. As the song concluded, Danielle stood and washed off the final handprint, the one over her mouth, herself. The performance ended as she looked at the audience, having reclaimed her body, and drew a free breath. The goals of this new ending were to counter the blame the script assigns Beatrice-Joanna, to restore dignity to a woman who had been abused, to show that a woman is more than her assault, and to provide a ritual of healing catharsis, both for the actors and the audiences who had been engaged with this difficult material.

BST's rehearsal practices drew on the skilled vision of survivors, on knowledge acquired from daily navigations of the threat of sexual violence, as a resource for staging strategies that exposed rape culture for critique without inflicting harm on performers or audience members. The fact that we did this mainly by working with and not against the grain of the text is of secondary importance. Theatre makers have an ethical responsibility to audiences not scripts. Textual fidelity does not justify sexist production choices. Nevertheless, our historicized reading of the play and engagement with feminist scholarship enabled us to draw precise and resonant connections throughout the performance with contemporary manifestations of its villain's misogyny. Production choices that ironized damaging views validated in the script were informed, tactical decisions based in deep engagement with (not casual disregard for) the play's language in its original social context. The revised ending invented by Charlene in BST's production exercised what Dorinne Kondo calls 'reparative creativity'. As she describes the value of this practice: 'We need visions of possibility [...] of a world imagined otherwise, so that we might attempt to remake the world'.[33] Our process was to draw out the elements in the play that served our critique of rape culture, to provide visual counterpoints that challenged damaging ideas affirmed in the dialogue, and to offer healing for survivors unavailable in a 400-year-old script that calls for a raped woman's death. Plays only stay alive if we use them to tell the stories that we need to live.

# Notes

1 To watch an archive film of this production, visit https://youtu be/EXi6Rs9jC0U. For supplementary documents from the production, see https://www.bravespiritstheatre.com/productions/the-changeling/

2 For a sixty-page guide to the company's working practices of text analysis, see Charlene V. Smith, *'Brave Spirits Theatre's Approach to Early Modern Verse, Rhetoric, and Text Analysis'*, Brave Spirits Theatre, https://www.bravespiritstheatre.com/wp-content/uploads/2019/10/BST-Text-Analysis-2019-3.pdf

3 Roberta Barker and David Nicol, 'Does Beatrice Joanna Have a Subtext?: *The Changeling* on the London Stage', *Early Modern Literary Studies* 10.1 (2004): 1–43, http://purl.oclc.org/emls/10-1/barknico.htm; Kim Solga, 'Beatrice Joanna and the Rhetoric of Rape', in Kimberly Jannarone (ed.), *Vanguard Performance Beyond Left and Right* (Ann Arbor: University of Michigan Press, 2005), 246–63; Kim Solga, *Violence Against Women in Early Modern Performance* (New York: Palgrave Macmillan, 2013); Sarah Dustagheer, 'New Directions: Performing *The*

*Changeling*: 2006–2015', in Mark Hutchings (ed.), *The Changeling: A Critical Reader* (London: Bloomsbury Arden Shakespeare, 2019), 143–63; Nora J. Williams, 'Resources', in Mark Hutchings (ed.), *The Changeling: A Critical Reader* (London: Bloomsbury Arden Shakespeare, 2019), 187–210.

4 'Victims of Sexual Violence: Statistics', RAINN.org, Rape, Incest, and Abuse National Network, 2021, https://www.rainn.org/statistics/victims-sexual-violence (accessed 29 April 2021).

5 See 'Victims of Sexual Violence: Statistics', RAIIN.org.

6 See Evelyn Byrd Tribble and John Sutton, 'Cognitive Ecology as a Framework for Shakespeare Studies', *Shakespeare Studies* 39 (2011): 94–103 (97).

7 'Sexual Assault', RAINN.org, Rape, Incest, and Abuse National Network, 2021, https://www.rainn.org/articles/sexual-assault (accessed 29 April 2021).

8 Jennifer Panek, 'A Performance History', in Mark Hutchings (ed.), *The Changeling: A Critical Reader* (London: Bloomsbury Arden Shakespeare, 2019), 35–66.

9 Williams, 'Resources', 203.

10 Jesselyn Cook, 'Inside Incels' Looksmaxing Obsession: Penis Stretching, Skull Implants And Rage', *Huffington Post*, 27 July 2018, https://www.huffpost.com/entry/incels-looksmaxing-obsession_n_5b50e56ee4b0de86f48b0a4f

11 For an overview of incel ideology, see Sara Brzuszkiewicz, 'Incel Radical Milieu and External Locus of Control', *Evolutions in Counter-Terrorism* 2 (November 2020): 1–20.

12 Elliot Rodgers, 'YouTube Video: Retribution', *New York Times*, 24 May 2014, https://www.nytimes.com/video/us/100000002900707/youtube-video-retribution.html

13 'recompense n. 2a; 2b; 3' *Oxford English Dictionary Online*, March 2021, Oxford University Press. http://www.oed.com/viewdictionaryentry/Entry/11125 (accessed 30 April 2021).

14 'Nice Guys', Know Your Meme, https://knowyourmeme.com/memes/nice-guys

15 'Transcript: Donald Trump's Taped Comments About Women', *New York Times*, 8 October 2016, https://www.nytimes.com/2016/10/08/us/donald-trump-tape-transcript.html

16 'Updates from the Riveting Testimonies of Christine Blasey Ford and Brett Kavanaugh', *New York Times*, 27 September 2018, https://www.nytimes.com/2018/09/27/us/politics/kavanaugh-hearings-dr-ford.html

17 Though I refrain from naming the actor, this comment was made during a session of the Fall 2018 Folger Shakespeare Institute's Center for Shakespeare Studies program, 'What Acting Is'.

18 Gretchen York, '*The Duchess of Malfi* and *The Changeling* at the Brave Spirits Theatre', *Shakespeare Newsletter* 68.1 (Fall/Winter 2018–19), https://shakespearenewsletter.com/the-duchess-of-malfi-and-the-changeling-at-the-brave-spirits-theatre/

19 The terms 'ableist' and 'ableism', Simi Linton explains, are used to explain the way in which the experience of non-disabled people has been privileged over the experience of disabled people. While the term points out discriminatory practices, Linton adds, '*ableism* also includes the idea that a person's abilities or characteristics are determined by disability or that people with disabilities as a group are inferior to non-disabled people' (9). See Linton, *Claiming Disability: Knowledge and Identity* (New York: New York University Press, 1998).

20 Steven Mullaney, *Reformation of Emotions in the Age of Shakespeare* (Chicago: University of Chicago Press, 2015), 74; Bertolt Brecht, 'Theater for Pleasure or Theater for Instruction?', in *Brecht on Theatre*, trans. John Willet (London: Methuen, 1964), 71. Cf. Dorrine Kondo's description of 'affective violence' in *Worldmaking: Race, Performance, and the Work of Creativity* (Durham, NC: Duke University Press, 2018), 18.

21 Williams, 'Resources', 206.

22 For the discussion of Isabella and Beatrice as intertwined characters, see Douglas Bruster's essay 'Isabella' in this volume.

23 Email message to author, 1 April 2021.

24 Email message to author, 15 September 2020.

25 Email message to author, 4 April 2021. For more information of the relatively new position of intimacy choreography in theatre and entertainment, see Holly L. Derr, 'The Art of Craft of Intimacy Direction', Howlround Theatre Commons, 30 January 2020, https://howlround.com/art-and-craft-intimacy-direction

26 1.1.151, Jasperino to Diaphanta; 3.3.194, Antonio to Isabella; 3.3.242, Lollio to Isabella; 3.4.92, De Flores to Beatrice-Joanna; 4.3.129, Isabella repeating Antonio's aggression back to him. Editors will make various decisions on whether the text in these moments is calling for a kiss, an attempted kiss, or a grope of some sort, a variation that could affect the perceived danger of each of these moments.

27 'Riveting Testimonies', *New York Times*. At the time, a chilling cartoon circulated on the internet showing Lady Justice held down with Republican hands covering her mouth, see Michael Cavna, 'Viral Kavanaugh cartoon powerfully depicts the assault of Lady Justice', *Washington Post*, 29 September 2018, https://www.washingtonpost.com/news/comic-riffs/wp/2018/09/29/viral-kavanaugh-cartoon-powerfully-depicts-the-assault-of-lady-justice/

28 Lydia Zoells, 'Reinterpreting Sexual Assault in "The Changeling"', *Electric Eel* 8 (8 January 2019), https://www.mcdbooks.com/electric_eel/issue-008

29 Email message to author, 12 September 2020 .

30 'Dissociation', RAINN.org, https://www.rainn.org/articles/dissociation

31 Email message to author, 1 April 2021.

32 As Deborah G. Burks puts it, 'Beatrice-Joanna's death is framed by these men, her survivors, as the necessary prerequisite to their formation of a more perfect family, an all male family', '"I'll Want My Will Else": "The Changeling" and Women's Complicity with Their Rapists', *ELH* 62, no. 4 (1995): 782.

33 Kondo, *Worldmaking*, 91.

# SELECTED BIBLIOGRAPHY

Aebischer, Pascale, 'Bend it like Nagra: Mainstreaming *The Changeling* in Sarah Harding's *Compulsion*', in *Screening Early Modern Drama beyond Shakespeare* (Cambridge: Cambridge University Press, 2013), 187–216.

Baird, Caroline, 'From Court to Playhouse and Back: Middleton's Appropriation of the Masque', *Early Theatre* 18:2 (2015): 57–85.

Barker, Roberta, and David Nicol, 'Does Beatrice Joanna Have a Subtext?: *The Changeling* on the London Stage', *Early Modern Literary Studies* 10.1 (May, 2004): 1–43. http://purl.oclc.org/emls/10-1/barknico.htm

Boehrer, Bruce, 'Alsemero's Closet: Privacy and Interiority in *The Changeling*', *The Journal of English and Germanic Philology* 96.3 (1997): 349–68.

Bromham, A.A., and Zara Bruzzi, *The Changeling and the Years of Crisis, 1619–1624: A Hieroglyph of Britain* (London: Pinter, 1990).

Burks, Deborah G., '"I'll Want My Will Else": *The Changeling* and Women's Complicity with Their Rapists', *ELH* 62.4 (1995): 759–90.

Cahill, Patricia, 'The play of skin in *The Changeling*', *postmedieval: a journal of medieval cultural studies* 3 (2012): 391–406.

Calbi, Maurizio, *Approximate Bodies: Gender and Power in Early Modern Drama and Anatomy* (London: Routledge, 2005).

Chakravorty, Swapan, '"Give Her More Onion": Unriddling the Welsh Madman's Speech in *The Changeling*', *Notes and Queries* 241 (1996): 184–7.

Daalder, Joost, 'Folly and Madness in *The Changeling*', *Essays in Criticism* 38.1 (January 1988): 1–21.

Daalder, Joost, 'The Closet Drama in *The Changeling*, V.iii', *Modern Philology* 89 (1991): 225–30.

Daalder, Joost, 'The Role of Isabella in *The Changeling*,' *English Studies* 73. 1 (1992): 22–9.

Dolan, Frances, *Dangerous Familiars: Representations of Domestic*

*Crime in England 1550–1700* (Ithaca, NY: Cornell University Press, 1994).

Dolan, Frances, 'Re-reading Rape in *The Changeling*', *Journal for Early Modern Cultural Studies* 11:1 (2011): 4–29.

Dustagheer, Sarah, 'New Directions: Performing *The Changeling*: 2006–2015', in Hutchings, (ed.), *The Changeling*, 143–63.

Eaton, Sara, 'Beatrice-Joanna and the Language of Love in *The Changeling*', *Theatre Journal* 36 (1984): 371–82.

Eliot, T.S., 'Thomas Middleton', in *Selected Essays*, 'New Edition' (New York: Harcourt Brace, 1950), 140–8.

Garber, Marjorie, 'The Insincerity of Women', in Valeria Finucci and Regina Schwartz (eds), *Desire in the Renaissance: Psycholoanalysis and Literature* (Princeton, NJ: Princeton University Press, 1994), 19–38; also in Margreta de Grazia, Maureen Quilligan and Peter Stallybrass (eds), *Subject and Object in Renaissance Culture* (Cambridge: Cambridge University Press, 1996), 349–68.

Gossett, Suzanne (ed.), *Thomas Middleton in Context* (Cambridge: Cambridge University Press, 2011).

Haber, Judith, '"I(t) Could Not Choose But Follow": Erotic Logic in *The Changeling*', *Representations* 81 (2003): 79–98.

Heinemann, Margot, *Puritanism and the Theatre: Thomas Middleton and Opposition Drama under the Early Stuarts* (Cambridge: Cambridge University Press, 1982).

Higgins, John, '"Servant obedience changed to master sin": Performance and the Public Transcript of Service in the Overbury Affair and *The Changeling*', *Journal of Early Modern Studies* 4 (2015): 231–58.

Hirschfeld, Heather, *Joint Enterprises: Collaborative Drama and the Institutionalization of English Renaissance Theater* (Amherst: University of Massachusetts Press, 2004).

Howard, Jean E., *The Stage and Social Struggle in Early Modern England* (London: Routledge, 1994).

Hutchings, Mark, 'De Flores Between the Acts', *Studies in Theatre and Performance* 31.1 (2011): 95–111.

Hutchings, Mark, '*The Changeling* at Court', *Cahiers Elisabéthains* 81 (2012): 15–24.

Hutchings, Mark (ed.), *The Changeling: A Critical Reader*, Arden

Early Modern Drama Guides (London: Bloomsbury Arden Shakespeare, 2019).

Jackson, Kenneth S., *Separate Theaters: Bethlem ('Bedlam') Hospital and the Shakespearean Stage* (Newark: University of Delaware Press, 2005).

Jones, Edward, 'The Confined World of *The Changeling*', *Cahiers élisabéthains* 39 (April 1991): 47–8.

Kistner, A.L. and M.K. Kistner, 'The Five Structures of *The Changeling*', *Modern Language Studies* 11.2 (1981): 40–53.

Lake, David J., *The Canon of Thomas Middleton's Plays* (Cambridge: Cambridge University Press, 1975).

Lehmann, Courtney, 'Taking back the night: Hospitality in *The Changeling* on Film', *Shakespeare Bulletin* 29:4 (2011): 591–604.

Luttfring, Sara D., 'Bodily Narratives and the Politics of Virginity in *The Changeling* and the Essex Divorce', *Renaissance Drama* 39 (2011): 97–128.

McManus, Clare, '"Constant Changelings", Theatrical Form, and Migration: Stage Travel in the Early 1620s' in Clare Jowitt and David McInnis (eds), *Travel and Drama in Early Modern England: The Journeying Play* (Cambridge: Cambridge University Press, 2018), 207–29.

McMillin, Scott, 'Middleton's Theatres', in Taylor and Lavagnino, eds, *Thomas Middleton*, 79–85.

McMullan, Gordon, '*The Changeling* and the dynamics of ugliness', in Emma Smith and Garrett Sullivan (eds), *The Cambridge Companion to English Renaissance Tragedy* (Cambridge: Cambridge University Press, 2010), 222–35.

Malcolmson, Cristina, '"As tame as the ladies": politics and gender in *The Changeling*', *English Literary Renaissance*, 20. 2 (1990): 320–39.

Middleton, Thomas and William Rowley, *The Changeling*, ed. Joost Daalder, New Mermaids (London: A&C Black, 1990).

Middleton, Thomas, and William Rowley, *The Changeling*, ed. Michael Neill, revised edition, New Mermaids (London: Methuen Drama, 2019).

Mayberry, Susan Neal, 'Cuckoos and Convention: Madness in Middleton and Rowley's *The Changeling*', *Mid-Hudson Language Studies* 8 (1985): 21–32.

Mooney, Michael E., '"Framing" as Collaborative Technique: Two

Middleton-Rowley Plays,' *Comparative Drama* 13 (1979): 127–41.

Neely, Carol Thomas, *Distracted Subjects: Madness and Gender in Shakespeare and Early Modern Culture* (Ithaca, NY: Cornell University Press, 2004).

Neely, Carol Thomas, '"Distracted Measures": Madness and Theatricality in Middleton', in Gossett (ed.), *Thomas Middleton in Context*, 306–13.

Neill, Michael, '"Hidden Malady": Death, Discovery, and Indistinction in *The Changeling*', *Renaissance Drama* 22 (1991): 95–121.

Neill, Michael, *Issues of Death: Mortality and Identity in English Renaissance Tragedy* (Oxford: Clarendon Press, 1997).

Nicol, David, *Middleton and Rowley: Forms of Collaboration in the Jacobean Playhouse* (Toronto: University of Toronto Press, 2012).

Nicol, David, '"Exit at one door and enter at the other": The Fatal Re-Entrance in Jacobean Drama', *Shakespeare Bulletin* 37.2 (2019): 205–29.

Nochimson, Richard L., '"Sharing" *The Changeling* by Playwrights and Professors: The Certainty of Uncertain Knowledge about Collaboration', *Early Theatre* 5 (2002): 41–2.

O'Callaghan, Michelle, *Thomas Middleton, Renaissance Dramatist* (Edinburgh: Edinburgh University Press, 2009).

Panek, Jennifer, 'Shame and Pleasure in *The Changeling*', *Renaissance Drama* 42.2 (2014), 191–215.

Panek, Jennifer, 'A Performance History', in Hutchings (ed.), *The Changeling*, 35–66.

Paster, Gail Kern, 'The Ecology of the Passions in *A Chaste Maid in Cheapside* and *The Changeling*', in Gary Taylor and Trish Thomas Henley (eds), *The Oxford Handbook of Thomas Middleton* (Oxford: Oxford University Press, 2012), 148–63.

Patterson, Annabel, 'Introduction' to *The Changeling*, ed. Douglas Bruster, in Taylor and Lavagnino (eds), *Thomas Middleton*, 1632–6.

Pollard, Tanya, 'Drugs, Remedies, Poisons, and the Theatre', in Gossett (ed.), *Thomas Middleton in Context*, 287–94.

Reed, Robert Rentoul, *Bedlam on the Jacobean Stage* (Cambridge, MA: Harvard University Press, 1952).

Ricks, Christopher, 'The Moral and Poetic Structure of *The Changeling*', *Essays in Criticism* 10.3 (1960): 290–306.

Ryner, Bradley D., 'Anxieties of Currency Exchange in Middleton and Rowley's *The Changeling*', in Julianne Vitullo and Diane Wolfthal (eds), *Money, Morality and Culture in Late Medieval and Early Modern Europe* (Aldershot: Ashgate, 2010), 109–25.

Slater, Michael, '"Shameless Collaboration": Mixture and the Double Plot of *The Changeling*', *Renaissance Drama* 47. 1 (2019): 55–8.

Solga, Kim, 'Playing *The Changeling* Architecturally', in *Violence Against Women in Early Modern Performance: Invisible Acts* (Basingstoke: Palgrave Macmillan, 2009), 56–76; reprinted in Susan Bennett and Mary Polito (eds), *Performing Environments: Site-Specificity in Medieval and Early Modern English Drama* (London: Palgrave Macmillan, 2014), 56–76.

Solga, Kim, 'Beatrice Joanna and the Rhetoric of Rape', in Kimberly Jannarone (ed.), *Vanguard Performance Beyond Left and Right* (Ann Arbor: University of Michigan Press, 2015), 246–63.

Stachniewski, John, 'Calvinist Psychology in Middleton's Tragedies', in R.V. Holdsworth (ed.), *Three Jacobean Revenge Tragedies: A Casebook* (Basingstoke: Macmillan, 1990), 226–47.

Taylor, Gary and Andrew J. Sabol, 'Middleton, Music and Dance', in Taylor and Lavagnino, (eds), *Thomas Middleton*, 119–81.

Taylor, Gary, and John Lavagnino (gen. eds), *Thomas Middleton: The Collected Works* (Oxford: Oxford University Press, 2007).

Williams, Nora J., '"Cannot I keep That Secret?": Editing and Performing Asides in *The Changeling*', *Shakespeare Bulletin* 34.1 (2016): 29–45.

Williams, Nora J. 'Resources', in Hutchings, ed., *The Changeling*, 187–210.

Zysk, Jay, 'Relics and Unreliable Bodies in *The Changeling*', *English Literary Renaissance* 45.3 (2015): 400–24.

# INDEX

Illustrations are indicated by '*ill.*'

actors 79, 170, 188 *see also* boy actors
   cross-gender casting 244–5
   safety of 247–50, 252
affection 119, 121, 123–4, 131
agency 78, 90–1, 92, 119, 160, 247
Alibius 54–5, 99
   description of madmen's performance 164–5
   jealousy 80–1, 86, 104, 108
   name 47, 103
   neglect of asylum 103–4
   parallels with Helkiah Crooke 101–3
   repentance and reformation 111, 163
Alicante 23, 25, 45, 47–9, 219
Allderidge, Patricia 100
Alonzo 150
   affection for Beatrice-Joanna 121
   ghost of 129, 149, 151
   murder 30, 33, 220
   severed finger 139, 139–40, 147–8, 149–50, 225
Alsemero
   arrival in Alicante 23–4
   death of Beatrice-Joanna 251
   and Diaphanta 25–6, 50, 191, 209
   final speech 211, 252
   imprisonment of Beatrice-Joanna 29, 54
   philosophy 49, 70, 117–18, 128
   relationship with Beatrice-Joanna 46, 69, 122–4, 141, 149, 189, 192, 208
   as substitute heir to Vermandero 210
   virginity test 29, 33, 70, 170
Antonio/Tony
   feigned foolishness 82, 85, 158
   as iconic character 171
   name 47
   reformation 163
   seduction by Isabella 87, 88–9, 106–7
Anzaldúa, Gloria 16, 218
Astington, John H. 183
asylum 24, 25, 27, 34, 47–8 *see also* hospital plot
   mismanagement of 101–3, 107–9
   as parody of castle 110
   as setting 45
   spaces in 28
   staging of 70
audiences 28, 30, 31
   complicity 244

female 181, 193
  imagination of 45–7, 56
  imitation of actors 170–1
  as judges 201–4
  modern 119
  reactions 36–7, 193, 252
  safety of 247, 250, 252
  as witnesses 197–200, 202, 208, 211, 242
authorship 63–72, 152
auto-eroticism 146–7

Baird, Caroline 48
Barker, Roberta 182, 238
Beatrice-Joanna 205–6
  death of 36, 54, 203, 209, 222
  feminist portrayal of 250, 251–2
  final speech 198, 204–10
  glove 139–44, 146–52, 241
  imprisonment 29, 54
  movement of 33, 36
  name 50, 218, 222
  rape 35, 90, 192, 218, 220–2, 238
  relationship with Alsemero 46, 69, 122–4, 141, 149, 189, 192, 208
  relationship with De Flores 53–4, 123–4, 130, 149, 192, 225–6
  representation in *Compulsion* 226–7
  as role for boy actors 187–9
  sexuality 128, 221
  virginity 30, 191, 218, 222, 240, 241
  wedding of 34–5, 54–5, 109, 149–50, 158, 164, 242, 249–50

bed trick 33, 42, 79
Bedlam 47–9, 51, 97–101, 118, 161–2
Beierle, Scott 240
Belknap, Madeline 248
Belsey, Catherine 150
Bethlehem Hospital *see* Bedlam
Birken, William 100, 101
*Black Lady, The* 189–90
blackmail, sexual 90, 238
blackness 189
blood 37, 205–6, 220
borderlands, sexual 218, 221, 224, 232–3
boy actors
  in female roles 179–82
  portraying subjectivity 189–92
  reaction of female spectators to 193
  training and support 183–8
bracelet 229, 231
Brave Spirits Theatre (BST) 237, 239, 252, 253
bridal procession 90, 249–50
Bridewell 100–1
Bright, Timothy: *A Treatise on Melancholy* 103
Bruster, Douglas 42, 119, 165, 246
  *Oxford Middleton, The* 48, 122, 141, 158–9
Bühler, Karl 44–5
Bullen, A.H. 63
Burbage, Richard 188
Butler, Judith 219

cabinets 25, 181, 190–1
Calvinism 62, 116, 128, 130, 181, 182

Camporesis, Piero 102–3
Cane, Andrew 183, 184, 188, 193
Canetti, Elias 201–2
Carroll, William C. 98
castle 25, 26, 27, 28, 67–9
castle plot 80, 152, 159 *see also* hospital plot
   authorship 63–6
   comparison with hospital plot 108, 118, 157, 170, 171, 247
   sexual violence in 158
Catholicism 42, 107–8, 123
'changeling,' identity of 50, 118, 171, 225, 226
charity 101, 107–9, 112
chivalry 50, 85
choreography, consent-based 248–50
closet 25, 29–30, 35–7, 70, 127, 204, 250
clown role 62
Cockpit/Phoenix Theatre 24, 27, 70, 98, 181
code switching 246
coercive control 225
Coker-Durso, Lauren 151
comedy 87, 88, 107, 118, 160, 168
confessions 198, 208
confinement 24–5, 28, 33–4, 36, 78, 86
Copjec, Joan 221
cosmetics *see* make-up
costume design 248–9
Cranmer, Archbishop Thomas 204, 207
Cromwell, Thomas 205–6

Crooke, Dr Helkiah 51, 98–9, 100–3
cue-lines 185–8
cures 103–5, 157, 167–8

Daalder, Joost 108
Dante 50, 218
Darwin, Charles 125
Davidson, Genna Beth 246–7, 248
De Flores
   casting 184
   death of 54, 203, 204
   dismemberment of Alonzo 139–40, 147–8
   freedom of movement 31–2
   glove scene 139–44, 146–52
   incel characteristics 240–1
   name 51
   obsession with Beatrice-Joanna 51, 124–5
   portrayal by woman 243–5
   as proxy for Beatrice-Joanna 141–4, 146, 149
   rape of Beatrice-Joanna 35, 149, 192, 209, 238–9, 248
   ugliness 243
deixis 44, 45, 49
Dekker, Thomas and Middleton, Thomas: *The Patient Man and the Honest Whore* 97, 102
Dekker, Thomas and Webster, John: *Northward Ho!* 252
Derrida, Jacques 217, 222
devils 68, 69, 70
Diaphanta

and Alsemero 25–6, 50, 191, 209
bed trick 33, 79
death of 26, 32, 188
as role for boy actors 185–6
virginity test 25, 30
disability
in early modern drama 161–2
feigned 163, 169
as link between plots 159
as narrative prosthesis 162, 168
portrayal using puppetry 245–6
representation of 157, 159–61, 171–2
staging of 151, 152, 159–60
theatrical signification of 169–70
'disability drag' 140, 151, 152
Dixon, Thomas 119
*double entendres* 43, 87, 107, 108
Drouet, Pascale 51, 118
Dufourmantelle, Anne 231
Dustagheer, Sarah 238

emotions 116–17, 119, 181
enclosure 24, 28, 29–30, 31, 98
executions, public 200–1, 204, 207
eyes 191–2

*fabliau* 85
femininity 227
feminism 233
feminist productions 237, 250, 252

Fenton, Geffraie: *Tragical Discourses* 125
film adaptations 218, 220
*The Changeling (2006)* 218, 223–6
coercive control in 225–6
*Compulsion (2008)* 218–19, 226–32
female sexuality in 219–20, 228
'foreign women' in 223, 225, 228, 232–3
horror in 220
locations 219, 224
*Middleton's Changeling (1998)* 218, 219–23
morality in 223–4
Neorealism in 220
'pornotroping' in 219–23
race in 221
representation of Beatrice-Joanna 218–21, 224
sexual violence in 218, 222, 230–2
suicide in 225
virgin-whore trope in 218–19, 222, 223, 226–7
Fineman, Joel 183
finger, severed 139–40, 148, 149, 150, 225
Flecknoe, Richard 188
Fletcher, John and Rowley, William: *The Maid of the Mill* 81
Fletcher, John: *The Pilgrim* 97, 107
Floyd-Wilson, Mary 122, 127
foolishness 159, 161–3
feigned 82, 158, 160, 162, 168–9

fools 24, 82, 102, 171, 187
*see also* madmen
  agency 160
  changing attitudes to 109
  main characters as 110–11
  mockery of 106–7
  movement of 34–5
  as puppets 245–6
Ford, Dr Christine Blasey 238, 239, 242, 244, 248
foreignness 217–19, 222, 223, 228, 232–3
Foucault, Michel 104, 108–9, 112
  *Histoire de la folie à l'àge classique* 105
Franciscus 82, 88, 158, 163
Freudian reading 182
Frisch, Andrea 199

Garber, Marjorie 197
Gayton, Edmund 170, 171
gender *see also* boy actors
  of actors 244–5
  patriarchalized 229
  and performance 181, 182, 190
  politics 85
gender relations 51
ghost, of Alonzo 129, 149, 151
gloves 139, 139–44, 140*ill.*, 146–52, 228, 240
Green, Thomas 200
Gresham, Sir Richard, Mayor of London 99–100
Grey, Lady Jane 204, 207
Gurnis, Musa 237, 240, 248, 249

hand, prosthetic 144, 145*ill. see also* prostheses

Harding, Sarah: *Compulsion* (film) 218–19, 226–32
Hartman, Saadiya 220, 228–9, 232
Henry VIII 99–100
honour 206–7, 209
Horace 51
horror, in film adaptation 220
hospital *see* asylum
hospital plot 78, 79, 80–1, 98, 118, 152, 157–8 *see also* castle plot
  authorship 63–5
  and disability 160–70
  effect on audience 170–2
  in film adaptations 219
  as metatheatre 159
  and puppetry 247
  purpose of 158
hospitality 230, 231, 233
Howard, Frances 53
Howard, Jean E. 181, 204
Hoy, Cyrus 64, 65
humours, bodily 117
hunger 102–3
Hutson, Lorna 199

imagination, of audience 44–6, 47, 49, 56
imprisonment 29, 35–6
incel culture 240–1
insanity 37, 97–8 *see also* madness
  and charity 108–9
  as disguise 109
  and hunger 102–3
  instrumentalization of 104–7
  meaning of 110–11
  moral status 118
  social awareness of 112

Isabella
  agency 78, 90–1, 119
  character 85–6
  confinement 70, 86–7
  disguise as madwoman 109, 158, 164
  importance of 79–80
  and Lollio 80–3, 85–91, 108, 157–8, 187, 191–3
  movement of 34
  name 81
  portrayal using puppetry 246–7
  as role for boy actors 186–7
  seduction of Antonio 91–2, 106–7
  sexuality 82–3, 87, 88–91
  social standing 84
  wedding 158

Jackson, Ken 101, 107, 108, 161–2
Jackson, MacDonald P. 64
James I 100, 101
Jasperino 117
Jenner, Thomas 100
jokes 87, 118, 163, 164, 244
Jones, Ann Rosalind 147
Jones, Inigo 27, 28
Jonson, Ben 181
judgement 197, 200–2, 204, 205, 208, 210–11

Kaiser, Walter 109
Kaleba, Casey 248
Karim-Cooper, Farah 189
Kavanaugh, Brett 238, 239, 242, 244, 248
keys 24, 28–9, 31, 32, 33, 34, 87, 232

Knapp, Adrienne 247, 252
Kondo, Dorinne 252–3
Kubrik, Stanley: *A Clockwork Orange* 230

labyrinths 181, 190–3
Lady Elizabeth's Men 27, 62, 180, 183, 189
Lake, David J. 64
Lander, Jesse 181
language 44, 86
*Last Tango in Paris* (film) 229, 230
limbs
  disembodied 139
  phantom 150, 152
  prosthetic 140–1, 143–6, 145*ill.*, 148, 149–51
Lipsius, Justus 118, 130
location 23, 45, 46–9, 219, 224
Lollio
  and asylum inmates 104–7, 168–9
  casting 183, 184
  and comedy 87, 88, 107, 118
  and Isabella 80–3, 85–91, 108, 157–8, 187, 191–3
  as keyholder 28, 32, 34
  name 51
Lollius, Marcus 51
London 46–7, 55, 100
Loomba, Ania: *Gender, Race, Renaissance Drama* 182
Low, Jennifer 181
Lupton, Donald: *London and the Countrey Carbonadoes and Quartred into Severall Characters* 105

madhouse *see* asylum
madmen 24, 70, 110–11, 171
    *see also* fools
  agency 160
  as background figures 109, 169–70
  as entertainment 34–5, 48–9, 54–5, 89, 105–7, 109, 164–5
  mistreatment of 102–7
  portrayal using puppetry 245–6
madness 52, 53–4, 55, 82, 118–19 *see also* insanity
  'cure' for 103–5, 157, 167–8
  feigned 91, 151, 162–4
  and passion 166
  staging 160–2
  theatrical signification of 168–9
magic 127, 128
make-up 189, 249
Manente, Briana 243, 249
Marmion, Shakerley: *Holland's Leaguer* 183
marriage 30, 34, 78, 121
  arranged 227
masculinity, toxic 237
masks, black 189–90
masques 48
Matthews, Steve 228
Mayberry, Susan Neal 110
McDonald, Michael 161–2
McMillin, Scott 28, 184
memory 198–9, 211
mental illness *see* foolishness; insanity; madness
metaphors, sexual 82
metatheatre 148, 151, 159, 162, 163, 182, 211

#MeToo movement 6, 239
Middleton, Thomas and Rowley, William: *The Changeling* 97
  contribution of authors 63–72, 152
  dramatic texts 79
  ending 54, 252–3
  feminist productions 237
  first staging of 24, 27, 98
  Freudian reading of 116, 239
  location 45, 46–9
  modern critical acclaim 171–2
  origins 62–7
  texts 121
Middleton Thomas 62–7, 71–2
  contribution to text 152, 161
  *A Game at Chess* 71
  *The Nice Valour; Or, The Passionate Madman* 160–1, 166–8
  'Spanish Trilogy' 61
  style of writing 64
mimesis 44
misogyny 51, 238–41, 243–6, 252, 253
Mitchell, David 150–1
Mooney, Michael E. 65
Moors 67–8, 70
morality 84, 118, 163, 209, 223, 229
movement, of characters 23–4, 31–7
Mukherji, Subha 210
Mullaney, Steven 244
murder 29, 30, 33
mutilation 139, 140, 141, 147, 148
mythology 52, 88

names 47, 51, 81, 103, 218, 222, 232–3
Nardizzi, Vin 148
Ndiaye, Noémie 190–3
Neely, Carol Thomas 109
Neill, Michael 35, 70, 98, 104, 108, 129
Neorealism 221
Nicol, David 48, 152, 182, 184, 238

occult 127–8
O'Donoghue, Edward G. 100, 101, 102
orgasm, female 121, 221

Paré, Ambrosius 144, 145*ill.*, 150
parricide 222, 231
passion 119, 122, 123–4, 131
Passionate Lord, The 166–8
Paster, Gail Kern 116–17, 119
patriarchy 229, 232
Patterson, Annabel 42–3, 141, 158–9, 165, 209, 209–10
Pearson, Meg F. 202
performance 43, 201–2
　of boy-actors 180–2, 193
　at Cockpit/Phoenix theatre 28–9
　and disability 159–61, 168–72
　feminist 238, 252
　and gender 181, 190
　and Isabella 84–5, 91, 92
　and race 190
　of rape 243, 246–8
Petrarchanism 85, 88, 124, 209, 240
phallic imagery 139, 148, 150

Phoenix Theatre *see* Cockpit/Phoenix Theatre
Piracquo, Tomazo de *see* Tomazo
play-boys *see* boy actors
playhouses 43 *see also* theatres
plots *see* castle plot; hospital plot
politics, Jacobean 42, 45–6
'pornotroping' 219–23
poverty 98, 106
pregnancy test 127–8
props 28, 139, 148, 149, 150
prostheses 139–41, 143–6, 145*ill.*, 148, 149–51
Protestantism 128
psychology 119
puppetry 245–7, 249

race 189–90, 218, 221, 228, 232–3
rape 67–8, 218, 228, 231
　of Beatrice-Joanna 35, 90, 192, 218, 220–2, 238
　performance of 243, 248
　staging of 245, 249–50
　survivors 239, 252
Rape, Abuse and Incest National Network (RAINN) 239
rape culture 237–8, 252, 253
Read, Timothy 183–4
Reed, Robert Rentoul 97
　*Bedlam on the Jacobean Stage* 161–2
reformation, of characters 163
Reynolds, John 47, 68
　*Triumphs of God's Revenge, The* 61–2, 120, 150
rhetorical theory 171

Roach, Joseph R. 171
roles 79, 170, 181, 184
Rome 51
rooms 25, 26, 68, 69–70
Row-Heyveld, Lindsey 151
Rowley, William
   *All's Lost by Lust* 61–2, 64, 67, 71
   contribution to text 63–72, 152, 158–9
Ryan, Marie-Laure 45, 49

safety 247–9, 250, 252
Salgádo, Gámini 98
Salkeld, Duncan 161–2
satire 107, 118
Saville, Arthur 184
Schwarz, Katherine 224, 227
Scott, Danielle 248, 249
secrets 24–6, 70, 80, 190
Seed, Patricia 232
sex, metaphors for 82
sexual economy 89–90
sexual violence 218, 238–9, 240
   *see also* rape
sexuality 25, 30, 34, 50, 91–2, 230–1
   assumptions about 78
   of Beatrice-Joanna 128, 221
   criminalization of 230
   female 164, 219
   and folly 111
   modern 116
Shakespeare, William 52, 125
   *Hamlet* 98, 129, 147, 161
   *A Midsummer Night's Dream* 88
   *Othello* 35–6, 37
   *The Tempest* 48, 55
Slater, Michael 66

slavery 221, 229
Smith, Charlene V. 237, 244, 247, 249, 250, 252–3
Snyder, Sharon 150–2
Snyder, Susan 160
Solga, Kim 25, 238
spaces 24–5
   enclosed 31–2, 36, 37
   locked 52
   private 25, 26, 33
   theatrical 27–30, 43–6
Spain 61, 64, 67–72, 189, 233
spectators *see* audiences
Spillers, Hortense 221, 229
Sprot, George 204
spying 23–4, 26, 31, 33, 34, 37, 181, 202–3
St. Johnson, Joshua 226
Stachniewski, John 182
staging 25, 26, 27, 28, 29–31, 37, 198
   of disability 152
   feminist 237–8
   non-realistic 245–7
   playhouse facade 70
stalking 242–3
Stallybrass, Peter 147
Stanton, Elizabeth Cady 226
Staynoe, Thomas 184
Stern, Jay: *The Changeling* (film) 218, 223–6
stoicism 117–18, 130, 130–1
subjectivity, female 181, 182, 184, 189–92
suicide 225
Sullivan, Erin 119
supernatural 128, 131
surveillance *see* spying
Swanston, Elliard 184, 188, 193

Teague, Frances 141–2
temporality 164–5, 167–8, 170
theatres 25, 28, 29, 202
theatrical signification 168–9
Thompson, Jasmine 252
Thompson, Marcus:
    *Middleton's Changeling*
    (film) 218, 219–23
Tichbourne, Chidiock 207
time *see* temporality
Tomazo
    and death of Alonzo 126–7
    final speech 203
    suspicion of Beatrice-Joanna
    33, 50, 120, 121–2
Tony *see* Antonio/Tony
Topsell, Edward: *History of
    Four-Footed Beasts* 125
tragedy 160, 197
trials 198, 199, 200

Vermandero
    adoption of Alsemero 210
    movement of 32
    as patriarch 50
    possessiveness 224
    response to Beatrice-Joanna's
    death 69, 203, 222
    secrecy 24
victim-blaming 252
violence 218, 230, 238–9, 240
virginity 191, 227, 230, 240,
    241
virginity test 25, 28, 29, 30, 33,
    70, 170
virgin-whore trope 218–19,
    222, 223, 226–7

Walsham, Alexandra 120
*Warning for Fair Women, A* 210

Webster, John: *The Duchess of
    Malfi* 97, 148, 161, 209
wedding 147, 158
    Alibius' speech 54–5, 164
    feminist staging of 242,
    249–50
    performance of madmen and
    fools 34–5, 48–9, 105,
    109, 164–5
    silent procession 90, 149–50
Whately, William: *A Bride-Bush*
    121
white privilege 228
whiteness 189
Whyatt, Sir Thomas 205
Wiggin, Pauline 63–4, 66
Willemsen, Annemarieke 142
Williams, Nora 182, 238, 239,
    245
Witen, Michelle: *Shakespeare
    and Space* 43–4
witnessing
    by audiences 197, 202, 208,
    211, 242
    by characters 203
    definitions of 198–9
    of executions 200–1
women
    agency 90–1, 92
    in audience 36–7, 181, 193
    of colour 218, 228
    constraints on 24, 79
    foreign 217–19, 222, 223,
    228, 232–3
    as property 36
    rape victims 239
    sexual threats towards 246–7
    status 50
    subjectivity 181, 182, 184,
    189–92

violence towards 240, 252
worlds, fictional 43, 44, 45–7
　　fractured 48, 49–52, 54
Wright, Thomas: *The Passions of the Mind* 119, 119–20

Wroth, Mary
　　*Love's Victory* 181
　　*Urania* 179–80, 190–1, 193

Zysk, Jay 143, 147

www.ingramcontent.com/pod-product-compliance
Lightning Source LLC
Chambersburg PA
CBHW052216300426
44115CB00011B/1703